The Book of
LITERARY LISTS

By the same author:

Dipped in Vitriol   1981
A Letter Does Not Blush   1984

The Book of
LITERARY LISTS

A collection of annotated lists of fact, statistic
and anecdote concerning books

Compiled and written by

NICHOLAS PARSONS

SIDGWICK & JACKSON
LONDON

First published in Great Britain in 1985
by Sidgwick & Jackson Limited

Compilation copyright © 1985 Nicholas T. Parsons

ISBN 0–283–99171–2

Typeset by Scarborough Typesetting Services
Printed in Great Britain by
The Garden City Press, Letchworth, Hertfordshire
for Sidgwick & Jackson Limited
1 Tavistock Chambers, Bloomsbury Way
London WC1A 2SG

Contents

III Publishers

IV Readers and Reviewers

V Books and Their Enemies

For Ilona

Author's Acknowledgements

I would like to express my thanks to those who contributed their lists to this book, despite the competition for their time from business and personal commitments. In alphabetical order they are: Jeffrey Archer, Professor Sir Alfred Ayer, Brigid Brophy, Barbara Cartland, Sir Hugh Casson, Shirley Conran, Professor Bernard Crick, Quentin Crisp, Clare Francis, Dick Francis, General Sir John Hackett, the Rt Hon. Denis Healey, Professor Richard Hoggart, P. D. James, H. R. F. Keating, Miles Kington, Sir Michael Levey, Professor Peter Levi, Joanna Lumley, John Julius Norwich, Charles Osborne, the Rev. Ian Paisley, Dr Magnus Pyke, Tom Rosenthal and Professor Mary Warnock.

The following publishers gave interesting information, again sacrificing valuable time to answer my queries: Philip Attenborough, Anthony Blond, Anthony Cheetham, Norman Franklin, William Kimber, the late James Mitchell, Peter Owen, Charles Pick, Christopher Sinclair-Stevenson and Rayner Unwin.

I grateful to the staff of these libraries for help and consideration at all times: the British Library, the libraries of the Royal Borough of Kensington and Chelsea, the British Council Library in Vienna, the Library of the Academy of Arts and Sciences, Budapest, and the London Library, to whom part of my royalties will be donated. I would also like to thank Peter Harland and his staff at Bookwatch.

I owe much to the persistence and patience of those who typed the manuscript: Leo Clark, Peta Murray, Angela Petford and Helen Swansbourne.

A special note of thanks is due to Margaret Payne at the Mark Longman Library of the National Book League, whose efficiency and knowledge are only equalled by her enthusiasm and helpfulness. Personal thanks are also due to Karen Elder and to my brother Louis Parsons, for providing a roof over my head at crucial periods of gestation and completion of the manuscript; and to Andrew Hilton for research.

Last, but certainly not least, I would like to thank Margaret Willes and her colleagues at Sidgwick & Jackson, in particular Esther Jagger. None of them, it should be said, bears any resemblance to Barabbas.

Introduction

André Maurois once remarked that 'in literature, as in love, we are astonished at what is chosen by others'. The favourite reading of well-known contemporaries that forms the core of this book may or may not astonish, but it certainly gives an intriguing insight into the power and influence of the printed word. This influence is also illustrated in much of the anecdote and statistic that comprises the rest of the book and which highlights various aspects of authorship and publishing. Notable among these are 'bestsellerdom' from earliest times, censorship, and the trials and tribulations of publishers and authors, especially those which each endures at the hands of the other. Success and failure − financial, artistic or personal − are recurring themes, even where the text concerns itself with literary cranks and curiosities: hoaxers, forgers, unreadable but incredibly persistent poets, bizarre terminology and so forth.

A maker of literary lists is inevitably a bit of an Autolycus, a snapper-up of unconsidered trifles; cumulatively, however, such information as that the author of *Bambi* let off steam by writing a kind of Viennese *Fanny Hill*, or that the Oxford University Press took fifty years to bring out the definitive edition of the works of the Latin poet Ennius, builds up a picture of the literary marketplace through the ages. Writers emerge as dedicated and slothful, naïve and cunning, generous and grasping, kindly and choleric; publishers emerge as choleric and kindly, grasping and generous, cunning and naïve, slothful and dedicated. In no other profession, surely, do the roles of Don Quixote and Sancho Panza so subtly intermingle; and in few other professions are the rewards so seemingly arbitrary and unpredictable − though the modern manufacturers of bestsellers are doing their best to remove the unpredictability. Literary and publishing history are therefore full of heroism and absurdity, tales of amazing luck or extraordinary misfortune.

I hope that others will share my fascination with the curious and colourful in the history of books and their makers, and that they will be entertained by this compilation. As for writers, aspirant or otherwise, it may be consoling for them to be reminded that they are not alone. Ditto publishers.

Nicholas Parsons
Vienna, 1985

I
Authors

All writers are vain, selfish and lazy, and at the very bottom of their motives lies a mystery. Writing a book is a long, exhausting struggle, like a long bout of some painful illness. One would never undertake such a thing if one were not driven by some demon whom one can neither resist nor understand.

George Orwell,
Why I Write – England Your England

∿

Writing is not a profession, but a vocation of unhappiness.

Georges Simenon

∿

Style and Structure are the essence of a book; great ideas are hogwash.

Vladimir Nabokov, *Writers at Work*

∿

Six of the Best –
Poets for a Desert Island

PETER LEVI

I have often been on the equivalent of desert islands, and experience has confirmed that it is not the greatest poets you usually need at such a time, except for Shakespeare and from time to time (not every year) Dante. If it happened now I would have a volume of Shakespeare's tragedies, and the poems of Marvell and of Raleigh, highly quirky and strongly flavoured poets, whose musical English I admire; then I think Virgil, a fascinating writer about whom I can never make up my mind, George Seferis, a modern Greek poet I admire greatly, and either Lorca, from whom I could learn Spanish, or the *Penguin Hebrew Verse* or *Russian Verse*. Maybe if this is to be a long stay, I would not after all take Virgil, but Horace, a more familiar and austere text which I find has a less even and dazzling surface and is more nourishing, and I would not take Lorca, or any anthology, but Theokritos, who is full of strange and inexhaustible eddies, and apprentice myself to him as I have never dared to do, because so many false feelings and conventions separate us from Theokritos and his goats. On a desert island they might drop away. It pays on a desert island to take strongly individual writers rather than the very greatest or smoothest, but I do not suppose any of these writers are much less than great: though Raleigh is so in a very few poems.

~

One afternoon in March at half past three
When walking in a ploughed field with a friend,
Kicking a little stone, he turned to me
And said, 'Tell me do you write poetry?'
I never had, and said so, but I knew
That very moment what I wished to do.
                                        W. H. Auden

~

Some Bestselling Poets of the Nineteenth and Early Twentieth Centuries

~

There's no money in poetry, but then there's no poetry in money either.

Robert Graves, BBC TV, 1962

~

Sir Walter Scott   1771–1832   After the success of 'The Lay of the Last Minstrel' Scott could command unheard of prices. Constable offered him £1000 for 'Marmion' before reading a single line. 'It was a price', Scott is reported to have said, 'that made men's hair stand on end.' The poem appeared in 1808 selling at a guinea and a half and rapidly established itself as a major success. By 1825 it had sold 31,000 copies, which made Scott a hot property; by the time he published 'The Lady of the Lake' in 1810 the price for his copyright had risen to £4000. It had sold 44,000 copies by 1830, when the attractions of Byron were beginning to eclipse those of Scott. Scott spent money – chiefly on Abbotsford, his house – as quickly as he earned it; the collapse of his publishing interests left him hugely in debt which he paid off by writing novels with incredible industry.

Thomas Moore   1779–1852   Byron's friend Thomas Moore, the author of many enchanting lyrics such as 'The Last Rose of Summer', was paid the then enormous sum of 3000 guineas in 1814 for the copyright of 'Lalla Rookh' (his actual earnings are given on p. 63). Moore, hopeless about money, rapidly spent this windfall; later, given a post in Bermuda, he turned it over to a deputy and went on a tour of America. The deputy embezzled vast sums and Moore was held responsible; to escape arrest he spent several years abroad.

Lord Byron   1788–1824   'I awoke one morning and found myself famous.' Thus did Byron record the success of 'Childe Harold's Pilgrimage' after its publication in 1812 in a small edition of 500 copies, which sold out in three days. The next two editions, of 3000, rapidly disappeared and the £600 that his publisher, John Murray, had paid appeared to be a bargain. Murray then offered Byron 1000 guineas for 'The Giaour' and 'The Bride of Abydos', which the poet, having written them in all of two weeks, turned down. In February 1814 'The Corsair' was published, and sold 10,000 copies on the day of publication. The publisher's office was full of people who had read it and came round to say how much they liked it, a practice which seems to have died out.

Felicia Dorothea Hemans   1793–1835   Few poets nowadays manage to hit the jackpot, but in the nineteenth century there was money to be made even out of a single poem − Mrs Hemans was the authoress of 'Casa Bianca', in which poem 'The boy stood on the burning deck/ Whence all but he had fled.' Less well known is her 'Early Blossoms', published precociously before she was fifteen, which drew a letter from Shelley. Unfortunately the Muse rather deserted her after this and by 1817 she was requesting John Murray, the publisher, to suggest 'any subject, or style of writing likely to be more popular'. 'Her poem on the "Elgin Marbles"', observes Samuel Smiles carefully in his *Memoirs of John Murray*, 'had not been satisfactory; and she seemed at a loss how to employ her pen.'

Mrs Hemans is also the progenitrix of verses which have enjoyed a cumulative existence since she first wrote:

> *The stately homes of England!*
> *How beautiful they stand,*
> *Amidst their tall ancestral trees*
> *O'er all the pleasant land.*

By 1881 E. V. Knox had transformed this to:

> *The stately homes of England,*
> *How beautiful they stood*
> *Before their recent owners*
> *Relinquished them for good.*

He may have been pulling Mrs Hemans's leg a little, as he was also the author of such works as *Parodies Regained*. The *coup de grâce* was delivered by Noel Coward with his elegant:

> *The stately homes of England*
> *How beautiful they stand*
> *To prove the upper classes*
> *Have still the upper hand.*

Thomas Babington Macaulay 1800–59 In 1842 Macaulay made what seems in retrospect an insanely quixotic gesture: he gave the copyright of 'The Lays of Ancient Rome' *gratis* to the publisher Thomas Longman. Macaulay imagined that the poem would have little commercial success and the understanding was that Longman would bring out a small edition, and that there should be 'no puffing of any sort'. This poem actually sold 100,000 copies over the next twenty-five years. Longman not only returned the copyright but paid Macaulay and his heirs a share of the vast profits.

Macaulay was a famous orator and talker — occasionally too much so: Sydney Smith remarked: 'He has occasional flashes of silence, that make his conversation perfectly delightful.'

Alfred, Lord Tennyson 1809–92 Some of Tennyson's subsequently most renowned works — 'The Lady of Shalott', 'The Lotus Eaters' — appeared in 1832 (but dated 1833) and were ignored. Revised versions, together with such mature work as 'Ulysses', were published in 1842 and the poet's fame began to grow; by the time he succeeded Wordsworth as Poet Laureate, in 1850, he had begun to command higher prices for his work. In that year he published the massive 'In Memoriam', which sold 60,000 copies in a few months. In 1859 'Idylls of the King' sold 10,000 copies in a week (out of an edition of 40,000); in 1864 'Enoch Arden' sold a first edition of 60,000 rapidly and in 1869 'The Holy Grail' sold 40,000 copies before publication. His income in 1870 from his poetry was £10,000 and his relationship with his second publisher, Moxon, with whom he shared his profits equally, was so cordial that he never even had a written agreement with him. He once received £1000 for a poem of three stanzas published in the USA, and just before he died in 1892 Macmillan were selling 20,000 copies a year of his collected works.

Tennyson's rise from absolute financial failure (his earliest volume brought him £11, and his first two books sold only 800 copies in two years) to untold riches is remarkable, even given the bestselling potential in Victorian times of poetry that caught the national mood. He once remarked: 'I don't think that since Shakespeare there has been such a master of the English language as I,' but added in the same breath: '. . . to be sure, I have nothing to say.'

Rudyard Kipling 1865–1936 In terms of sales Kipling's poem 'If' is one of the most successful ever written; it has been translated into twenty-seven languages and anthologized again and again. An indication of its particular appeal, which transcended poetry and made it more like a universal prayer, is given by this letter to the publishers from the superintendent of the Buffet at Waterloo Station during World War I (quoted in Simon Nowell Smith (ed.), *Letters to Macmillan*, Macmillan, 1967).

Dear Sir, *12 November 1916*

As hon. Superintendent of this buffet which serves hundreds of men going to the Front each day, I am writing to ask you if you would be good enough to grant me permission to have 30,000 copies of your poem 'If' struck off in leaflet form, for presentation to every man going out, as a Xmas and New Year card.

Working amongst the men as we have done, I realize what a tremendous influence for good the poem would have on them and how it would help them to endure the hardships of the trenches during the coming winter.

Hoping to receive a favourable reply, yours sincerely

Beryl C. M. Wilson

Kipling was a shrewd businessman. He could be tough on terms and resourceful in planning ways of marketing his works. Eventually author and publisher overplayed their hands with the costly limited leather-bound Sussex Edition, during the preparation of which Kipling died. Unsold stock was destroyed in an air raid in World War II, and the surplus red leather was used to upholster the chairs in Macmillan's offices — a monument to a publisher's one bite too many at the same cherry.

Gabriele d'Annunzio 1863–1938 Seldom has such a successful poet, who chimed so well with many of the more disagreeable attitudes of his fellow countrymen while he was alive, descended so abruptly in public esteem after his death. 'The vast edifice of d'Annunzio's work,' writes Martin Seymour-Smith in *Who's Who in Twentieth Century Literature* (Weidenfeld and Nicolson, 1976), 'much of it based on a crude misunderstanding of Nietzsche, has rotted away . . . a crass sensualist for whom an unconsidered death was the final ideal . . . he did clear the air of Italian letters — but he also made it uninhabitable.'

D'Annunzio shocked and titillated the Italian public at the same time. His novel *Il Fuoco* created a sensation because of its frankness about his affair with the actress Eleanora Duse. When, at the head of a band of adventurers, he seized the port of Fiume in 1919, many Italians were thrilled. His books sold rapidly — never mind if in literature, as in life, he was bombastic, affected and frequently ridiculous.

Exposure to the man himself rapidly corrected the more absurd pretensions of his work. As his wife put it: 'When I married my husband I thought I was marrying poetry itself. I would have done better to buy, at three francs fifty, each volume of poetry he published.' That, indeed, is what Italians did in their tens of thousands.

Other Men's Weeds

There is a crowded field from which to judge absolutely the worst poetry to appear in print; many of the candidates for the wooden spoon award have been dignified with an anthology of their own compiled by D. B. Wyndham Lewis and Charles Lee; it was entitled *The Stuffed Owl* (Everyman, 1930, 1948), after the memorable lines of Wordsworth:

> *Yet, helped by Genius – untired comforter*
> *The presence even of a stuffed Owl for her*
> *Can cheat the time. . .*

Lewis and Lee concentrate on the great names who are happily not immune from lapses. But there have been other connoisseurs of the genre who have explored the lesser or the unknown amongst the flat-footed bards. Here are six of the best discoveries:

Julia A. Moore   1847–1920   By general consent the worst American poetess, and perhaps the worst in English, she was satirized by Mark Twain in *Huckleberry Finn* as Emmeline Grangerford. Her unhappy knack of linking an awkward style to an inappropriate subject was expertly parodied in the 'Ode to Stephen Dowling Bots, Dec'd':

> *No whooping cough did rack his frame,*
> *Nor measles drear, with spots;*
> *Not these impaired the sacred name*
> *Of Stephen Dowling Bots.*

Her first volume, *The Sweet Singer of Michigan Salutes the Public*, was rapturously received, not least by Twain who admitted that the book had given him joy for twenty years. Another critic, Bill Nye, referring to her penchant for violent deaths, observed that: 'Julia is worse than a Gatling gun; I have counted twenty-one killed and nine wounded in the small volume she has given to the public.' It is hard to choose from so much richness, but after hovering between 'Byron: A Critical Survey':

> 'Lord Byron' was an Englishman
> A poet I believe
> His first works in old England
> Was poorly received.
> Perhaps it was 'Lord Byron's' fault
> And perhaps it was not.

and 'Little Libbie', I chose the latter as most characteristic of Julia Moore's delight in undeserved deaths and sudden bathos.

> While eating dinner, this dear little child
> Was choked on a piece of beef
> Doctors came, tried their skill awhile
> But none could give relief . . .
> Her friends and schoolmates will not forget
> Little Libbie that is no more;
> She is waiting on the shining step
> To welcome home friends once more.

Frederick J. Johnston-Smith   A turn-of-the-century master of the inappropriate image and the unfortunate use of colloquialism, and a hopeless slave to the exigencies of rhyme and metre, Johnston-Smith was celebrated by Sir John Squire in his essay *The Beauties of Badness*. In 'The Captain of the Dolphin' by this remarkable lyricist may be found the following couplet:

> *A balminess the darkened hours had brought from out the South;*
> *Each breaker doffed its cap of white and shut its blatant mouth.*

The same poet produced:

> Reluctant I leave, like a lover who goes
> From the side of the maid of his choice
> By whom he is held with a cord actuose
> Spun out of her beauty and voice.

'Actuose', says Squire, is 'very characteristic' of the poet, who uses enormous numbers of astonishing words of which he does not tell us the meaning, although he gives us a glossary containing such definitions as:

Derelict = an abandoned ship

Outward-bound = sailing from home

Yo-heave-ho! = a phrase used by sailors when two or more pull in concert on the same rope.

Johnston-Smith's glossary brings to mind another improbable work supplied with an equally impressive apparatus of additional information: Solyman Brown's 'Dentologia — A Poem on the Diseases of the Teeth' (1840). Footnotes to the poem supplied sensible advice on dental care and an appendix gave a list of 300 qualified dentists practising in America.

William McGonagall   1825–1902   In 1877, while sitting 'lonely and sad' in his room, William McGonagall was consumed with creative fervour and recognized with apocalyptic insight his true vocation: he was to be a poet. 'Throughout the remaining twenty-four years of [his] life,' writes Derek Wilson in *Extraordinary People* (Pan, 1983),

> a torrent of verse poured from him; bad verse, excruciatingly bad verse, devoid of all metre and scansion, never dignified by any flash of poetic insight, seldom rising above the utterly banal. The poetry of his verses was in stark contrast to the magnificent subjects which usually inspired them. For, above all things, McGonagall was moved by epic events, stirring spectacles and outstanding catastrophes.

Here is an extract from his long poem in celebration of the opening of the Tay railway bridge:

> *Beautiful Railway Bridge of the Silvery Tay!*
> *And prosperity to Messrs Bouche and Grothe,*
> *The famous engineers of the present day,*
> *Who have succeeded in erecting the Railway*
> *Bridge of the Silvery Tay*
> *Which stands unequalled to be seen*
> *Nearby Dundee and the Magdalen Green.*

McGonagall was pleased to be able to celebrate the dramatic collapse of the same bridge a little later.

The poet once walked from Dundee to Balmoral in foul weather in the hope of presenting his verses to Queen Victoria and giving her a recitation; but he was turned away at the castle gates. He went to America and was met with massive indifference. Back home he was pelted with rotten vegetables during his performances; but neither indifference nor abuse could stop the mouth of the bard. Posthumously he has had his reward, becoming a minor cult figure whose appalling works are frequently reprinted, and stacked up in the smallest room in houses all over the realm.

Richard Le Gallienne   1866–1947   Le Gallienne, whose prolific output of decadent verse has been unkindly dubbed 'Wilde-and-water', is the most engaging of the over-ripe nineties' poets. His unrepentantly over-the-top poem 'Beauty Accurst' has a certain bizarre attraction, such as might accrue from one of Keats's odes made into a film by Ken Russell:

> *I am so fair that whereso'er I wend*
> *Men yearn with strange desire to kiss my face,*
> *Stretch out their hands to touch me as I pass*
> *And women follow me from place to place.*

Moreover . . .

> *Lo! when I walk along the woodland way*
> *Strange creatures leer at me with uncouth love,*
> *And from the grass reach upward to my breast,*
> *And to my mouth lean from the boughs above*
>
> *The sleepy kine move round me in desire*
> *And press their oozy lips upon my hair,*
> *Toads kiss my feet and creatures of the mire;*
> *The snails will leave their shells to watch me there.*

The Rev. E. E. Bradford   According to Charles Osborne's biography of W. H. Auden, the poet rejoiced in the works of the Rev. Bradford whose lyrical descriptions of

> *Brave Scottish boys with naked knees*

inspiring:

> *Love that fills the human heart*
> *Flooding every secret part*

took a certain section of the reading public by storm in 1913. His innocent celebrations of teenage boys, interspersed with fierce swipes at womankind, make him as eminently quotable as *The Public School Hymn Book*, and much more down to earth. In a powerful didactic poem illustrating the intrusion of feminine sensuality into a relationship where the masculine version is functioning perfectly satisfactorily, the Rev. Bradford describes two boys whose naked forms adorn the seashore. The one is 'bright haired with beryl-coloured eyes' whose 'slender naked form.' lies 'bleak and bare'; the other is distinctly earthy:

> Close by his side a lusty lad lay prone
> With brawny back, broad loins and swelling thighs
> All dimpled o'er with muscle, thew and bone:
> His curly head half-raised was turned slantwise
> Propt on one arm, to let his thoughtful eyes
> Drink in the radiant beauty of the boy
> Who, though his gaze was fixed upon the skies,
> Perceived and thrilled with shy and modest joy –
> The bliss of friendship pure – a bliss without alloy.

That, at any rate, is their story. But they are not alone:

> And I who passed, with well-approving eye
> In silence watched . . .

Perhaps it was these lines that *The Commonwealth* had in mind when it observed that the 'atmosphere [of the poem] is healthy and vigorous, and shows that the author has not only an intimate acquaintance with the ways of boys, but also sound knowledge of how to meet and deal with the minor vices of boyhood'.

Indeed the Rev. Bradford's success was well earned. He was moral and versatile or, as the *Glasgow Herald* put it, the purveyor of 'serene wisdom served in a silver spoon – silver, for there is no mistaking the value of the verse form'. This is true whether he is writing in sub-Wordsworthian vein:

> In a sense a bee may be
> Equal to an elephant
> Seeing she can certainly
> Do a score of things he can't:
> All the same the fact remains
> She has not his force or brains.

or whether he is anticipating the work of Betjeman and Pevsner:

> *Her spacious church is picturesque*
> *Built not in one style but in all:*
> *The nave is Norman Romanesque,*
> *The later choir, transitional:*
> *The tower's a stunted nondescript*
> *In Cromwell's time, 'tis said, 'twas stript*
> *Of parapet and pinnacles;*
> *But still it serves to hold the bells.*

Altogether the Rev. Bradford is a delightful poet and seldom produces a dull page; but he is not a good poet.

C. Day-Lewis 1904–72 Becoming Poet Laureate is not necessarily a guarantee of badness, and much of Day-Lewis's poetry is still read with pleasure and respect. Unfortunately he sometimes got carried away during the period of mutual admiration amongst left-wing poets before World War II. His proficiency of technique, on these occasions, only makes the awful obsequiousness of the message more embarrassingly vivid, as in these lines to W. H. Auden, surely amongst the most fatuous and sycophantic written in modern times:

> *Look West, Wystan, lone flyer, birdman, my bully boy!*
> *Plague of locusts, creeping barrage, has left earth bare:*
> *Suckling and centenarian are up in the air*
> *No wing-room for Wystan, no joke for kestrel joy.*

And the poem winds up with:

> *Gain altitude, Auden, then let the base beware!*
> *Migrate, chaste my kestrel, you need a change of air!*

This is not, admittedly, as bad as earlier exercises in eulogy; we should be glad that this Poet Laureate was incapable of writing:

> *And thou Dalhousie, the great God of War,*
> *Lieutenant-Colonel to the Earl of Mar*

or:

> *Dust to dust, and ashes to ashes*
> *Into the tomb the Great Queen dashes.*

or even:

Along the wires the electric message came
He is no better, he is much the same.

William Wilkie 1721–72 Honourable mention for industry with
uniformly poor results should be made of the eccentric Scots poet and
clergyman, William Wilkie. His *Epigoniad* (1757) consisted of nine
books of heroic couplets in the style of the *Iliad*, and was politely
ignored by the critics, except for one who mocked Wilkie's notions of
prosody. This drew a passionate defence from David Hume; not, to be
sure, on the grounds of poetic merit, but rather because Wilkie 'was a
Scotsman, who had never been out of his own country'. Even this novel
criterion by which to judge the *Epigoniad* and the *Moral Fables in
Verse* (1768) has not rescued the reputation of Wilkie for posterity. He
is better remembered for his eccentricities, which included a refusal to
sleep between clean sheets (he always insisted that his hostess supply
dirty ones), and his habit of absent-mindedly leaving before the end
the services at which he was officiating.

Amanda McKittrick Ros 1860–1939 This remarkable lady was
really more celebrated as a dreadful novelist whom heartless critics
such as Barry Pain and Wyndham Lewis could not resist baiting. Each
hostile review of her work – and they were all hostile – elicited a satisfying volley of abuse from Larne, Co. Antrim, where Mrs Ros resided;
doubting reviewers were labelled 'donkeyosities', 'egotistical earth-
worms', 'evil-minded snapshots of spleen', 'poisonous apes', 'talent
wipers of wormy order', and 'clay crabs of corruption'.
    Despite the regrettable failure of critics to see her merits, Amanda
Ros had her following who savoured her works as masterpieces of
unintentional humour, and read them aloud to each other at weekly
meetings of the Oxford Amanda Ros Society (established 1907).
Aficionados were delighted by the alliterative bang and crash of her
style, and by the names of her characters, of which a representative
sample appears in her novel *Helen Huddleston*; they include Lord
Raspberry and his sister Cherry, Sir Peter Plum, the Earl of Grape and
Sir Christopher Currant, while the maid is given a name appropriate
to her status – Lily Lentil.
    Although she has been called 'the world's worst novelist' (which did
not deter her from contemplating an application for the Nobel Prize
for Literature in 1930), her verse should not be overlooked by lovers of

lyrical bathos. She published two volumes, of which the titles give promise of appealing content: *Poems of Puncture* (1912) and *Fumes of Formation* (1933). This promise is not disappointed: here, for example, are her couplets 'On Visiting Westminster Abbey':

> *Holy Moses! Take a look!*
> *Flesh decayed in every nook,*
> *Some rare bits of brain lie here,*
> *Mortal loads of beef and beer.*

Ella Wheeler Wilcox 1850–1919 The poetry of moral exhortation has never found a more determined or more popular practitioner than Ella Wheeler Wilcox, who had completed a novel before reaching the age of ten, and subsequently wrote at least two poems a day. Her first collection, the appropriately titled *Drops of Water* (1872), promoted the cause of temperance; but it was in 1883 that she first aroused public enthusiasm and moral censure with her less appropriately titled *Poems of Passion*. After that there was no stopping her, and forty volumes of cloudy spiritualism tinged with naïve eroticism poured from her pen.

Unlike many appalling poets, Ella Wheeler did manage to produce some quotable lines which have provided an invaluable standby for the makers of Christmas crackers ever since:

> *Laugh and the world laughs with you:*
> *Weep, and you weep alone*

This is from her most famous poem, 'Solitude'.

Some of Ella Wheeler's titles have suffered from the distressing decay of language that has been so marked in the years since her death, and this renders a few of them open to misconception. 'The Old Stage Queen', for instance, one of her most powerfully felt offerings, ends:

> *She rises to go. Has the night turned colder?*
> *The new Queen answers to call and shout;*
> *And the old Queen looks back over her shoulder,*
> *Then all unnoticed she passes out.*

Another poem celebrates 'The Queen's Last Ride': but this is about Queen Victoria.

Admirers of Ella Wheeler Wilcox will be glad to know of an edition fairly recently published, a selection made by Lalique, Lady L'Endell, described as 'the only edition authorized by [her] for sale in the British Empire' (Arlington Books, 1971).

～

. . . a daisy – and don't you forget it.
Copywriter's line for Walt Whitman's *Leaves of Grass*.
The copywriter was fired.

～

Bestselling Modern Writers

～

As far back as in the time of Rome it was remarked that often books have their own very strange fates: consisting in failure, notwithstanding their high merits, and in enormous success, notwithstanding their triviality.

Tolstoy on Shakespeare,
whose works he regarded with contempt

～

In his interesting study *Bestsellers* (Routledge, 1981), John Sutherland lists the following authors whose collective sales had achieved stratospheric status by the beginning of the 1980s:

Harold Robbins, 200 million
Alistair Maclean, 150 million
Frederick Forsyth, 50 million
Mickey Spillane, 150 million
Barbara Cartland, 100 million
Jacqueline Susann, over 6 million in USA alone
Peter Benchley, over 10 million in USA alone
Richard Bach, over 2 million in USA alone

Maclean is title for title the most successful novelist ever in English. His books notably eschew the love element; when asked about this in an interview he replied briskly: 'Sex? No time for it. Gets in the way of the action.'

Outstandingly Prolific Authors

It is alleged that the Spaniard **Lope de Vega** (1562–1635) wrote 2200 plays, though only 500 survive, and that Dumas *père*'s complete works would run to 1500 volumes. A modern wordsmith who seems to have even the well-known romantic novelists licked is a South African, **Kathleen Lindsay** (1903–73), who clocked up 904 novels, writing under six pen-names. Here is an annotated list of other amazingly prolific writers.

Hilaire Belloc   1870–1953   In 1927 Belloc issued his hundredth title, and wrote to the poet and novelist Maurice Baring: 'The more enormous one's output the more the publishers get to regard you as a reliable milch cow.' Belloc is celebrated for (among other things) the witty couplet:

> *When I am dead, I hope it may be said:*
> *'His sins were scarlet, but his books were read.'*

His industry even attracted the attention of the great E. C. Bentley, who felt compelled to denounce him in the verse form he invented, the clerihew:

> *Mr Hilaire Belloc*
> *Is a case for legislation ad hoc.*
> *He seems to think nobody minds*
> *His books being all of different kinds.*

Dorothy Richardson   1873–1957   One of the most sustained achievements of fictional output is Dorothy Richardson's twelve-volume stream of consciousness novel *Pilgrimage* (1915–38). There are signs that she never really wanted to finish it, for after her death an unfinished thirteenth volume was discovered. To some the work is a worthy predecessor to Joyce's *Ulysses* and the work of Virginia Woolf. Others find it difficult to suppress a yawn as the heroine's self is laboriously unpicked and examined, and the critic Frank Swinnerton wrote: '. . . If I am asked whether I consider such impressionism anything more than a marvellous feat of memory or reproduction, I must answer there comes a moment in which one wishes that Miriam had died young or that she had moved through life at a less even and ample pace.'

Charles Hamilton, alias Frank Richards 1875–1961 Hamilton created Billy Bunter and was so prolific that George Orwell accused him of being a composite name covering several industrious hacks. In his celebrated reply Hamilton wrote: 'In the presence of such authority, I speak with diffidence: and can only say that, to the best of my knowledge and belief, I am only one person, and have never been two or three.'

For over thirty years he produced 1½ million words annually, mostly as Frank Richards but also as Martin Clifford, Clive Clifford, Ralph Redway, Owen Conquest and Hilda Richards; there were nineteen other pen-names. He even had a plan to write a series about a French school with a hero named Raoul — and to write it in French. Although he immortalized and romanticized a public school where boys played up and played the game, and muffins were toasted over study fires at teatime, Hamilton himself had not been to such a school.

∾

I teach sportsmanship according to the British idea . . . I teach that decent behaviour wins in the end as a natural order of things.

Captain W. E. Johns, creator of Biggles

∾

The bulk of my readers are the cleanly-minded, virile, outdoor sort of people of both sexes, and the books are widely read in the Army, the Navy, the Universities, the Public Schools and the Clubs. . . . Although I now make a good many thousands per annum, I still am not a 'professional novelist', nor a long-haired literary cove. I prefer the short-haired executive type.

P. C. Wren, creator of Beau Geste

∾

Edgar Wallace 1875–1932 Wallace wrote over 170 novels and plays and in his heyday averaged six major books a year. The *canard* that he used a ghost writer was quite untrue. He is perhaps best remembered for his novel *The Four Just Men* (1905), a huge success in print and on film, and the inspirer of a TV series. He once wrote a book of 80,000 words over a weekend. In a letter to his wife about the time of *The Four Just Men* he wrote: 'Religion and immorality are the only things that sell books nowadays. I am going to start a middle course and give them crime and blood and three murders a chapter; such is the insanity of the age that I do not doubt for one moment the success of the venture.'

Wallace's devotion to work may well have stemmed from some underlying insecurity. He was found abandoned in Greenwich, south London, when only nine days old and brought up by a Billingsgate fish porter. When he grew rich he ran two Rolls-Royces and used to hire the entire restaurant of the Carlton Hotel for supper parties.

His huge output, which included seventeen plays on the London stage in six years, earned him as much as £50,000 a year, but he managed to die £140,000 in debt. Films, broadcasting and paperbacks cleared the debt by 1937, and thirty years after his death his books still sold over a million copies annually.

Thomas Wolfe   1900–38   In 1929 Wolfe wrote engagingly to his editor Maxwell Perkins at Scribner's, who had demanded some reduction in the vast, sprawling manuscript of *Look Homeward, Angel*: 'My efforts to cut out 50,000 words may sometimes result in my adding 75,000. . . .' Legend has it that Wolfe wrote the novel standing up, using the top of his refrigerator. The finished pages fell to the floor unrevised, were scooped up at the end of the day, crated and sent to the publisher. Wolfe produced 330,000 words, and Perkins asked for cuts; after several weeks he received a manuscript eight pages shorter – Wolfe had made the required cuts, then written another 100,000 words to fill in the gaps. Wolfe got an advance of $500, less 10 per cent for his agent – about $0.00104 per word.

Georges Simenon   b. 1903   Simenon has written over 400 novels, 200 as Simenon and the rest under twenty-three pseudonyms. He was seventeen when his first popular novel, *Au Pont des Arches*, was published under the name of Georges Sim. He has also written over 1000 stories and fifteen volumes of autobiography and memoirs. The Maigret novels, which started in 1929 with *Inspector Maigret Investigates*, ran until 1973 – at one stage he was producing one a month. A 1970 study estimated that his books had sold 50 million copies, been translated into twenty-seven languages and read by 600 million people. He was described by André Gide as 'the best novelist in French literature today'. 'Literature with a capital L', Simenon once wrote, perhaps with a nod at Gide, 'is rubbish.' His prolific output was not limited to words – in his autobiography he stated that he had had sexual relations with a thousand women, most of them prostitutes.

John Creasey   1908–73   This indefatigable thriller writer wrote 565 books (some writers say more) over forty years for a large number of publishers. His pen-names – of which there were twenty-five –

ranged from Tex Riley via Henry St John Cooper to Elise Fecamps. In the single year of 1937 he wrote twenty-six novels.

Romantic Novelists – A Prolific Breed

In *The Purple Heart Throbs* (Hodder, 1974), her amusing survey of the romantic novel, Rachel Anderson gives the following astonishing statistics for some of the leading writers in the field up to 1974:

Denise Robins d. 1985 162 books published; sales of 300,000 paperbacks a year.

Barbara Cartland b. 1901 135 books published; total sales estimated at 14 million.

Ursula Bloom 1892–1984 With 420 books published out of 468 written, she is quoted in *The Guinness Book of Records* as the author with the greatest number of published books.

Earlier romantic novelists were no less prolific. **Ruby M. Ayres (1883–1933)**, for instance, clocked up 143 novels, and **Annie S. Swan (1860–1943)** managed 183.

Catherine Cookson b. 1905 In a class of her own, she sharply repudiates the tag 'romantic novelist', whatever the booksellers' classification of her work may be. An interview by Catherine Stott in the *Sunday Telegraph* of 24 February 1985 (to which I am indebted for these statistics) described her as the 'most-borrowed, the best-selling, and probably possessed of the highest annual income of any writer in Britain'. All sixty-two of her books are still in print. Over 85 million copies have been sold; in the Public Lending Right figures for 1984 thirty-three of her books were in the top 100 most borrowed titles. Cookson statistics are impressive, especially since her writing career, like that of Conrad, only began at the age of forty. Self-made, the survivor of a nervous breakdown and a dangerous bleeding disease, Catherine Cookson is a literary and statistical phenomenon.

~

Those perfectly happy in their affections never read novels, because real love is so much more fascinating than that described.
O. S. Fowler, *Sexual Science*, 1875

~

Men want pure women.
Barbara Cartland, in conversation with Noel Edmonds,
BBC 1, August 1985

~

Six of the Best

BARBARA CARTLAND

These are the books which for reference I have found most inspiring and exciting.

Lesley Blanch, *The Sabres of Paradise*. When I first read *The Sabres of Paradise* I was thrilled and enthralled by her very vivid story of Shamyl, the leader of the Caucasus, who fought the Russians for forty years. It inspired my novel *As Eagles Fly* and years later I was thrilled to find that the Earl Mountbatten of Burma had at Broadlands Shamyl's personal Koran, which the Earl's father, Prince Alexander of Hesse, had picked up on the battlefield. It is a strangely shaped little book which I held in my hands and felt I was really holding a page of history.

Robert Payne, *The Splendour of Greece*. This book has inspired dozens of my novels and I have quoted it again and again, most especially in *Kiss the Moonlight*. Robert Payne's descriptions of the 'light' of Greece are so moving that it made me understand how the Ancient Greeks taught the world to think and how we can still learn from them today.

Sir Arthur Bryant, *The Years of Victory*. Sir Arthur Bryant, who is one of my most beloved friends and favourite author, has inspired me to write and to think with every historical book he has ever written. *The Years of Victory* is perhaps one that has produced more of my novels than any of the others, but every book he has ever written has pride of place in my heart, and I refer to them week by week, day by day.

Christopher Hibbert, *George IV* (two volumes): *The Prince of Wales* and *The Prince Regent*. Here again are two history books which have meant an enormous amount to me and whose descriptions of Carlton House and the Prince Regent himself, with his following, have been of inestimable value. Not only does Christopher Hibbert write accurately — everything he says is true — but he also makes it so real that it is easy to translate into a novel. I have read hundreds, perhaps thousands, of books on this period, which is my particular favourite, and I have never met anyone who writes better or more inspiringly than Christopher Hibbert.

Joanna Richardson, *La Vie Parisienne*. This again is a book I cannot be without and which has helped me so tremendously to understand the beauty, the excitement and the extravagance of the

Second Empire in France. It is so well laid out that it is easy to use as a reference book, and the illustrations are delightful. It keeps authors like myself from making mistakes about what was one of the most fascinating periods in history. I have read all Joanna Richardson's books and I only wish she would write another one set out in the same way as *La Vie Parisienne*.

Barbara Cartland, *The Magnificent Marriage*. I never read any novels except my own. When I feel worried, agitated or upset, I read one and find the last pages soothe me and leave me happy. I quite understand why I am popular in hospitals. When I very nearly died my sons brought me the history books, which I enjoy, but I was too ill to read them. Instead I read my own novels, in particular *The Magnificent Marriage*, 'fell asleep in the Duke's arms' and got well very quickly! The backgrounds of all my novels, for which I read twenty to thirty history books for research, have to be accurate as they are used in universities and schools. *The Magnificent Marriage* is a story of the development of Singapore, which I wrote after I had been there, and every detail of Chinese customs, the pirates and Singapore itself is absolutely correct.

The Top Twenty Translated Authors

The *UNESCO Statistical Yearbook* collects figures for the most translated authors in the world. In 1978, the latest year for which figures are available, the top twenty translated authors were:

Author	Country of origin	No. of translations 1978	No. of translations 1961–70
V. I. Lenin	USSR	413	2354
Agatha Christie	UK	282	920
Jules Verne	France	279	1102
Walt Disney (Productions)	USA	269	352
L. I. Brezhnev	USSR	210	279
Karl Marx	Germany	186	819
Hans Christian Andersen	Denmark	153	611
Barbara Cartland	UK	137	38
C. Perrault	France	136	169
Leo Tolstoy	USSR	136	1063
Mao Tse-tung	China	121	203

Enid Blyton	UK	117	974
Jack London	USA	115	539
J. Grimm	Germany	110	571
Georges Simenon	Belgium	105	1076
William Shakespeare	UK	93	1227
R. L. Stevenson	UK	86	465
Pearl Buck	USA	83	659
Alistair Maclean	UK	83	387
Mark Twain	USA	83	642

Authors favoured by the Russians have a built-in advantage over their competitors in that many of the translations are into the various tongues of the USSR; hence the startling performance of Mr Brezhnev.

In 1978 the Bible was translated 309 times in twenty-three countries (2126 times in 1961–70); the *Arabian Nights* was translated ninety-six times in eighteen countries (288 times between 1961 and 1970).

Lexicographers

Dr Johnson 1709–84 Sitting in the bookseller Dodsley's shop one day, Dr Johnson was cunningly presented with the idea of a work suitable to his genius when Dodsley casually remarked that a dictionary of English would be valuable. At first Johnson was enthusiastic; then doubts, or, more likely, his habitual indolence, began to assail him. After a pause he remarked: 'I believe I shall not undertake it.'

Thus began the great project at which he slaved in solitude from 1747 to 1755. A magnificent plan was produced and addressed to Lord Chesterfield who, however, forgot all about it until the *Dictionary* was nearing publication and he wrote two rather airy recommendations in *The World*. Johnson, full of hurt pride and contempt, then penned his famous letter: 'Is not a patron, my lord, one who looks with unconcern on a man struggling for life in the water, and when he has reached ground, encumbers him with help?'

Johnson's method was to read massively amongst what he considered were the best English authors, and underline every sentence that he wished to quote. The material was then given to assistants who arranged the quotes alphabetically under the head-words which they defined. Asked how he proposed to compile his dictionary unaided in three years, since the forty-strong Académie Française had taken forty years to compile theirs, the old chauvinist replied: 'Sir, thus it is: this is the proportion; forty times forty is sixteen hundred. As three to sixteen hundred, so is the proportion of an Englishman to a Frenchman.'

Eccentricities and prejudice were probably a selling point as much as a drawback for potential purchasers; 'pension', for instance, is said to be (in England) the 'mean pay given to a state hireling for treason to his country'. (Johnson had not yet been awarded his own pension.) It is also hard to resist the definition of 'excise' — 'A hateful tax levied upon commodities, and adjudged not by the common judges of property, but wretches hired by those to whom excise is paid.' (Johnson's father had had trouble with excise officers.)

The *Dictionary* appeared in 1755 in two large folio volumes and maintained its position as the authoritative lexicon of the English language for nearly a century. Johnson received £1575 from Dodsley for his labours and gave his profession an ironically modest definition in the work itself: 'Lexicographer: A writer of dictionaries, a harmless drudge that busies himself in tracing the origin and detailing the signification of words.'

Henry George Liddell 1811–98 Robert Scott 1811–87 Liddell and Scott's *Greek-English Lexicon*, the scourge of schoolboys and a most enduring monument of scholarship, started life as a translation and revision of Passow's *Greek-German Lexicon*. The first edition, of 3000 copies, appeared in 1843. Passow's name was on the title page for four editions. 'Thereafter', says Peter Sutcliffe in *The Oxford University Press — An Informal History* (OUP, 1978), 'Liddell and Scott went hand in hand to eternity.' Liddell was a remarkable Oxford figure who holds the record for length of tenure as Dean of Christchurch (thirty-six years). It was his daughter, Alice, for whom the Rev. Charles Dodgson, alias Lewis Carroll, wrote *Alice's Adventures in Wonderland*. Scott later became Master of Balliol.

A refreshing aspect of Liddell and Scott is that they were not prudes. For many years the *Lexicon* is said to have featured a certain Greek word, which more sensitive editors appear subsequently to have removed, meaning: to thrust a radish up the fundament (a punishment for adulterers in ancient Athens).

Sir James Murray 1837–1915 Murray is the greatest figure in English lexicography, and surely the most industrious. He was appointed in 1879 as editor of the *New English Dictionary on Historical Principles* which he undertook to complete for the Clarendon

Press in ten years; it actually took fifty years, and Murray lived to edit only half of it. *The Oxford English Dictionary*, its final title, was an advance on all previous lexicography and a model for its successors.

Murray's total payment was to be £9000, and he was to send at least 800 pages to the press every year. This optimistic arrangement failed to take into account the unreliability of voluntary helpers who were to read books in search of quotations to illustrate the meanings of words. (The brothers Grimm, who had used a similar system when preparing their great German dictionary, had found that of eighty-three helpers only six were satisfactory.) Some of the volunteers simply scribbled down lists of words that they supposed to have first appeared in the works of a certain author, like Mrs Potts's list of words in Bacon. 'I find in your pages words as old as Hengist and Horsa, words introduced before Simon de Montfort was born, words that Caxton was printing,' wrote Murray to the erring lady. Many of Murray's contributors, however, were efficient, intelligent, educated ladies who were underemployed because of the Victorian reluctance to allow middle-class women to work. Some of them were more than a little taken with the toiling scholar who wrote them such elegant letters, and timidly confessed to remembering him in their prayers. One even left him a legacy of £1000.

Henry Fowler 1858–1933 Frank Fowler 1871–1918 The Fowler brothers are two hallowed names of lexicography, although they had little in the way of obvious academic qualifications for the task of preparing the *Concise Oxford Dictionary*. Henry had been a schoolmaster and then an industrious journalist. He was rather a hearty character, bathing in the Serpentine every day when he lived in London; he was also mildly eccentric and had a recurrent dream of taking tea with Queen Victoria. His brother Frank was a failed tomato grower in Guernsey.

The chemistry of their partnership certainly had beneficial results – *The King's English* (1906) and *The Concise Oxford Dictionary* (1911). Henry on his own produced his bossy masterpiece, *The Dictionary of Modern English Usage* (1926), which is, as one critic puts it, 'sometimes as mannered as the mannerisms Henry set out to eradicate'. Yet it established itself as a most useful reference book; like Dr Johnson, Fowler relieves any potential tedium of the subject matter with agreeable wit.

The Digesta Anti-Shakespeariana

~

With the single exception of Homer, there is no eminent writer, not even Sir Walter Scott, whom I can despise so entirely as I despise Shakespeare when I measure my mind against his. The intensity of my impatience with him occasionally reaches such a pitch, that it would positively be a relief to me to dig him up and throw stones at him, knowing as I do how incapable he and his worshippers are of understanding any less obvious form of indignity.

George Bernard Shaw,
after seeing Irving's production of *Cymbeline*

~

'True' Authors of Shakespeare's Works – the Bacon Lobby

It was the Rev. James Wilmot who first 'discovered' that Shakespeare's work was written by Sir Francis Bacon. Unfortunately he burned his research material as an act of cultural responsibility, but communicated its substance to James Corton Cowell, who reported the discovery to the Ipswich Philosophical Society on 7 February 1805. It was another half century before the flames from this spark began to consume the whole shabby and fraudulent edifice of the Shakespeare hoax. The chief proponents of Baconian authorship were:

Delia Bacon   In 1857 this lady (no relation) published *The Philosophy of the Plays of Shakespeare Unfolded*, in which it was explained that the dramas were coded versions of political ideas and that the Shakespearian *nom de plume* hid the identities of Bacon, Raleigh, Spenser and Sidney. She made one prize convert in Ralph Waldo Emerson and persuaded Nathaniel Hawthorne to write an introduction to her book. Shakespeare's grave contained proof of her theory, according to Mrs Bacon, but though she spent many hours lurking in Stratford-on-Avon churchyard by night, she never plucked up courage to open the grave. She died in a lunatic asylum in Connecticut in 1859.

William Henry Smith *Bacon and Shakespeare. An Inquiry Touching Players, Playhouses, and Play-writers in the Days of Elizabeth* appeared in the same year as Delia Bacon's work. Smith's major catch was Lord Palmerston who, Schoenbaum remarks in *Shakespeare's Lives*, 'towards the close of a long life, rejoiced in three triumphs: the reunification of Italy, the opening up of China and Japan, and the "explosion of the Shakespearian illusions"'.

Nathaniel Holmes In 1866 the first of a long line of eccentric Baconians from the legal profession comes on the scene with this American, who wrote *The Authorship of Shakespeare*. The appeal of this topic for the legal mind seems to be that while most of the necessary evidence is altogether lacking, what there is can be subjected to ingenious distortion based on violent prejudice.

Mrs Windle Holmes was followed by the first of many cryptographers, who demanded Letters Patent from the British Museum giving her exclusive rights to reveal the Baconian cipher. In a postscript to her work Mrs Windle casually added that Bacon was also the author of Montaigne's *Essays*, no such Frenchman as Montaigne ever having existed.

Ignatius Donnelly Mrs Windle's line of approach was greatly enriched by Donnelly in *The Great Cryptogram: Francis Bacon's Cipher in the So-called Shakespeare Plays* (1888). He enlarged the Baconian canon to include, among others, not only Montaigne's *Essays*, but also Burton's *Anatomy of Melancholy* and the works of Marlowe. It was hard to know which to admire more – Bacon's industry or his modesty.

American Supporters There was no reason why the USA should have a monopoly of truth. In 1878 J. Villeman wrote: '*Tout ce qu'il y a de bon dans les drames de Shakespeare, est de Bacon; tout ce qu'il y a de mauvais dans les drames de Bacon, est de Shakespeare.*' All the same, the Americans seemed the most gullible and enthusiastic supporters of the Baconian heresy. Henry James was half convinced by it, and Mark Twain wholly so. Dr Orville Owen, a Detroit doctor, produced five volumes of complicated but absurd analysis. In 1899 Mrs Elizabeth Wells Gallup published a decipherment based on a misunderstanding of the way founts were used in Elizabethan printing. And a Mrs Clark invented a 'dial' consisting of a marine compass superimposed on a clock face with the alphabet written round the intersections. By twiddling the dial you could work out the cipher.

William and Elizabeth Friedman   In 1957, however, the work of the cipher enthusiasts was subjected to a rather penetrating analysis in *The Shakespearian Cyphers Examined*. The Friedmans pointed out, with great tact, that the evidence the Baconians wished to find could indeed very often be deduced from the application of ciphers. Indeed, the work of the cryptologists was miserably incomplete: for example, a study of Shakespearian anagrams showed that the plays were the work of Lewis Carroll, President Theodore Roosevelt and Gertrude Stein.

Sir Edward Durning-Lawrence   A new departure in Baconianism was the work of a British Baconian of sufficient diligence and stature to hold his own with the Americans. Durning-Lawrence's attachment to anagrams and numerology is revealed in *The Shakespeare Myth* (1910). Any combinations of letters that could be found in rough proximity in Shakespeare's text and which, if extracted, spelled either backwards or forwards (or any other way) such words as 'pig', 'hog' or 'swine' were grist to Sir Edward's mill. Sir John Squire played an unkind hoax on the learned paddler of the Baconian canoe. To the paper in which Durning-Lawrence had been expounding his thesis he sent a letter under the suspicious signature of P. O. R. Ker. The letter drew Sir Edward's attention to a quotation in Elizabethanese which Squire had invented and ascribed to Shakespeare's contemporary, Robert Greene. The quotation was pregnant with piggish references and made it clear that Shakespeare was merely the mouthpiece of Bacon. Durning-Lawrence at once wrote in (not even bothering to check the reference) to say that Mr P. O. R. Ker's reference was yet another demonstration of the facts that Shakespearians refused to accept. Like many of his colleagues, Sir Edward was filled with an irrational personal animosity towards Shakespeare, as evidenced by some of his epithets for him: the 'drunken illiterate clown of Stratford', 'the sordid money-lender of Stratford' and 'the mean, drunken, ignorant, and absolutely unlettered rustic of Stratford'.

Other Authors of Shakespeare

Francis Bacon is not the only person who indisputably wrote the works of Shakespeare. Researchers have produced many rival candidates, twenty-seven of whom appear below.

Francis Bacon   1561–1626
Robert Burton   1577–1640
Robert Cecil, Earl of Salisbury
  c. 1563–1612
Sir Edward Dyer   c. 1545–1607
Michael Agnolo Florio (? father of John
  Florio)
Ben Jonson   1572 1637
Roger Manners, Earl of
  Rutland   1576–1612
Christopher Marlowe   1564–93
Sir Walter Raleigh   1552–1618
William Stanley, Earl of Derby
  1575–1627
Edward de Vere, Earl of Oxford
  1550–1604
Cardinal Thomas Wolsey
  c. 1475–1530
The Jesuits

Barnabe Barnes   c. 1569–1609
William Warner   c. 1558–1609
John Donne   1572–1631
Samuel-Daniel   c. 1562–1619
Mary, Countess of Pembroke (Sir Philip
  Sidney's sister)   c. 1555–1621
Robert Devereux, Earl of Essex
  1566–1601
William Seymour   1588–1660
Patrick O'Toole
Anne Whateley (who wrote
  Shakespeare's sonnets); also known
  as . . .
Anne Hathaway   c. 1555–1623
King James I   1566–1625
Daniel Foe
Sir Philip Sidney   1554–1586
Edmund Spenser   c. 1552–99

Unfortunate names seemed to plague the anti-Shakespeare researchers — after J. Thomas Looney, who indignantly refused a *nom de plume* less likely to provoke hilarity, came Sherwood E. Silliman and George M. Battey.

Alert readers will be able to find Shakespeare substitutes in the most unexpected corners of literature. Who would have expected Colonel Joseph C. Hart's *The Romance of Yachting* (1848) to contain a tirade against the plagiarist and pornographer, William Shakespeare? This remarkable work seems to have been overlooked by students of literature; and indeed by students of sailing.

Shakespeare Today

There are 150,000 works on Shakespeare, and new ones are coming out at the rate of over 3000 a year. To keep abreast one would have to read ten papers a day on Shakespeare. An American professor, interviewed on Radio 4 in 1985, plans to put the entire Shakespeare industry productions on a computer to which anyone can apply for information on their special subject.

~

> *Joyce is read as obscene instead of successfully past obscenity: Shakespeare instead of being read as past lust is not even read as lusting.*

> Robert Graves, *Lars Porsena*
> *or the Future of Swearing and Improper Language*, 1927

~

Hidden Talents —
Mystery Writers' Other Roles

~

Generally speaking people are plagued with problems that they are unable to solve. To escape them they pick up a detective story, become completely absorbed, help bring the investigation to a successful conclusion, switch off the light and go to sleep.
Erle Stanley Gardner

~

John Bingham b. 1908   Lord Clanmorris, a retired intelligence officer, Bingham is thought to be the model for John Le Carré's George Smiley.

Nicholas Blake 1904–72   Blake was really Cecil Day-Lewis, left-wing poet of the Auden generation and subsequently Poet Laureate, 1968–72. His hero, Nigel Strangeways, was based on W. H. Auden and his stories are redolent with literary allusion. Day-Lewis also translated *The Aeneid* (1952).

Edgar Box b. 1925   Box turns out to be none other than that coruscating wit, novelist and Democratic politician, Gore Vidal. Vidal inhabits the border country between fact and fiction, or between politics and reality. He once observed (in *Encounter*, 1967): 'It is the spirit of the age to believe that any fact, however suspect, is superior to any imaginative exercise, no matter how true.'

~

The thriller is an extension of the fairy tale. It is melodrama so embellished as to create the illusion that the story being told, however unlikely, could be true.
Raymond Chandler, *Raymond Chandler Speaking*

~

Erskine Childers 1870–1922   The author of that great spy classic, *The Riddle of the Sands* (1903), became an irreconcilable Sinn Fein supporter after World War I, and was subsequently executed by the Irish Free State for treason.

G. D. H. Cole 1889–1959 Margaret Cole 1893–1980 A social-ist economist, G. D. H. Cole made his name with his advocacy of workers' control in *The World of Labour* (1913). He also wrote biographies, notably one of Cobbett (1924). After contracting diabetes in 1931 he took to writing detective stories in collaboration with his wife Margaret, and between then and 1942 twenty-nine appeared. Cole's political career was distinguished – he was chairman of the Fabian Society and Vice-President of the Workers' Educational Association. Margaret Cole wrote a book on Beatrice Webb (1945) and a history of Fabian socialism (1961).

Edmund Crispin 1921–78 Under his real name, Bruce Montgomery, he was a prolific composer who wrote concert material and scores for some forty films; he was also much in demand for radio and TV.

Glyn Daniel b. 1914 A donnish detective story writer (as Dilwyn Rees he wrote *The Camridge Murders*), Daniel is better known as an archaeologist and television performer. However, looking for clues in the past as an academic activity is perhaps not so far removed from looking for murder clues.

Paul Erdman b. 1937 The well-heeled young men who staff international banks sport a 'uniform' – the discreet but expensive suit, the *Wall Street Journal* and *Financial Times* in the expensive briefcase, the BMW (medium-sized model), and the latest novels by Paul Erdman or Robert Ludlum. Erdman was himself a banker and economist, but after being cast as the 'fall guy' in a financial swindle he ended up in a Swiss prison, where he wrote his first successful book, *The Billion Dollar Killing* (1972).

Michael Innes b. 1906 Another don writing with great professionalism in the genre, Innes is J. I. M. Stewart, Reader in English Literature at Oxford. In 1936 he wrote *Death at the President's Lodgings*, and since then has delighted his fans with fifty or more books. He has also written straight novels since 1954, including a five-volume panorama of modern Oxford life, *A Staircase In Surrey*.

Ronald Knox 1888–1957 Knox came from a writing family but was best known as a don, a theologian and latterly a Monsignor. He joined the Church of Rome in 1917 and held various important posts. His great work was the translation of the Bible from the Vulgate, completed in 1950. Though fascinated by the detective genre, he later became afraid that his lighter writing might detract from the prestige and dignity that he felt he should embody as a prominent English member of the Catholic Church, and gave it up. But happily he never repressed his love of limericks, parody and literary hoaxing.

Ivy Litvinov   d. 1977   A curiosity amongst writers of the genre, she was the British-born wife of Maxim Litvinov, who became Soviet ambassador in Washington. The curiosity lies in the fact that her only detective story, *His Master's Voice* (1930), was written under hypnotic instruction. It was therefore, at least in part, the work of the hypnotizer, a German specialist who had gone to Moscow to examine the brain of the recently deceased Lenin.

Gypsy Rose Lee   *The G-String Murders* sounds as though it might be good fun for a rainy afternoon. According to Julian Symons in *Bloody Murder* (Faber, 1972), the tone of this 'cheerfully ribald book about the murder of stripper La Verne in the lavatory with its newly acquired throne . . . is set by the backstage notice: "Full Net Pants. No Bumps. No Grinds. Keep Your Navel Covered."' The celebrated artiste Gypsy Rose Lee published this well-documented thriller in 1941. She wrote one more in the genre, *Mother Finds a Body* (1942), which, says Symons, contains a superb malapropism spoken by a woman leaving a party: 'I'm going. I find the company very uncongenital.' Apparently these two books were not sufficiently money-spinning to tempt the authoress into full-time writing, and she went back to stripping. This can only be a source of regret to her readers. A lady of unlikely erudition and wit, Gypsy Rose Lee also composed splendid off-the-cuff verses such as:

> *To the music of Rimsky-Korsakoff*
> *I could never take my corset off;*
> *And where are the sailors who would pay*
> *To see me strip to Massenet?*

She also once observed aphoristically: 'God is love — but get it in writing.'

My Choice of the Six Greatest Masters or Mistresses of the Detective Genre

P. D. JAMES

Wilkie Collins 1824–89 T. S. Eliot described *The Moonstone* as 'the first, the longest and the best detective story', and certainly Wilkie Collins deserves his place for that book alone. The complicated plot is deftly handled, his characters are real people, he is scrupulously accurate in his descriptions of contemporary medical, forensic and police procedure, and in Sergeant Cuff he has created the prototype of the realistically portrayed professional detective.

Sir Arthur Conan Doyle 1859–1930 Creator of the best-known amateur detective in fiction, the immortal Sherlock Holmes, and one of the founding fathers of the genre, Conan Doyle was a superlative storyteller whose books, although redolent with the ethos and spirit of their age, are timeless in their appeal. *The Hound of the Baskervilles* is typical of his power to evoke atmosphere and create terror.

Dashiell Hammett 1894–1961 Hammett was the most famous, important and vigorous of the American 'hard-boiled' school of detective fiction whose tersely written, cynical and violent books have extended the boundaries of the crime novel and set an indelible stamp on American fiction. His most famous book, *The Maltese Falcon*, is a classic of the genre.

Agatha Christie 1890–1976 The undisputed Queen of Crime, her name is virtually synonymous with the cosy, middle-class, British detective story. Compulsively readable, prolific and highly ingenious, she is outsold only by the Bible and Shakespeare. Her quality is uneven, but at her best she is an unsurpassed fabricator of mystery. *The Murder of Roger Ackroyd* breaks all the rules and succeeds brilliantly.

Dorothy L. Sayers 1893–1957 Detective writer, playwright and Christian apologist, she boasted wit, originality and intelligence which did much to make the 'golden age' detective story intellectually respectable. Her aristocratic detective, Lord Peter Wimsey, arouses passions in those critics who deplore his snobbery, arrogance and omniscience, but he is an enduring creation in the tradition of the eccentric amateur. *The Nine Tailors*, with its powerful evocation of the Fen country, has claims to be among the best half dozen detective stories ever written.

Margery Allingham 1904–66 A brilliant exponent of the classical English detective story whose later novels (her best) are cleverly plotted, closely observed and sophisticated studies of the English scene. She is particularly strong in the creation of eccentrics and in the use of the setting to evoke atmosphere and enhance the plot. *The Tiger in the Smoke*, the story of a manhunt in fog-shrouded London, refutes the common assertion that the great absolutes of good and evil are outside the range of the detective novelist.

H. R. F. KEATING

Choosing, as the little girl sniffing the camellias in the G. F. Watts painting must be thinking, is effing appalling. I have cheated in selecting six by having one list of writers here and another of books by a second lot (p. 108). And I have confined myself strictly to mystery stories (none of your vulgar private eyes). Even so, all the writers and the books I have left out. . . .

Edgar Allan Poe Margery Allingham
Sir Arthur Conan Doyle Rex Stout
Georges Simenon P. D. James

Authors Who Wrote Secret Erotica

Pietro Aretino 1492–1556 Unlicensed jester, gossip, poet and writer of witty plays, Aretino was patronized by the Pope, Francis I, Giovanni de' Medici, the Bishop of Vicenza and the Emperor Charles V. His *Sonnetti Lussuriosi* (1524) was a collection of verses and erotic drawings that demonstrated positions for sexual intercourse. The book was extremely popular and got Aretino into trouble with the Pope, who discontinued his patronage. However, the complaint of the poet John Donne was of a different order: he objected that some positions were missing.

Norman Douglas 1868–1952 Pagan, epicurean and, as a consequence of his sexual preferences, all too often in trouble with the police and thus constantly having to cross borders with undignified haste, Douglas is remembered for his superb travel book *Old Calabria* and his entertaining pagan novel *South Wind*. Not surprisingly, he also wrote two works of erotica, one a book of aphrodisiac recipes enticingly called *Venus in the Kitchen*; and the other a splendid book of outrageous limericks (*Some Limericks*, privately printed in Florence, 1928). Irreverent, scatological and erotic, the limericks are 'ensplendoured' with scholarly notes. These are an extremely funny send-up of literal-minded PhD scholarship long before that lugubrious phenomenon had become so distressingly widespread. As for the limericks, they are among the best of the genre, as an example will show:

> *The frequenters of our picture palaces*
> *Have no use for psychoanalysis;*
> *And although Doctor Freud*
> *Is distinctly annoyed*
> *They cling to their old-fashioned fallacies.*

W. S. Gilbert 1836–1911 Sir Arthur Sullivan 1842–1900
The impish humour of Gilbert and Sullivan was extended to the field of erotica, a fact not stressed in the abundant literature on the operatic duo. They wrote *The Sod's Opera*, among the characters of which are Count Tostoff, the Brothers Bollox (a pair of hangers on) and Scrotum, a wrinkled old retainer. This opera scarcely sounds as if it had come from the author of the Bab Ballads and the composer of 'Onward Christian Soldiers'. There are no records of a public performance, more's the pity.

Anais Nin b. 1903 *The Delta of Venus* and other works from the pen of Henry Miller's friend were commissioned by a wealthy patron. One of the very few straight erotic works by a woman, they are highly professional. Anais Nin and a whole army of impoverished writers formed a porn factory to earn some quick literary bucks. She is probably better known as a stream of consciousness novelist and as a prolific diarist.

Felix Salten (Siegmund Salzmann) 1869–1947 The Viennese critic and writer made his name in the anglophone world with the enchanting children's story *Bambi* (1929) — the tale of an orphaned deer struggling for survival in the hostile woods, later immortalized on celluloid by Walt Disney. Salten, however, despite his impeccable credentials as a provider of sentimental family entertainment, indulged another side of his nature when he wrote an anonymous novel entitled *Josefine Mutzenbacher*. This was the frankly written supposed memoir of a prostitute, and achieved a status in the German-speaking world roughly equivalent to that of *Fanny Hill*. Connoisseurs regard it as greatly superior to run-of-the-mill erotica, exhibiting an exact knowledge and sharp observation of the language and lifestyle of the Viennese proletariat and petit bourgeoisie at the turn of the century.

Algernon Charles Swinburne 1837–1909 A Victorian conspiracy of silence concealed the real nature of Swinburne's sexual preferences. Men such as Edmund Gosse, Max Beerbohm and A. E. Housman had seen the evidence but discreetly shielded the general public from the rather sordid truth. For Swinburne's reaction to the curious public school obsession with beatings administered by sadistic elder boys or masters who were latent homosexuals was to become incurably addicted to them. He was also addicted to the works of the Marquis de Sade, and did not limit himself to the enjoyment of his taste for flagellation in literary fantasy; a house in London's notorious Circus Road was regularly visited, and there the tiny, exotic poet submitted happily to vigorous flogging by two heavily made-up ladies.

The British Museum possesses Swinburne's lugubrious literary tribute to his obsession, a lengthy poem entitled 'The Flogging Block'. The author is sheltered behind the pseudonym 'Rufus Rodworthy Esq.' and there are annotations by 'Barebum Birchingham Esq.'. Two lines will give an indication of the tone of the poem:

> *What a great fleshy bottom, both fleshy and brawny,*
> *As plump as two peaches, not skinny and tawny . . .*

Mark Twain 1835–1910 In 1876 Mark Twain wrote a piece of erotica for his friend the Rev. Joseph Twitchell with the less than promising title of *1601 or A Fireside Conversation in ye Time of Queen Elizabeth*. The American Secretary of State, John Hay, somehow got hold of the manuscript in 1880 and sent it to a friend of his, Alexander Gunn, who proposed to have it printed. At this Hay piously protested – but asked Gunn to save him a copy all the same. In the end the book was privately printed in several countries and became a collector's item.

1601 is as much scatological as erotic, the first part consisting of a long discussion between Elizabeth I, Ben Jonson, Beaumont, William Shaxpur (*sic*) and the Duchess of Bilgewater as to who has just been responsible for a monstrous fart that has polluted the atmosphere of the room. It then proceeds to a discussion of fornication at the court. 'If there is a decent word findable in it,' wrote Twain, 'it is because I overlooked it.'

Authorial Gaffes

There are many instances of authors being the victims of their own innocence. Here are six of the best:

Jane Austen 1775–1817

Mrs Goddard was the mistress of a School – not of a seminary, or an establishment, or any thing which professed, in long sentences of refined nonsense, to combine liberal acquirements with elegant morality upon new principles and new systems – and where young ladies for enormous pay might be screwed out of health and into vanity. . . .

Emma

Robert Browning 1812–89

. . . *Then, owls and bats*
Cowls and twats,
Monks and nuns, in a cloister's moods
Adjourn to the oak-stump pantry
'Pippa Passes'

In the preface to his complete edition of Browning in 1896, Augustine Birrell promised to explain any words that 'if left unexplained' might 'momentarily arrest the understanding of the reader'. Thus he explains such impenetrable words as 'lutanist' and 'fugue'; but not 'twat'. When collecting examples of usage, the editors of the *Oxford English Dictionary* wrote politely to Browning inquiring the meaning he intended for 'twat' in the poem. Browning said it meant a piece of headgear for nuns, the equivalent of cowls for monks. To illustrate his definition he thoughtfully provided the source, which he remembered from youthful reading – two lines in *Vanity of Vanities*, published in 1659:

They talk't of his having a Cardinall's Hat;
They'd send him as soon an old Nun's Twat.

That seems clear enough.

Arthur Hugh Clough   1819–61

The laurels for the best authorial gaffe should surely be awarded to Arthur Hugh Clough, the highly moral poet of 'The Latest Decalogue' and a civil servant who finished up as the secretary of a commission on military schools. In 1848 he published 'The Bothie of Toper-Na-Fuosich', the words of the title being Gaelic. 'Bothie' meant 'hut' or 'booth', and 'Toper-Na-Fuosich' meant something else – Clough wasn't too sure what; he had simply lifted the name from an old map. After a while a Gaelic-speaking friend enlightened him. The phrase apparently meant 'bearded well' and was unmistakably a metaphor for the 'twat' of Browning's seventeenth-century source. The unfortunate Clough was greatly dismayed by this unwelcome information and is said to have lost all pleasure in reading what was probably his best poem.

George Eliot   1819–80

Mrs Glegg had doubtless the glossiest and crispest brown curls in her drawers, as well as curls in various degrees of fuzzy laxness.

The Mill on the Floss

Henry James   1843–1916

'Oh, I can't explain!' cried Roderick impatiently, returning to his work. 'I've only one way of expressing my deepest feelings – it's this.' And he swung his tool.

Roderick Hudson

Dr Johnson   1709–84

That confidence which presumes to do, by surveying the surface, what labour can perform, by penetrating the bottom.

Preface to Shakespeare

∿

Authors have a very feeble grip of reality. . . . .

George Bernard Shaw

∿

Calamities of Authors

~

. . . He is a man of 35, but looks 50. He is bald, has varicose veins and wears spectacles, or would wear them if his only pair were not chronically lost. If things are normal with him, he will be suffering from malnutrition, but if he has recently had a lucky streak, he will be suffering from a hangover. At present it is half past eleven in the morning, and according to his schedule he should have started work two hours ago; but even if he had made any serious effort to start he would have been frustrated by the almost continuous ringing of the telephone bell, the yells of the baby, the rattle of an electric drill out in the street, and the heavy boots of his creditors clumping up the stairs. The most recent interruption was the arrival of the second post, which brought him two circulars and an income tax demand printed in red.

Needless to say this person is a writer.

George Orwell, *Confessions of a Book Reviewer*

~

Orwell describes the usually calamitous situation of being an author. The title of this section is taken from Isaac D'Israeli's vivid catalogue of authorial disasters, first published in 1812.

The following pages include some authors who were imprisoned for their writings; others who suffered an even worse fate will be found in Part V.

Torquato Tasso 1544–95 Tasso's poverty is well known. According to Isaac D'Israeli in *Curiosities of Literature* he once entreated his cat to assist him with his night-time labours with the lustre of his eyes, since he had no candles. Tasso was for some time imprisoned in Ferrara on the Duke's orders because he was supposed to be insane. For seven years he languished, producing a quantity of verse and philosophical dialogues, the fame of which ultimately secured his release when Vincenzo Gonzaga, the Duke of Milan, intervened on his behalf.

Tasso was dogged by the critics all his life, and indeed rewrote his masterpiece *Gerusalemme Liberata* (1575) taking into account critical objections. The result was *Gerusalemme Conquistata* (1593). At the end of his life his sufferings were rewarded as the Pope wished to crown him as Poet Laureate; but he died after arriving in Rome for the ceremony.

Galileo Galilei   1564–1642   Condemned for his assertion that the Copernican system more accurately reflected the realities of physical science than did the prevailing biblical orthodoxy espoused by the Church, Galileo was imprisoned in 1633 and possibly tortured. The Inquisition tried to make his imprisonment permanent – they were especially outraged by his *Dialogo sopra i due massimi sistemi del mondo*, written after he had agreed to refrain from promoting his theories. Later he was released and finished his days at Arcetri above Florence. In prison he was visited by Milton, an admirer, who describes him at that time as poor and old. To add insult to injury, his widow's confessor took advantage of her piety to go through the manuscripts that Galileo had left, and destroy such as he deemed not fit to be circulated in the world.

Theodore Reinking   Seventeenth century   After the Thirty Years' War had resulted in his native country, Denmark, being made subject to Sweden, the patriotic Reinking lamented the subject status of his fellow countrymen in a book entitled *Dania ad exteros de perfidia Suecorum* (1644). Not surprisingly, this was ill received by the Swedes, who put him into prison. After many years he was offered his freedom on one condition – that he literally ate his book first. It is said that he managed to do this after concocting a palatable sauce to help him get the book down. . . .

Thomas De Quincey   1785–1879   After a bohemian, vagrant and drug-taking youth, De Quincey matured into a reclusive, disorganized and unpredictable old age. The latter period was partially eased by the solicitude of his children, who would tell him when his hair or clothing were on fire from the candle – De Quincey never noticed such trifles himself. After a while his papers would multiply to such an extent as to render habitation no longer possible; he then simply abandoned his dwelling and moved on.

De Quincey's arrival in London as a young man and his meeting with Ann, the prostitute waif, are described in *Confessions of an Opium Eater* (1822). And opium was indeed the calamity that helped to ruin him for any systematic literary work – most of his prolix output was occasional writing. He started taking the drug for toothache when briefly up at Oxford, and soon became an addict. In 1813 he was taking between 8000 and 12,000 drops daily (opium could be openly purchased and cost only a few pence); he lost his teeth and was obliged to live on liquids, and his sleep was tormented by horrible dreams. He therefore worked at night or indulged in solitary starlit rambles, and tried to sleep during the day.

De Quincey's finances were chaotic, burdened by moneylenders and absurd quixotic gestures. He was so impressed by Coleridge that he gave the poet an anonymous £500 which he could ill afford.

Fyodor Dostoevsky 1821–81 Many of Dostoevsky's calamities were due to his courageous but imprudent character. Part of his youth was spent in a Siberian labour camp because of his dissident politics; he even faced a mock execution. After his release he soon contracted substantial debts which he hoped to redcem at the gaming tables of Wiesbaden. Borrowing heavily from the Fund for Assisting Needy Men of Letters (a sort of tsarist Arts Council Literature Panel), he set off for the West with an unsatisfactory mistress. Inevitably, he lost at roulette; and then he lost his companion.

Back in Moscow, Dostoevsky's troubles multiplied. His wife Marya died, as did his brother, leaving him a pile of debts, a widow and children. Dostoevsky shouldered responsibility for that family as well as for an extravagant stepson, Pasha.

At this point, he signed an iniquitous contract with a publisher called Stellovsky, giving the latter the right to bring out editions of all his works to date. The author also had to deliver a new novel to a deadline; if he failed to do so, Stellovsky had an option on everything Dostoevsky wrote for the next nine years. On signature of this grotesque document, the author got 3000 roubles; he promptly went back to Wiesbaden and lost the lot.

Dostoevsky was rescued by Anna Grigoryevna Snitkina, who encouraged him and attempted to discipline him. Under her aegis *The Gambler* was completed and handed over to the vulture Stellovsky in time. *Crime and Punishment* followed, and was an enormous success, though Dostoevsky's royalties failed to meet the demands of his creditors. To escape them and his grasping relatives, in 1867 he and Anna began a wandering existence in Germany, Switzerland, Italy and Austria; but he frittered away his money in gambling and quarrelled with his new wife.

Ouida (Louise de la Ramée) 1839–1908 In the late 1860s Ouida's income from her absurd novels reached the dizzy heights of £5000 a year, enabling her to move permanently into the Langham Hotel where she held court with her mother and innumerable dogs.

She surrounded herself with splendidly virile men, having a special penchant for the Guardsmen types that appear in her fiction. After an embarrassing episode at Covent Garden, when she flung a bouquet containing passionate verses at an Italian tenor, she set off for Europe.

Her period in Florence began glitteringly but ended in decline and the now-perennial emotional embarrassments. Probably her best works were produced at this time, since she was writing about what she knew rather than what her girlish fancy had imagined. (One of the more excruciating aspects of Ouida is that her pen-name was chosen from her childhood mispronunciation of 'Louise', a fact that should be sufficient warning to the prospective reader.)

From the 1880s Ouida's life became a succession of misery and financial distress aggravated by the decline in her popularity as an author. There were law suits, which she usually lost, and sordid wranglings with publishers, which gained her nothing. In 1894 she retired to Lucca with a retinue of forty dogs. Friends did manage to obtain a Civil List pension for her – an ironic fate for a novelist whose reputation had been built on breaking the mould of polite respectability in English fiction. She died utterly alone, from the effects of pneumonia.

Ouida's reputation is hard to understand now – Max Beerbohm said she was one of the 'miracles of modern literature' and Wilfrid Scawen Blunt compared her to Balzac – but her readers were attracted by the flamboyance and fantasy gratification in her writing. 'I do not object to realism in fiction,' she wrote. 'What I object to is the limitation of realism in fiction to what is commonplace, tedious and bald – is the habit, in a word, of insisting that the potato is real and that the passion flower is not.'

Edgar Wallace 1875–1932 It is always unwise to offer to the public prizes connected with books – the prizes attract the attention of prize hunters as much as book buyers, as Edgar Wallace discovered. He offered £500 to anyone who could find the correct solution to the puzzle at the end of *The Four Just Men* (1905) – namely who had killed the Foreign Secretary. Sheafs of correct answers arrived immediately, and the pay-out destroyed any possibility of profit on the book.

Six Works of Science

MAGNUS PYKE

The six scientific works which I have listed below have changed irre-vocably the way we look at the world, but only two of them are books. The rest are short contributions which appeared in the periodic 'literature' in which the discoveries of science, great and small, are published.

There are two main reasons why there are so few books. First, it is only rarely that a scientist can foresee the significance of his dis-covery. More frequently, only after other workers have built on his foundations does the importance of his work become apparent. The second reason why great scientific ideas so seldom burst on the world from books is that scientists today are so steeped in the jargon of science that many of them lose the capacity to write intelligible, stylish prose in which to convey to their generation the nature and significance of an important discovery.

Here then is my selection, even if it is mainly of non-books.

Nicholas Carnot *Reflexions sur la Puissance Motrice du Feu et sur les Machines Propres à Développer Cette Puissance*, 1824. With-out this development of the 'Carnot cycle' we might never have had freezers to give us frozen food or liquid hydrogen to fuel our rockets to the moon, and the world would therefore have been a different place.

Charles Babbage Reports by Lady Lovelace of the lectures delivered by Babbage during a lecture tour of Italy in 1822. These lectures constitute the best account of the principles, which Babbage had worked out, of the computer which is revolutionizing our lives today. Although Babbage's principles were sound, his computer, being mechanical not electronic, did not actually work.

John Bardeen, Walter Brattain and William Shockley Nobel Prize for Physics, 1956. The work of these men was primarily respon-sible for the invention of the transistor, from which the silicon chip and all that it comprises developed. This at last made computers possible as well as cash dispensers, robots, quartz watches, American Express credit cards and much else that makes modern life what it is.

Ernest Rutherford *The Newer Alchemy*, 1937. During a long series of fruitful researches at McGill, Manchester and Cambridge universities, Rutherford demonstrated some of the first examples of splitting the atom, which at the end of his life he described in his last book. It is interesting to note that, although his work was the basis of modern understanding of nuclear energy, Rutherford himself never considered it to be of any practical significance.

Charles Darwin *The Origin of Species*, 1840. This is a rare and striking example of a scientist being able to write a book, intelligible to any educated reader, describing a revolutionary conception which shed a fresh light on the world as it is. The book was a bestseller.

A. A. Michelson and E. W. Morley 'The Michelson-Morley Experiment', 1887: *Philosophical Magazine* 24, 449. The Michelson-Morley Experiment is described in physics textbooks, but very few people who consider themselves well informed have ever heard of it or recognize how dramatically it changed our true understanding of the universe. Common sense tells those well-educated citizens that light speeds towards the earth and that, as we rush towards the light, in our flight around the sun the combined speed of the incoming light and the inswinging earth must be greater than when the earth at a different stage of its orbit is flying away from the light source. But what the two American physicists Michelson and Morley, and all who followed them up to Einstein and beyond, showed was that this is not so. The universe is not as uninformed reason would suggest; regardless of common sense, light always travels at the same speed.

Lost Manuscripts

Ultramarine On 2 October 1932 the publisher Ian Parsons parked his Bentley outside the Chatto and Windus offices and went in to make a telephone call, leaving a suitcase in the back seat. When he returned the suitcase was gone, together with the manuscript of Malcolm Lowry's *Ultramarine* which was inside it. Lowry, whose personal life was pretty chaotic, had kept no copy. Chatto undertook to pay him a weekly stipend until it had been rewritten. Lowry set to work, but despite his attempts to recapture his throught flow by revisiting all the places where the original had been written, he soon dried up. The situation was saved by a friend of Lowry's who, unbeknown to the struggling author, had rescued the original manuscript which Lowry had thrown into the wastepaper basket while making a fair copy. When the author revisited the friend on his inspiration-seeking tour, he triumphantly produced this manuscript.

To his credit Lowry did not want Chatto to publish purely out of a sense of obligation after what had happened. There was some uncertainty about the book, and in the end it was published by Cape.

The French Revolution, **Vol. I** Probably the most famous example of a lost manuscript is that of the first volume of Thomas Carlyle's *The French Revolution.* John Stuart Mill, the philosopher, had borrowed the manuscript to write notes on it. Some time later, the Carlyles were interrupted at tea one evening by a rap on the door. When they opened it they found Mill, white-faced and inarticulate, on the doorstep. After a while he was coaxed into explaining himself. He had left the manuscript out and his tidy-minded maid, taking the tattered leaves for waste paper, had burnt the lot. Carlyle remarked forlornly in a letter describing the incident:

> The thing was lost, and perhaps worse; for I had not only forgotten all the structure of it, but the spirit it was written with was past; only the general impression seemed to remain, and the recollection that I was on the whole well satisfied with that, and could now hardly hope to equal it. Mill, whom I had to comfort and speak peace to, remained injudiciously enough till almost midnight, and my poor Dame and I had to sit talking of indifferent matters; and could not till then get our lament freely uttered.

Carlyle heroically set to work to rewrite it, and it appeared in 1837 to much acclaim. Mill offered Carlyle £200 compensation for the manuscript, and Carlyle accepted half that sum.

Crocodile Avid for Literature The sequel to Jack Reynolds's successful and mildly spicy *A Woman of Bangkok*, which dealt with a man's obsession with a courtesan called White Fox in that city of fabled lubricity, failed to arrive on his publisher Frederic Warburg's desk, despite increasingly anxious inquiries. Eventually the elusive author wrote, perhaps truthfully, perhaps to get the importunate Warburg off his back: 'Recently I was crossing the river here (S.E. Asia) in a punt; I had the novel, almost complete, in my despatch case. In mid-stream I stumbled and lost my balance, the case fell into the water, and a crococile swallowed it.'

Dickens and the Railway Disaster The story of the part-manuscript of Dickens's *Our Mutual Friend* is, in fact, the story of a barely averted catastrophe, and although the manuscript was recovered, both it and the author were within a hair's breadth of being lost completely. Dickens had been ill and had taken a cure in France. Revived and relieved, he travelled back by train on 9 June 1864; just outside

Staplehurst in Kent, the train left the rails and all the carriages plunged over a bridge except the one in which Dickens was travelling. After rescuing the two ladies in his carriage, Dickens remembered with dismay that the next part of *Our Mutual Friend* in manuscript was still in the carriage, together with his brandy flask, and he bravely climbed back in to recover these two vital objects. The brandy he then offered amongst the injured. He was later to complete the manuscript — but with great difficulty. He seems to have suffered from delayed shock following this horrific experience, and from that time writing induced fainting fits and nausea. In the autumn he went to Paris and struggled to the end of *Our Mutual Friend* — the last novel that he actually completed.

Seven Pillars of Wisdom The first draft of Lawrence's work was completed in 1919 from notes that the author had kept during his desert campaign in World War I. After the book was finished, Lawrence destroyed the notes. Unfortunately, around Christmas 1919 Lawrence managed to leave the manuscript at a railway station on a journey to Oxford, where he had a fellowship at All Souls. He changed trains at Reading, where he spent some time in the refreshment room, and having put the bag containing the manuscript under the table he promptly forgot it. The author, who had something of a love-hate relationship with his work, joyously announced to friends: 'I've lost the damned thing!' He was prevailed upon to rewrite it, without notes a formidable task. Using his outline diaries and some recently published documentary material, he succeeded in doing so, the manuscript in fact being rewritten twice. Only the Introduction and the last two 'books' had survived the dreadful moment of absent-mindedness on Reading railway station. By spring 1920 the eight lost 'books' had been rewritten and the surviving two revised. Lawrence then revised it further and burned most of the first revision with a blowlamp in Epping Forest. The new manuscript, incorporating a few pages of the previous one, was printed verbatim on the press of the *Oxford Times* in an edition of eight copies. Demand led to a subscribers' edition at the then astronomical price of £90 a copy, in a run of a little more than a hundred. This in turn led to a public edition, in part to pay for the limited one, which had cost £13,000 to produce. Yet again Lawrence revised, and *Seven Pillars of Wisdom* eventually appeared in 1926. It is said that one bookseller was offering the book at £700. The abridged version, *Revolt In The Desert*, came out in 1927 and ran through five printings. Lawrence refused to take any money from the proceeds, which all went to a trust.

Six of the Best

SIR JOHN HACKETT

I look back over seventy-odd years and ask which books have meant most to me in that time, and which have stayed with me longest, as enduring elements of the *mise en scène* in which my own little drama has been played through.

Above everything else is the King James Bible. For as long as I can remember that has been a part of my life. No one day telleth another, no night certifieth another, without some echo from it, good, bad, funny, sad, elegant or ugly. I am certainly not a religious maniac, still less a fundamentalist. I am a Christian, but with some respect for the views of Bishop David Jenkins of Durham, and a pretty regular churchgoer who sometimes wonders whether his observances are not, at least in part, a matter of civility and long habit. My deep and abiding devotion to the Authorized Version might almost be said to have less to do with religion than with other things. But that book is there and dominates the scene.

Next there is Shakespeare. I think of his plays as one book. I read them straight through, some more than once, in four months spent as a fugitive after the battle of Arnhem, hurt and hidden in occupied Holland, rediscovering much that I knew and treasured already and finding much more. If I must single out one play it would be *Hamlet*, as penetrating a comment on the human condition (mine, yours), if from a different angle, as anything done by Charlie Chaplin and Laurel and Hardy. I should like the Sonnets too, but must not be greedy.

Seven Pillars of Wisdom comes next, of which the condensed version, *Revolt in the Desert*, read by me as a sixteen-year-old when the whole book was still a collector's piece worth a mint of money, was the first book I ever read straight through twice.

There are many more contenders for a place on this little list and choice is hard. I have no excuse, however, to omit Plato's *Republic* and Herodotus, which have remained more firmly with me than anything else I read at Oxford all those years ago. I should like to add *Paradise Lost*, the *Odyssey* and Ovid's *Metamorphoses*, but only got to know these well during the latter part of my life. I should also like to put in Chaucer and Bunyan, though a close companionship here had slipped apart by the middle of the century. I feel a little disloyal at leaving out Toynbee's huge *Study of History*, which I read with deep interest and much benefit in the late forties, but then put by in a failure of confidence. I should like to include Maeterlinck's *Blue Bird*, which haunted my childhood and can haunt me still, but dare not for I have not looked at it for very many years and cannot guess what I would find there now.

My last choice would be *Henry Esmond*, read with a thrill of pleasure at Geelong Grammar School when I was fifteen, and with me still. This marvel of lucidity, humanity and grace comes last in my list only because, whatever else found its way there, its own place was secure from the start.

Remarkable Deaths of Authors

Pietro Aretino   1492–1556   The libeller, satirist, licentious poet and hatchet-wielding critic Aretino is supposed to have died of mirth. He laughed so heartily at a droll and obscene adventure concerning one of his sisters that he fell off his stool and struck his head with sufficient violence to kill himself.

Robert Greene   ?1560–92   The dramatist and pamphleteer died after a surfeit of Rhenish wine and pickled herrings at a fatal banquet of authors.

Lord Byron   1788–1824   Byron became ill in April 1824 with a fever brought on, it was said, by rowing an open boat across a lagoon after getting very hot from riding, and at the same time being drenched in a thunderstorm. Harold Nicolson, however, in *The English Sense of Humour* (Constable, 1958) mentions that Byron had a convulsive fit (possibly epileptic) three months earlier. He treated himself with 'enormous quantities of cider laced with insertions of brandy. . . . I cannot believe,' writes Nicolson, 'that in the paludal climate of Missolonghi that was a wise thing to do.'

The poet's death, as had his life, created a sensation. 'It seemed an awful calamity,' wrote Tennyson later. 'I remember I rushed out of doors, sat down by myself, shouted aloud, and wrote on the sandstone "Byron is dead".' A Royal Navy warship took the body to England for burial.

Oscar Wilde   1854–1900   The death of Oscar Wilde in France, from complications of middle ear disease, is graphically described by his friend Robert Ross in a letter. The scene was macabre; the district doctor arrived some hours after the event and inquired if Wilde had been murdered or committed suicide. There was a danger that the putrefying corpse would have to be taken to the morgue because of Wilde's notoriety and the fact that he was living under the assumed name of Sebastian Melmoth. However, 'after examining the body . . . and after a series of drinks and unseasonable jests, and a liberal fee, the District Doctor consented to sign the permission for burial. Then arrived some other revolting official; he asked how many collars Oscar had, and the value of his umbrella.'

Lionel Johnson   1867–1902   The poet and Roman Catholic convert died 'after a fall in Fleet Street', as one biographical entry chastely puts it. Actually he had taken to drink and fell off a bar stool, fracturing his skull. In his most famous poem, 'By the Statue of King Charles at Charing Cross', Johnson wrote:

> *Vanquished in life, his death*
> *By beauty made amends.*

This, but for the bar stool, might have been a suitable epitaph for this nervous, reclusive and talented man.

Rupert Brooke   1887–1915   Brooke died on a French hospital ship of blood poisoning resulting from an infected mosquito bite aggravated by sunstroke. He left his money to three poets – Wilfred Gibson, Lascelles Abercrombie and Walter De La Mare, hoping it would enable them to write poetry and plays. He had been on his way to fight in the World War I Dardanelles campaign, and was buried on the island of Skyros.

> *If I should die, think only this of me:*
> *That there's some corner of a foreign field*
> *That is forever England.*
> > 'The Soldier'

Arnold Bennett   1867–1931   Bennett died from typhoid after drinking water from a carafe in a Paris hotel – in order to demonstrate that the local water was perfectly safe. 'Pessimism, when you get used to it', he once wrote, 'is just as agreeable as optimism.'

II
Books

Nine-tenths of existing books are nonsense, and the clever books are the refutation of that nonsense.

Benjamin Disraeli

~

In the main there are two sorts of books; those that no-one reads and those that no-one ought to read.

H. L. Mencken, *Prejudices*

~

There are no bad books any more than there are ugly women.

Anatole France

~

Six Works of History

JOHN JULIUS NORWICH

For six works of history that have changed our ideas I would choose the following:

Barbara Tuchman, *A Distant Mirror*. Most of us are fairly hazy about the fourteenth century, but after this book we no longer have any excuse to be. Mrs Tuchman is as perceptive and as illuminating when she writes about the Middle Ages as she is on what we have come to think of as her home ground — the turn of the present century and the events leading up to World War I.

Robert Byron, *The Byzantine Achievement*. It is perhaps the first totally successful attempt to rescue the reputation of the Byzantine Empire from the odium which it has suffered since the days of Gibbon. A young man's book written when the author was still in his early twenties, but not a jot the worse for that. If I were asked to compile a list of the six books which had influenced me most in the course of my life, it would be in that too. Why on earth has it never been reprinted in paperback?

Ernest Kantorowicz, *The Emperor Frederick the Second:* a majestic biography of one of the greatest rulers who ever lived. A trifle long-winded and over-Germanic in parts, it does not really do justice to the Italian side of Frederick, the first man, I believe, who effortlessly spanned the gulf between the Teutonic and the Latin civilizations. *Stupor Mundi*, he was called by his contemporaries — and with good reason. Kantorowicz captures his greatness brilliantly, and the sheer astonishment he aroused in everyone with whom he came into contact.

Ernest Renan, *The Life of Jesus*. Christ is seen here as a man rather than as a God: an exquisitely written biography by a superb historian who was also one of the leading Hebrew scholars of his day. A man of reason above all — although he studied for the priesthood, he could not bring himself to take his final vows — he never allows his scepticism to affect the sympathy and compassion of the narrative.

William Prescott, *The Conquest of Mexico*. (I might equally well have included the same author's *The Conquest of Peru*). Another *tour de force* of historical writing — the more remarkable in that the author was almost completely blind. Here is one of the most exciting — and tragic — epics in the whole history of the world, magnificently recounted. The nobility of Montezuma is emphasized as strongly as the courage of Cortes, both of them emerging as men of integrity and honour.

Garrett Mattingley, *The Defeat of the Spanish Armada*. One of the most gripping history books I know, it is written with a degree of gusto that carries one along on its surge and temporarily blinds one to the profound scholarship that lies beneath the sparkle of the style.

~

Ideology wants to convince you that its truth is absolute. A novel shows you that everything is relative.
Milan Kundera, *Comedy Is Everywhere*

~

Six of the Best

IAN PAISLEY

The six books that have most influenced me, both personally and as a politician, are:

The Bible
John Bunyan, *Pilgrim's Progress*
Philip Doddridge, *The Rise and Progress of Religion in the Soul*
John Foxe, *Acts and Monuments*
Cromwell's *Letters*
Thomas Carlyle, *Speeches*

~

The devil's instrument, church's enemy, people's confusion, heretic's idol, hypocrite's mirror, schism's broacher, hatred's sewer, lies' forger, flatteries' sink; who at his death despaired like Cain, and, stricken by the horrible of God, breathed forth his wicked soul to the dark mansion of the black devil!
Sir Thomas Walsingham on John Wycliffe

~

The Bible

Principal English Translations

~

Holy Bible
Writ Divine —
Bound in Leather
1/9
Satan trembles
When he sees
Bibles sold
As cheap as these
>   Early twentieth-century advertisement
>   by William Collins, Bible publishers

~

Seventh Century   The Venerable Bede translated St John's Gospel into Anglo-Saxon.

Ninth Century   King Alfred translated parts of the Bible.

Fourteenth Century   John Wycliffe's Version   As part of his campaign against the abuses of the Church Wycliffe stopped using Latin and began to write in English. By 1384 his translation of the Bible — the first English version, and the first complete one in the vulgar tongue — was completed and widely circulated. Like many who disseminate knowledge which some (in this case the clerics) consider their private preserve, Wycliffe's followers were persecuted.

1526   William Tyndale's Translation   After visiting Martin Luther (translator of the Bible into German) in 1524 he had 3000 copies of his translation of the New Testament into English printed at Worms. The Pentateuch and Jonah followed. Henry VIII's agents seized him in Antwerp in 1535, imprisoned him, and in 1536 strangled and burnt him after a 'trial'. Tyndale's 'crime' was not only that he made the Bible available in the common tongue, but that he went back to the original Hebrew and Greek, rather than translating from the officially accepted Latin of the Vulgate. Tyndale said: 'I will cause a boy that driveth the plough shall know more of the Scripture than thou [an opponent] dost.'

1535 **Miles Coverdale** published in Zurich the first full Bible in English, which was given a royal licence by Henry VIII in 1537. The so-called **Great Bible** appeared in London in 1539, and a second Great Bible, or **'Cranmer's Bible'**, was also edited by Coverdale (1540). The latter was the first English Bible to be officially set up in churches (May 1540). Coverdale's Bible became known as the Bug Bible because Psalms 12:5 is translated: 'Though shalt not nede to be afrayed for eny bugges by night.'

1560 **The Geneva Bible,** the first printed in verse divisions and using Roman type, was published with a dedication to Elizabeth I. Ninety-six editions appeared in England between 1560 and 1640, only eight of which came after the Authorized Version. It was the translation used by Shakespeare, and was popularly known as the Breeches Bible, because Genesis 3:7 was rendered: '. . . and they sowed figge-tree leaves together, and made themselves breeches'.

1568 **The Bishop's Bible** was issued on the initiative of Archbishop Parker. In 1562, under his stewardship, the Thirty-Nine Articles were passed by convocation.

1611 **The Authorized or King James Version** appeared, a revision of the Geneva Bible and the Bishops' Bible in the light of contemporary scholarship. The best scholars in Greek and Semitic languages worked in six groups, two groups each in Westminster, Oxford and Cambridge. It remains the only great literary work produced by a committee, a classic of literature as much as of theology, with a resonance and beauty seldom equalled.

1881 **The Revised Version** of 1881–95 revised the Authorized Version . . .

1952 . . . and the **Revised Standard Version** of 1946–1952 revised the Revised Version for American readers. The bestselling qualities of the Bible had not been in doubt since 1611, but even so it is startling to read that the Revised Version sold a million copies on publication day. According to the advertising agency handling the promotion, the first printing, if stacked in a single pile, would stretch upwards for twenty-four miles – higher than one hundred Empire State Buildings.

Not everyone greeted this blockbuster with applause. A Baptist minister in the Bible Belt burned a copy in front of his church, declaring it to be the 'material of Satan' (the phrase 'young woman' had been substituted for 'virgin' in a passage from Isaiah). And the critics were sometimes dismissive. For example, in the Song of Solomon, 'Thy navel is like a round goblet which wanteth not liquor' (Authorized Version) had been changed to: 'Your navel is like a rounded bowl that never lacks mixed wine.' 'This,' observed Dwight Macdonald in the *New Yorker*, 'disturbingly suggests a cocktail party.'

1961–70 The New English Bible The culmination (and, some would say, the nadir) of Protestant Bible translating. A committee of the Protestant Churches of Great Britain and Ireland produced this limp, spiritless and turgid version. Docile churchgoers gradually had it imposed on them by bishops and clergy who were doing for the Bible what property developers had done for London.

1982 The New King James Version/Revised Authorized Version The Authorized version updated to deal with changes in the language since 1611.

Catholic Translations

1383–1405 The Vulgate The *fons et origo* of Roman Catholic translations of the Bible into English is the fourth-century St Jerome. His version of the Bible, the Vulgate, was edited in 1516 by Erasmus. His many luminous aphorisms are irresistible, such as 'Avoid as you would the plague, a clergyman who is also a man of business.'

Wycliffe's Bible was translated from the Vulgate, though of course Wycliffe himself was regarded as a dangerous heretic by the orthodox.

1582 and 1609 The Douai Bible or the **Reims and Douai Version** was a translation by English Roman Catholics abroad, the New Testament being published in Rheims in 1582, the Old Testament at Douai in 1609.

1945 Monsignor Ronald Knox produced a new translation of the **Vulgate** for Roman Catholics, the New Testament being authorized in 1945 and the Old Testament 'for private use only' in 1949. Knox, a former don at Trinity College, Oxford, wrote detective stories as well as trenchant essays and a parody of Trollope. His mixture of donnishness and sincere faith made him an attractive ambassador for Catholicism and his translation of the Bible was a great success. He wrote in *Let Dons Delight*: 'It is so stupid of modern civilization to have given up belief in the devil, when he is the only explanation for it.'

Bizarre Bibles

Brewer's Dictionary of Phrase and Fable lists, among others, the following:

The Affinity Bible 1923 Contains an error in the table of affinity that declares: 'A man may not marry his grandmother's wife.'

The Camels Bible 1823 Records that 'Rebekah arose, and her camels' (Genesis 24:61). It should be 'damsels'.

The Ears to Ear Bible 1810 Matthew 13:43 reads: 'Who hath ears to ear, let him hear.'

The Fool Bible Printed during Charles I's reign. Psalm 14, verse 1 reads: 'The fool hath said in his heart there is a God.' The printers were fined £3000 (which must make the mouth water of many an author whose work has been mutilated in the press).

The Lions Bible 1804 Contained numerous errors of which the most entertaining was from I Kings 8:19, '. . . but thy son that shall come forth out of thy lions' (for loins).

The Printers' Bible 1702 David complains in Psalm 119, verse 161 that 'printers have persecuted me without cause'. It should be 'princes' − a Freudian slip, perhaps?

The Unrighteous Bible 1653 For I Corinthians 6:9 the words are: 'Know ye not that the unrighteous shall inherit the kingdom of God?' Otherwise known as **The Wicked Bible** (there is another: see below).

The Wicked Bible 1631 Exodus 20:14 records the seventh commandment as: 'Thou shalt commit adultery.' The printer was fined £300, which ruined him.

1782 Mrs Sarah Kirby Trimmer's *Sacred History* was a bowdlerized, abridged version of the Bible aimed at children between seven and fourteen. Mrs Trimmer had hit upon a goldmine. Adults were also keen to have the biblical pill suitably sugared; accordingly she produced a version from which all references to such matters as sodomy, onanism and incest were ruthlessly expunged, making certain sections of the Old Testament (Sodom and Gomorrah, Lot and his daughters) completely incomprehensible.

∾

. . . a moral vulture which steals upon our youth, silently striking its terrible talons into their vitals, and forcibly bearing them away on hideous wings to shame and death.

Anthony Comstock, on erotic literature

∾

Book Firsts

375–335 BC   Oldest known written text, Sumerian papyri written in Aramaic, found near Jericho.

1384   First English vernacular Bible – Wycliffe's translation, of which he himself probably did New Testament and part of Old, completed.

c. 1456   Gutenberg Bible appeared, first complete book printed from movable type in Europe, though *Donatus Latin Grammar* may be five years earlier. Printing from movable type was known in China before Europeans invented it, and dates from fourteenth century. Two claimants to be first ever are *The Family Sayings of Confucius* (1317 and 1324) and *Sun-tzu-shi-chia-chu*, Korea, 1409. An even earlier Korean scroll found in 1966 has been dated AD 704.

First in Europe dated and in a vernacular is *Eyn mannung der Christenheit widder die durken* (Appeal of Christianity against the Turks), probably printed by Gutenberg at Mainz in 1454.

1475   First illustrated Bible, printed by Jodocus Pflanzman in Augsburg.

1477   First book printed in England, produced by William Caxton – *The Dictes* or *Sayengis of the Philosophres*, folio volume of seventy-eight pages translated from French by Lord Antone Erle. Actual date on imprint is 18 November 1477.

1557   First English poetry anthology, *Songes and Sonnettes*, published by Richard Tottell.

1563   First children's book in England – *A Booke in Englyssh Metre, of the great Marchante Man called Dives Pragmaticus, very preaty for Children to read*.

c. 1576   First known autobiography in English: an account of Thomas Whythorne's childhood as a chorister at Magdalen College School, interspersed with songs and sonnets; followed by his career as a music teacher and finally as music master to Archbishop Parker.

1603   First book translated from English into other languages – James I's *Basilicon Doron*, written to instruct his son Henry in duties of kingship – done into French and Dutch.

1605   First printed 'modern' novel – Cervantes' *Don Quixote*. Origins of novel as genre go back to antiquity and examples of entertaining and (possibly) instructive fiction can be found in ancient Egypt, Greece and Rome.

1661–3   First translation of Bible into an American Indian language – by Sir John Eliot, into Mohawk. Later (1832) translated into Chippowa, Algonquin tongues, Massachusetts, Cree and Micmac.

1668   First poet officially awarded title of Poet Laureate – John Dryden.

1678   Joseph Moxon published first part-work, in thirty-eight instalments, entitled *Mechanic Exercises*.

1687   Aphra Behn, first woman novelist and playwright in England, published *The Wandering Beauty*, *The Unfortunate Bride*, *The Dumb Virgin* and *The Unhappy Mistake*. Between 1670 and 1687 she wrote nineteen plays, and between 1683 and 1688 eleven novels, five translations and many letters and poems.

1691   Earliest book reviews – by J. de la Crosse – began to appear in monthly *History of Learning*.

1719   First follow-up to a successful novel: *The Further Adventures of Robinson Crusoe*.

1773   First book by a negro author in English: Phyllis Wheatley, a slave from Boston, Massachusetts, published *Poems on Various Subjects, Religious and Moral* in London.

1786   First book for blind, printed in embossed type – Valentin Haüys's *Essai sur L'Education des Aveugles* – published in Paris.

1807   First book illustrated with lithographs – John Thomas Smith's *Antiquities of Westminster*.

1822   First clothbound book – Diamond Classics series produced in England in red calico binding by William Pickering.

1829   First book in Braille – *Procédé pour Ecrire les Paroles* – published by Louis Braille in Paris.

1833   First dustjacket issued (non-removable, monotone), with Longman's annual *The Keepsake*.

1836   First British author to receive royalties – Charles Knight for *The British Almanac*.

1841   First detective story – Poe's *The Murders in the Rue Morgue*, published in *Graham's Magazine*.

1841   Bernard Tauchnitz starts paperback Collection of British Authors series in Leipzig.

1842   First book set by type-composing machine – Edward Binn's *The Anatomy of Sleep*.

1886   First book set by linotype – *The Tribune Book of Open Air Sport*, New York.

1890s   First bestseller lists printed by London *Bookman*, and from 1895 by *Bookman* in New York.

1907   First novel in Esperanto – Dr Henry Vallienne's *Kastele de Prelongo*, published in Paris.

1932   Book tokens launched in Britain by National Book Council.
1936   Left Book Club started by Victor Gollancz – first book club in England, though in fact merely part of publisher's list.
1937   Readers' Union, first English book club in sense of offering selections from several publishers' lists.

Genesis of a Bestseller

CHARLES PICK

The literary agent, Ursula Winant, telephoned me in 1963 to say she had a marvellous first novel which she thought would be just right for my firm, Heinemann. However, before she sent the manuscript, if we decided to publish she wanted to be sure we would:

1   Publish within three months
2   Print 10,000 copies
3   Pay an advance of £500

We read the manuscript and agreed that the agent had found a superb new storyteller. I rang to tell her so but said we could not agree to any of her conditions. First, we would not want to publish until the following February, eight months ahead. Secondly, we would not print 10,000 copies but 15,000 copies. Thirdly, we would pay £1000, which we thought the book was worth.

Our offer for *When the Lion Feeds* was accepted, and to date Wilbur Smith has written seventeen books with world sales of approximately 35 million. His last book, *The Leopard Hunts in Darkness*, had at the time of writing sold 185,000 copies in hardback and will probably have an initial printing with Pan of a million copies.

By 1985 eight of Wilbur Smith's books had achieved sales of over a million copies each. The most widely read author Heinemann has ever published, at the age of fifty-one he is still writing a new book each year.

~

Wilkins's Coptic Gospels, *published in an edition of 500 by Oxford University Press in 1716, had sold 100 copies by 1760. In 1907 a copy from this printing was on the OUP list at 12s 6d, to which it had been reduced in the previous century.*

~

Six of the Best

SHIRLEY CONRAN

Here are my six books to take to a desert island:

The Superwoman books. Writing them made me much more efficient as I worked out how to be . . . ! In fact:

A rhyming dictionary (at least I can write poetry in the sand).

War and Peace (yes, really).

Collected de Maupassant (best shorts).

No Dickens.

Anthony Burgess, *The Malayan Trilogy*.

A really beautiful art book (the out-of-print Matisse in two volumes — can't remember the publisher but it was £42).

Proust's *A la Recherche du Temps Perdu*, the 1947 Gallimard edition, illustrated by Van Dongen.

∿

My editor told me that the second half of the book needed a damn good love scene, and there is nothing I dislike writing more. Love-making is such a non-verbal thing. I hate that explicit 'he stuck it in her' kind of thing because it is so boring. You can only say 'he stuck it in her' so many ways.

Guardian interview with Colleen McCullough,
1⁵ April 1977, talking about her novel *The Thorn Birds*.

∿

Bank Account Busters — Some Recent Record Breakers

Ragtime: 1976 saw a new record in fiction advances with $1.3 million paid for E. L. Doctorow's novel *Ragtime*, a panoramic novel of pre-1914 America.

The Bleeding Heart: Marilyn French, author of the autobiographical feminist bestseller *The Women's Room* (1977) was a hot property when her next book appeared. In 1979 Ballantine Books paid $1.9 million for it.

The Thorn Birds: Colleen McCullough's saga went to paperbackers Avon Books in the USA for $1.9 million in 1978.

The Devil's Alternative: Frederick Forsyth got a record British publishing advance in 1979 for his novel *The Devil's Alternative* — £250,000. And that was offered on the basis of the synopsis alone.

Princess Daisy: Judith Krantz's pulp novel fetched a record advance at an auction held in New York on 5 September 1979. Bantam books paid $3,208,875 for it. The British paperback house, Corgi, paid $450,000 for British rights.

Earnings from Fourteen Famous Works

In *Literary Byways* William Andrews gives the following earnings (in contemporary value of currency) from some famous works. The price paid for the copyright of 'Lalla Rookh' is given on p. 4.

Hamlet	William Shakespeare	£5
Paradise Lost	John Milton	£5
Northanger Abbey	Jane Austen	£10
The Vicar of Wakefield	Oliver Goldsmith	£60
The Beggar's Opera	John Gay	£400
Tom Jones	Henry Fielding	£700
'The Rape of the Lock'	Alexander Pope	£7
English Dictionary	Dr Samuel Johnson	£1575
The Vicar of Wakefield	Oliver Goldsmith	60 guineas
'The Lady of the Lake'	Walter Scott	£2100
'Lalla Rookh'	Thomas Moore	£3000
Phineas Finn	Anthony Trollope	£3200
Decline and Fall of the Roman Empire	Edward Gibbon	$10,000
'The Village Blacksmith'	Henry Wadsworth Longfellow	$15

Early Bestsellers in America

This list is taken from Hackett and Burke, *Eighty Years of Best Sellers* (Bowker, 1977), with minor modifications. The introduction reads:

> These are the titles, published before 1895, when the systematic recording of best sellers began, which have without question sold a total of a million copies or more through the years. It is impossible to arrive at definite sales figures for most of these because each has been issued by a variety of publishers. Many of these firms are no longer in existence and few accurate sales records are obtainable now, especially for the earliest books.
>
> Prayer books, hymn books, textbooks, and similar specialized volumes are not included in this list, although many of the titles that are included have appeared in school editions as well as in trade editions. The list is in chronological order according to American publication.

The Holy Bible
John Bunyan, *The Pilgrim's Progress*
Mother Goose
Aesop's *Fables*
Oliver Goldsmith, *The Vicar of Wakefield*
Daniel Defoe, *Robinson Crusoe*
Robert Burns, *Poems*
Jonathan Swift, *Gulliver's Travels*
Arabian Nights' Entertainment
Benjamin Franklin, *Autobiography*
William Shakespeare, *Plays*
Washington Irving, *The Sketch Book of Geoffrey Crayon, Gent.*
Sir Walter Scott, *Ivanhoe*
Sir Walter Scott, *Kenilworth*
James Fenimore Cooper, *The Spy*
James Fenimore Cooper, *The Last of the Mohicans*

Johann R. Wyss, *The Swiss Family Robinson*
Noah Webster, *American Dictionary of the English Language* (in various editions)
Edward Bulwer-Lytton, *The Last Days of Pompeii*
Charles Dickens, *Oliver Twist*
Edgar Allan Poe, *Tales*
Richard Henry Dana, Jr, *Two Years Before the Mast*
James Fenimore Cooper, *The Deerslayer*
Charles Dickens, *The Old Curiosity Shop*
Ralph Waldo Emerson, *Essays*
Alfred Tennyson, *Poems*
Charles Dickens, *A Christmas Carol*
Alexandre Dumas, *The Three Musketeers*
Alexandre Dumas, *The Count of Monte Cristo*

Henry Wadsworth Longfellow, *Poems*

Hans Christian Andersen, *Fairy Tales*

Charlotte Brontë, *Jane Eyre*

William Makepeace Thackeray, *Vanity Fair*

Emily Brontë, *Wuthering Heights*

Francis Parkman, *The Oregon Trail*

John Greenleaf Whittier, *Poems*

Charles Dickens, *David Copperfield*

Ik Marvell, *Reveries of a Bachelor*

Nathaniel Hawthorne, *The Scarlet Letter*

Susan Warner, *The Wide Wide World*

Nathaniel Hawthorne, *The House of the Seven Gables*

Herman Melville, *Moby Dick*

Charles Dickens, *Bleak House*

Harriet Beecher Stowe, *Uncle Tom's Cabin*

Charles Dickens, *Hard Times*

Mary Jane Holmes, *Tempest and Sunshine*

Henry David Thoreau, *Walden*

Thomas Bulfinch, *The Age of Fable*

John Bartlett, *Familiar Quotations*

Walt Whitman, *Leaves of Grass*

J. H. Ingraham, *The Prince of the House of David*

Mary Jane Holmes, *Lena Rivers*

Dinah Maria Mulock [Mrs Craik], *John Halifax, Gentleman*

Oliver Wendell Holmes, *The Autocrat of the Breakfast Table*

Charles Dickens, *A Tale of Two Cities*

Mrs Henry Wood, *East Lynne*

Jakob and Wilhelm Grimm, *Fairy Tales*

George Eliot, *Silas Marner*

Victor Hugo, *Les Misérables*

Mary Elizabeth Braddon, *Lady Audley's Secret*

Mrs E. D. E. N. Southworth, *Ishmael*

Mrs E. D. E. N. Southworth, *Self-Raised* or *Out of the Depths*

Mary Mapes Dodge, *Hans Brinker and His Silver Skates*

Augusta J. Evans, *St Elmo*

Edward Everett Hale, *The Man Without a Country*

Lewis Carroll, *Alice's Adventures in Wonderland*

Louisa May Alcott, *Little Women*

Edward Fitzgerald (trans.), *The Rubaiyat of Omar Khayyam*

Thomas Bailey Aldrich, *The Story of a Bad Boy*

Louisa May Alcott, *Little Men*

E. P. Roe, *Barriers Burned Away*

Mary Baker Eddy, *Science and Health with Key to the Scriptures*

Thomas Hardy, *The Return of the Native*

Mark Twain, *The Adventures of Tom Sawyer*

Cardinal Gibbons, *The Faith of Our Fathers*

Lew Wallace, *Ben-Hur*

Emile Zola, *Nana*

Gustave Flaubert, *Madame Bovary*

Margaret Sidney, *Five Little Peppers and How They Grew*

James Whitcombe Riley, *Poems*

Johanna Spyri, *Heidi*

Robert Louis Stevenson, *Treasure Island*

Robert Louis Stevenson, *A Child's Garden of Verses*

Mark Twain, *The Adventures of Huckleberry Finn*

Leo Tolstoy, *War and Peace*

Kate Douglas Wiggin, *The Birds' Christmas Carol*

H. Rider Haggard, *She*

Marie Corelli, *Thelma*

Mrs Humphry Ward, *Robert Elsmere*

Guy de Maupassant, *Stories*

Rudyard Kipling, *Barrack-Room Ballads*

Anna Sewell, *Black Beauty*

Rudyard Kipling, *Plain Tales from the Hills*

Jerome K. Jerome, *Three Men in a Boat*

A. Conan Doyle, *The Adventures of Sherlock Holmes*

Ellen G. White, *Steps to Christ*

Marshall Saunders, *Beautiful Joe*

William H. Harvey, *Coin's Financial School*

Hannah Whitall Smith, *The Christian's Secret of a Happy Life*

George du Maurier, *Trilby*

John Cleland, *Memoirs of a Woman of Pleasure (Fanny Hill)*

US Bestsellers 1895–1975: Combined Hardback and Paperback Sales

This list, also from *Eighty Years of Best Sellers*, is arranged in descending order of copies sold:

> This overall list of best sellers includes books published in the United States from 1895 through 1973 which have, over 80 years, sold at least 2,000,000 copies. The books on this list qualified when their hardbound and paperbound sales were combined. New Bible translations are not included but some new dictionaries are. Pamphlets are not included nor are encyclopedias, hymnals, prayer books, textbooks, picture books, and game books.
>
> The date of original publication [in the USA] follows the author's name. 'F' indicates fiction and 'J' indicates children's books.

	Title	Author	Year	Sales
	Pocket Book of Baby and Child Care	Benjamin Spock	1946	23,285,000
	Better Homes and Gardens Cook Book		1930	18,685,976
	Webster's New World Dictionary of the American Language			18,500,000
	The Guinness Book of World Records	Norris and Ross McWhirter	1962	16,457,000
	Betty Crocker's Cookbook		1950	13,000,000
F	The Godfather	Mario Puzo	1969	12,140,000
F	The Exorcist	William Blatty	1971	11,702,097
F	To Kill a Mockingbird	Harper Lee	1960	11,113,909
	Pocket Atlas		1917	11,000,000
F	Peyton Place	Grace Metalious	1956	10,672,302
	English-Spanish, Spanish-English Dictionary	Carlos Castillo and Otto F. Bond	1948	10,187,000
F	Love Story	Erich Segal	1970	9,905,627
F	Valley of the Dolls	Jacqueline Susann	1966	9,500,000
F	Jaws	Peter Benchley	1974	9,475,418
F	Jonathan Livingstone Seagull	Richard Bach	1970	9,055,000
	The Joy of Cooking	Irma S. Rombauer and Marion Rombauer Becker	1931	8,992,700
	The Sensuous Woman	'J'	1969	8,814,662
F	Gone with the Wind	Margaret Mitchell	1936	8,630,000
	New American Roget's College Thesaurus in Dictionary Form			8,442,200
	The Dell Crossword Dictionary	Kathleen Rafferty	1964	8,292,951
F	God's Little Acre	Erskine Caldwell	1933	8,258,400
F	1984	George Orwell	1949	8,147,629
	Everything You Always Wanted to Know about Sex but Were Afraid to Ask	David Reuben	1969	8,000,000
F	In His Steps	Charles Monroe Sheldon	1897	8,000,000 (est.)
	The American Heritage Dictionary of the English Language		1969	7,485,207
	Larousse French-English, English-French Dictionary		1961	7,340,000
	Mythology	Edith Hamilton	1930	7,272,600
F	The Carpetbaggers	Harold Robbins	1961	7,171,841
F	The Happy Hooker	Xaviera Hollander	1972	7,141,156
F	Animal Farm	George Orwell	1946	7,070,892
	Roget's Pocket Thesaurus		1923	7,020,000

	The Late Great Planet Earth	Hal Lindsey and C. C. Carlson	1970	7,000,000
	The New American Webster Handy College Dictionary			6,921,300
	How to Win Friends and Influence People	Dale Carnegie	1937	6,578,314
F	Lady Chatterley's Lover	D. H. Lawrence	1932	6,326,470
	30 Days to a More Powerful Vocabulary	Wilfred J. Funk and Norman Lewis	1942	6,299,161
	Chariots of the Gods?	Erich von Däniken	1970	6,200,000
F	Catch-22	Joseph Heller	1961	6,113,000
F	I, The Jury	Mickey Spillane	1947	6,096,700
F	The Great Gatsby	F. Scott Fitzgerald	1925	6,036,000
	I'm OK, You're OK	Thomas Harris	1969	6,005,000
	The Prophet	Kahlil Gibran	1923	6,000,000
	101 Famous Poems	R. J. Cook (comp.)	1916	6,000,000 (est.)
F	The Catcher in the Rye	J. D. Salinger	1951	5,985,626
J	Green Eggs and Ham	Dr Seuss	1960	5,940,776
J	One Fish, Two Fish, Red Fish, Blue Fish	Dr Seuss	1960	5,842,024
J	Hop on Pop	Dr Seuss	1963	5,814,101
F	The Big Kill	Mickey Spillane	1951	5,699,000
F	Rich Man, Poor Man	Irwin Shaw	1970	5,689,545
J	Dr Seuss's ABC	Dr Seuss	1963	5,648,193
	Doctor's Quick Weight Loss Diet	Irving Stillman and S. S. Baker	1967	5,608,491
F	Airport	Arthur Hailey	1968	5,474,949
F	Exodus	Leon Uris	1958	5,473,710
J	The Cat in the Hat	Dr Seuss	1957	5,394,741
F	My Gun Is Quick	Mickey Spillane	1950	5,296,000
F	One Lonely Night	Mickey Spillane	1951	5,274,900
F	Kiss Me, Deadly	Mickey Spillane	1952	5,259,100
F	The Long Wait	Mickey Spillane	1951	5,245,600
	The Diary of a Young Girl	Anne Frank	1952	5,213,441
	The Power of Positive Thinking	Norman Vincent Peale	1952	5,205,000
F	Vengeance Is Mine	Mickey Spillane	1959	5,176,300
F	Fear of Flying	Erica Jong	1973	5,072,800
F	Doctor Zhivago	Boris Pasternak	1958	5,010,520
	Modern World Atlas		1922	5,000,000
J	The Wonderful Wizard of Oz	L. Frank Baum	1900	5,000,000 (est.)
	Black Like Me	John H. Griffin	1961	4,918,479
F	I Never Promised You a Rose Garden	Joanne Greenberg	1964	4,913,100
F	Mandingo	Kyle Onstott	1957	4,905,000
	The Pocket Cook Book	Elizabeth Woody	1942	4,900,000
F	Never Love a Stranger	Harold Robbins	1948	4,854,180
F	The Adventurers	Harold Robbins	1966	4,847,000

F	*Tragic Ground*	Erskine Caldwell	1944	4,810,418
F	*The Ugly American*	William J. Lederer and Eugene L. Burdick	1958	4,794,776
	Profiles in Courage	John F. Kennedy	1956	4,784,324
F	*Once Is Not Enough*	Jacqueline Susann	1973	4,756,000
J	*Charlotte's Web*	E. B. White	1952	4,670,516
F	*The Good Earth*	Pearl S. Buck	1931	4,635,500
	The Sensuous Man	'M'	1971	4,572,877
F	*The Love Machine*	Jacqueline Susan	1969	4,493,000
	Folk Medicine	D. C. Jarvis	1958	4,488,000
	Let's Eat Right to Keep Fit	Adelle Davis	1954	4,446,200
F	*Rosemary's Baby*	Ira Levin	1967	4,411,055
F	*Return to Peyton Place*	Grace Metalious	1959	4,400,000
	Psycho-Cybernetics	Maxwell Maltz	1961	4,350,000
	RCAF Exercise Book		1962	4,330,000
	In Cold Blood	Truman Capote	1966	4,243,338
	Future Shock	Alvin Toffler	1971	4,213,585
F	*Thunderball*	Ian Fleming	1965	4,211,700
F	*79 Park Avenue*	Harold Robbins	1955	4,185,592
F	*The Other Side of Midnight*	Sidney Sheldon	1973	4,134,281
	The Boston Cooking School Cook Book	Fannie Farmer	1896	4,100,000
F	*The Winthrop Woman*	Anya Seton	1958	4,080,016
F	*Up the Down Staircase*	Bel Kaufman	1965	4,046,319
	A Message to Garcia	Elbert Hubbard	1898	4,000,000 (est.)
F	*Where Love Has Gone*	Harold Robbins	1962	3,976,000
F	*Hawaii*	James A. Michener	1959	3,913,341
F	*Journeyman*	Erskine Caldwell	1935	3,910,155
	Here Comes Snoopy	Charles M. Schulz	1973	3,900,000
F	*Portnoy's Complaint*	Philip Roth	1969	3,866,488
	The Greatest Story Ever Told	Fulton Oursler	1949	3,858,948
	Kids Say the Darndest Things!	Art Linkletter	1957	3,821,608
F	*Christy*	Catherine Marshall	1967	3,797,732
F	*Tobacco Road*	Erskine Caldwell	1932	3,756,796
F	*Goldfinger*	Ian Fleming	1959	3,747,000
F	*The Robe*	Lloyd C. Douglas	1942	3,724,391
F	*Lost Horizon*	James Hilton	1935	3,714,210
	Good Ol' Snoopy	Charles M. Schulz	1973	3,650,000
	Helter Skelter	Vincent Bugliosi and Curt Gentry	1974	3,650,000
F	*From Here to Eternity*	James Jones	1951	3,646,004
F	*Lolita*	Vladimir Nabokov	1958	3,633,467
	Love without Fear	Eustace Chesser	1949	3,627,900
	Better Homes and Gardens Meat Cook Book		1959	3,609,105
	All This and Snoopy, Too	Charles M. Schulz	1973	3,600,000

F	*The Other*	Thomas Tryon	1971	3,594,693
F	*Trouble in July*	Erskine Caldwell	1940	3,593,268
F	*Centennial*	James A. Michener	1974	3,591,763
F	*Butterfield 8*	John O'Hara	1935	3,577,729
	Xaviera	Xaviera Hollander	1973	3,572,000
F	*The Case of the Sulky Girl*	Erle Stanley Gardner	1933	3,564,334
F	*Mutiny on the Bounty*	Charles Nordhoff and James Norman Hall	1932	3,556,694
	The American Woman's Cook Book	Ruth Berolzheimer (ed.)	1939	3,549,276
F	*Duel in the Sun*	Niven Busch	1944	3,501,866
F	*Georgia Boy*	Erksine Caldwell	1943	3,501,281
	Four Days	American Heritage and UPI	1964	3,500,000
F	*The Case of the Lucky Legs*	Erle Stanley Gardner	1934	3,499,948
F	*The Arrangement*	Elia Kazan	1967	3,485,000
	Sybil	Flora R. Schreiber	1973	3,472,000
	Games People Play	Eric Berne	1965	3,470,000
F	*Pocket Book of Short Stories*	M. E. Speare (ed.)	1941	3,445,000
	Langenscheidt's German-English, English-German Dictionary		1960	3,440,000
F	*On Her Majesty's Secret Service*	Ian Fleming	1963	3,438,700
J	*The Cat in the Hat Comes Back*	Dr Seuss	1958	3,431,917
F	*The Razor's Edge*	W. Somerset Maugham	1944	3,430,505
F	*All Quiet on the Western Front*	Erich Maria Remarque	1929	3,425,000
F	*A Stone for Danny Fisher*	Harold Robbins	1952	3,409,391
F	*A House in the Uplands*	Erskine Caldwell	1946	3,408,361
F	*The Betsy*	Harold Robbins	1971	3,366,200
F	*From Russia with Love*	Ian Fleming	1957	3,365,100
F	*Couples*	John Updike	1968	3,330,858
F	*You Only Live Twice*	Ian Fleming	1964	3,283,000
	An Analysis of the Kinsey Report	Donald P. Geddes and Enid Currie (ed.)	1954	3,246,300
F	*Doctor No*	Ian Fleming	1958	3,239,500
F	*The Group*	Mary McCarthy	1963	3,230,047
F	*The Green Berets*	Robin Moore	1965	3,200,000
	It's for You, Snoopy	Charles M. Schulz	1973	3,200,000
	Let's Face It, Charlie Brown	Charles M. Schulz	1973	3,200,000
	We Love You, Snoopy	Charles M. Schulz	1973	3,200,000
	Better Homes and Gardens Baby Book		1943	3,180,808
F	*The Chinese Room*	Vivian Connell	1942	3,171,512

F	*The Vixens*	Frank Yerby	1947	3,170,056
F	*The Royal Box*	Frances Parkinson Keyes	1954	3,156,000
F	*The Dream Merchants*	Harold Robbins	1949	3,150,738
F	*The Case of the Haunted Husband*	Erle Stanley Gardner	1941	3,127,585
	Between Parent and Child	Haim G. Ginott	1965	3,108,677
F	*Captains and the Kings*	Taylor Caldwell	1972	3,105,045
F	*Anatomy of a Murder*	Robert Traver	1958	3,100,000
F	*The Case of the Curious Bride*	Erle Stanley Gardner	1934	3,077,368
F	*Casino Royale*	Ian Fleming	1953	3,037,253
	The Conscience of a Conservative	Barry Goldwater	1960	3,007,000
F	*Tropic of Cancer*	Henry Miller	1961	3,002,000
	Grosset Webster Dictionary		1956	3,000,000
	Hailey's Bible Handbook		1927	3,000,000
	The Story of the Bible	Jesse Lyman Hurlbut	1904	3,000,000
F	*The Red Badge of Courage*	Stephen Crane	1896	3,000,000 (est.)
F	*The Summer of '42*	Herman Raucher	1971	2,995,291
F	*Magnificent Obsession*	Lloyd C. Douglas	1929	2,974,030
F	*The Cardinal*	Henry Morton Robinson	1950	2,950,807
	Better Homes and Gardens Family Medical Guide		1964	2,941,443
	The I Hate to Cook Book	Peg Bracken	1960	2,929,782
F	*Forever Amber*	Kathleen Winsor	1944	2,925,268
F	*The Case of the Velvet Claws*	Erle Stanley Gardner	1933	2,924,756
F	*The Sure Hand of God*	Erskine Caldwell	1947	2,911,666
F	*The Case of the Rolling Bones*	Erle Stanley Gardner	1939	2,908,964
F	*The Fountainhead*	Ayn Rand	1943	2,905,109
	Hey, Peanuts	Charles M. Schulz	1973	2,900,000
F	*The Pirate*	Harold Robbins	1974	2,900,000
	Alive	Piers Paul Read	1974	2,884,368
F	*Live and Let Die*	Ian Fleming	1954	2,883,400
F	*Moonraker*	Ian Fleming	1955	2,877,500
	The Rise and Fall of the Third Reich	William L. Shirer	1960	2,872,000
	The Hidden Persuaders	Vance Packard	1957	2,867,523
F	*The Agony and the Ecstasy*	Irving Stone	1961	2,866,718
F	*The Case of the Silent Partner*	Erle Stanley Gardner	1940	2,850,904
	Fun with Peanuts	Charles M. Schulz	1973	2,850,000
	Good Grief, Charlie Brown	Charles M. Schulz	1973	2,850,000
F	*For Your Eyes Only*	Ian Fleming	1960	2,848,800
F	*The Case of the Counterfeit Eye*	Erle Stanley Gardner	1935	2,847,765
F	*Rebecca*	Daphne du Maurier	1938	2,820,313

F	*Tales of the South Pacific*	James Michener	1947	2,817,394
	The Total Woman	Marabel Morgan	1973	2,817,000
F	*The Naked and the Dead*	Norman Mailer	1948	2,816,662
F	*The Chapman Report*	Irving Wallace	1960	2,812,500
J	*The Little Prince*	Antoine de Saint-Exupéry	1943	2,811,478
F	*Never Leave Me*	Harold Robbins	1954	2,802,263
	Very Funny, Charlie Brown	Charles M. Schulz	1973	2,800,000
	Let's Get Well	Adelee Davis	1954	2,799,110
F	*The Spy Who Loved Me*	Ian Fleming	1962	2,798,400
	See Here, Private Hargrove	Marion Hargrove	1942	2,786,223
F	*The Case of the Caretaker's Cat*	Erle Stanley Gardner	1935	2,783,403
	Please Don't Eat the Daisies	Jean Kerr	1957	2,778,988
F	*The Best of Everything*	Rona Jaffe	1959	2,760,000
F	*The Case of the Substitute Face*	Erle Stanley Gardner	1938	2,750,710
	The Service Cook Book	Ida Bailey Allen	1933	2,750,000
	The Gulag Archipelago, I	Alexander Solzhenitsyn	1974	2,742,331
F	*The Case of the Baited Hook*	Erle Stanley Gardner	1940	2,737,397
J	*The Little House on the Prairie*	Laura Ingalls Wilder	1953 ed.	2,732,666
	The Pocket Book of Verse	M. E. Speare (ed.)	1940	2,719,500
F	*Around the World with Auntie Mame*	Patrick Dennis	1958	2,716,816
F	*The Foxes of Harrow*	Frank Yerby	1946	2,702,597
F	*The Case of the Stuttering Bishop*	Erle Stanley Gardner	1936	2,702,363
	Here Comes Charlie Brown	Charles M. Schulz	1973	2,700,000
F	*The French Lieutenant's Woman*	John Fowles	1969	2,696,400
F	*The Source*	James A. Michener	1965	2,687,734
F	*On the Beach*	Nevil Shute	1957	2,680,597
F	*Brave New World*	Aldous Huxley	1932	2,672,065
F	*Not as a Stranger*	Morton Thompson	1954	2,667,977
F	*Diamonds Are Forever*	Ian Fleming	1956	2,664,400
F	*The Odessa File*	Frederick Forsyth	1972	2,648,411
F	*The Case of the Sleepwalker's Niece*	Erle Stanley Gardner	1936	2,646,024
	Let's Cook It Right	Adelle Davis	1947	2,640,612
	Comparative World Atlas		1948	2,630,000
F	*The Inheritors*	Harold Robbins	1969	2,619,000
	Better Homes and Gardens Casserole Cook Book		1961	2,613,948
F	*Battle Cry*	Leon Uris	1953	2,611,000
F	*Of Human Bondage*	W. Somerset Maugham	1915	2,609,236
F	*Drum*	Kyle Onstott	1962	2,605,000

F	*Wheels*	Arthur Hailey	1971	2,604,614
F	*The Case of the Half-Wakened Wife*	Erle Stanley Gardner	1945	2,604,336
	Better Homes and Gardens New Garden Book		1951	2,601,288
	For the Love of Peanuts	Charles M. Schulz	1973	2,600,000
F	*The Case of the Black-Eyed Blonde*	Erle Stanley Gardner	1944	2,588,757
	The Weight Watchers' Program Cookbook	Jean Nidetch	1968	2,575,000
F	*The Glorious Pool*	Thorne Smith	1934	2,572,945
	Charlie Brown's All-Stars	Charles M. Schulz	1973	2,568,600
	Columbia Viking Desk Encyclopedia		1953	2,565,899
F	*Topper*	Thorne Smith	1926	2,560,806
	What Next, Charlie Brown	Charles M. Schulz	1973	2,550,000
F	*This Very Earth*	Erskine Caldwell	1948	2,546,252
F	*The Drifters*	James A. Michener	1971	2,528,342
	More Dennis the Menace	Hank Ketcham	1953	2,527,459
J	*The Little House in the Big Woods*	Laura Ingalls Wilder	1953 ed.	2,527,203
	The Nun's Story	Kathryn Hulme	1956	2,521,531
	Papillon	Henri Charrière	1970	2,510,000
	House Plants	Sunset Editors	1968	2,500,000
F	*Women's Barracks*	Tereska Torres	1950	2,500,000
F	*A Tree Grows in Brooklyn*	Betty Smith	1943	2,487,740
F	*The Case of the Dangerous Dowager*	Erle Stanley Gardner	1937	2,485,874
	Better Homes and Gardens Handyman's Book		1951	2,478,431
F	*The Case of the Lame Canary*	Erle Stanley Gardner	1937	2,476,145
	How to Stop Worrying and Start Living	Dale Carnegie	1948	2,471,140
	The Greening of America	Charles A. Reich	1971	2,462,982
	Honor Thy Father	Gay Talese	1971	2,462,000
F	*Advise and Consent*	Allen Drury	1959	2,456,718
F	*Fail-Safe*	Eugene Burdick and Harvey Wheeler	1962	2,452,000
	You Are Too Much, Charlie Brown	Charles M. Schulz	1973	2,450,000
	Dennis the Menace: Household Hurricane	Hank Ketcham	1957	2,434,336
F	*No Time for Sergeants*	Mac Hyman	1954	2,433,154
J	*My First Atlas*		1959	2,431,000
F	*So Well Remembered*	James Hilton	1945	2,414,460
	The Naked Ape	Desmond Morris	1967	2,411,136
	Betty Crocker's Good and Easy Cookbook		1954	2,400,000
F	*The Chosen*	Chaim Potok	1968	2,400,000

	I'll Cry Tomorrow	Lillian Roth, Mike Connolly and Gerold Frank	1954	2,400,000
	You're a Winner, Charlie Brown	Charles M. Schulz	1973	2,400,000
F	*The New Centurions*	Joseph Wambaugh	1970	2,382,316
	English through Pictures (The Pocket Book of Basic English)	I. A. Richards and C. M. Gibson	1945	2,380,000
	Scholastic World Atlas		1960	2,370,000
F	*The Jungle*	Upton Sinclair	1906	2,367,600
J	*Love and the Facts of Life*	Evelyn Duvall and Sylvanus Duvall	1950	2,360,000
F	*Singing Guns*	Max Brand	1938	2,360,000
F	*The Day of the Jackal*	Frederick Forsyth	1971	2,357,926
F	*Pavilion of Women*	Pearl S. Buck	1946	2,353,453
	Better Homes and Gardens Salad Book		1958	2,341,060
F	*The Passionate Witch*	Thorne Smith	1941	2,330,645
F	*Cannery Row*	John Steinbeck	1945	2,330,000
J	*Egermeier's Bible Story Book*	Elsie E. Egermeier	1923	2,326,577
	All the President's Men	Carl Bernstein and Bob Woodward	1974	2,320,000
F	*Strange Fruit*	Lillian Smith	1944	2,318,230
F	*B.F.'s Daughter*	John P. Marquand	1946	2,316,989
	Serpico	Peter Maas	1973	2,315,000
F	*The Crazy Ladies*	Joyce Elbert	1970	2,315,000
F	*The Pearl*	John Steinbeck	1947	2,310,000
F	*The Damned*	John D. MacDonald	1974	2,300,000
	We're on Your Side, Charlie Brown	Charles M. Schulz	1973	2,300,000
	A House Is Not a Home	Polly Adler	1953	2,286,000
	The Greatest Book Ever Written	Fulton Oursler	1951	2,282,322
F	*Kitty*	Rosamond Marshall	1943	2,273,841
F	*The Case of the Empty Tin*	Erle Stanley Gardner	1941	2,270,297
F	*This Is Murder*	Erle Stanley Gardner	1935	2,266,268
F	*The Case of the Careless Kitten*	Erle Stanley Gardner	1942	2,262,177
F	*2001: A Space Odyssey*	Arthur C. Clarke	1968	2,260,800
	Dennis the Menace Rides Again	Hank Ketcham	1955	2,254,960
F	*Dark Fires*	Rosemary Rogers	1975	2,250,000
	Family Reference Atlas		1956	2,250,000
	Gods from Outer Space	Erich von Däniken	1971	2,250,000
	The Wonderful World of Peanuts	Charles M. Schulz	1973	2,250,000
F	*Mr Roberts*	Thomas Heggen	1946	2,246,396
J	*Go Ask Alice*	Anonymous	1971	2,245,605

F	*The Case of the Cautious Coquette*	Erle Stanley Gardner	1949	2,244,552
	Kon-Tiki	Thor Heyerdahl	1950	2,237,449
F	*The Silver Chalice*	Thomas B. Costain	1948	2,236,004
J	*Benji*	Leonore Fleischer	1974	2,235,694
	Hiroshima	John Hersey	1946	2,230,000
F	*The Pocket Book of Erskine Caldwell Stories*	Henri Seidel Canby (ed.)	1947	2,229,000
	Body Language	Julius Fast	1970	2,227,000
	Better Homes and Gardens Sewing Book		1961	2,225,393
F	*Pride's Castle*	Frank Yerby	1949	2,214,669
F	*The Amboy Dukes*	Irving Shulman	1947	2,213,167
F	*The Clue of the Forgotten Murder*	Erle Stanley Gardner	1935	2,212,271
F	*Deliverance*	James Dickey	1970	2,201,244
F	*The Fan Club*	Irving Wallace	1974	2,200,000
	How to Be Your Own Best Friend	Mildred Newman and Bernard Berkowitz	1973	2,193,704
	Masters of Deceit	J. Edgar Hoover	1958	2,192,133
F	*The Young Lions*	Irwin Shaw	1948	2,185,201
F	*Myra Breckinridge*	Gore Vidal	1968	2,180,000
J	*The Little Engine That Could*	Watty Piper	1926	2,166,000
F	*Lord of the Flies*	William Golding	1962	2,165,000
F	*National Velvet*	Enid Bagnold	1935	2,152,210
	According to Hoyle	Richard L. Frey	1964	2,150,000
F	*The Black Rose*	Thomas B. Costain	1945	2,146,812
F	*The Seven Minutes*	Irving Wallace	1969	2,140,000
F	*The Stranger*	Albert Camus	1954	2,139,000
F	*Rally Round the Flag, Boys!*	Max Shulman	1957	2,134,289
F	*Prince of Foxes*	Samuel Shellabarger	1947	2,133,810
J	*Stuart Little*	E. B. White	1945	2,129,591
	Soul on Ice	Eldridge Cleaver	1968	2,125,335
F	*The Deep*	Mickey Spillane	1961	2,124,418
	Pregnancy, Birth and Family Planning	Alan F. Guttmacher	1973	2,122,600
F	*The Case of the Golddigger's Purse*	Erle Stanley Gardner	1945	2,121,708
F	*The Man*	Irving Wallace	1964	2,120,000
F	*Topaz*	Leon Uris	1967	2,105,751
	Wanted: Dennis the Menace	Hank Ketcham	1961	2,103,951
	The American College Dictionary	Clarence L. Barnhart (ed.)	1947	2,103,835
	The Song of Our Syrian Guest	William Allen Knight	1903	2,103,064
F	*The Revolt of Mamie Stover*	William Bradfor Huie	1951	2,102,600

F	*The Grapes of Wrath*	John Steinbeck	1939	2,100,908
	The Pocket Dictionary	W. J. Pelo	1941	2,100,000
F	*Karen*	Marie Killilea	1952	2,099,261
	The Boston Strangler	Gerold Frank	1967	2,089,800
J	*Freckles*	Gene Stratton Porter	1904	2,089,523
F	*Nevada*	Zane Grey	1928	2,087,837
F	*The Caine Mutiny*	Herman Wouk	1954	2,087,173
F	*Sanctuary*	William Faulkner	1931	2,080,985
F	*Seven Days in May*	Fletcher Knebel and Charles W. Bailey II	1962	2,073,434
	The Outline of History	H. G. Wells	1921	2,070,170
	Harlow	Irving Shulman	1964	2,068,000
	Expectant Motherhood	Nicholas J. Eastman	1940	2,063,775
F	*Another Country*	James Baldwin	1962	2,054,928
J	*The Girl of the Limberlost*	Gene Stratton Porter	1909	2,053,892
	Bible Readings for the Home Circle		1914	2,051,488
	Western Garden Book	Sunset Editors	1933	2,050,000
	All Things Bright and Beautiful	James Herriot	1974	2,044,374
F	*Leave Her to Heaven*	Ben Ames Williams	1944	2,031,210
F	*The Case of the Crooked Candle*	Erle Stanley Gardner	1944	2,029,248
	Listen to the Warm	Rod McKuen	1967	2,025,000
	Better Homes and Gardens Fondue and Tabletop Cooking		1970	2,022,529
F	*The Bramble Bush*	Charles Mergendahl	1958	2,007,000
F	*The Bridge on the River Kwai*	Pierre Boulle	1954	2,007,000
F	*The Case of the Borrowed Brunette*	Erle Stanley Gardner	1946	2,006,808
	The Elements of Style	William Strunk, Jr. and E. B. White	1959	2,000,000
	The Feminine Mystique	Betty Friedan	1963	2,000,000
	How to Prepare Your Income Tax	David Joseph	1941	2,000,000
	The New Compact Bible Dictionary	Thomas A. Byrant	1967	2,000,000
	Streams in the Desert	Mrs Charles E. Cowman	1925	2,000,000
F	*The Tight White Collar*	Grace Metalious	1960	2,000,000
	Webster's New School and Office Dictionary		1975	2,000,000

Six of the Best

MARY WARNOCK

The six books which I have most enjoyed are:

Lewis Carroll, *Alice in Wonderland* together with *Through the Looking Glass* (especially the latter). I first read it when I was about six, found it mysteriously funny and satisfactory, and read it over and over again. The more logic and philosophy I learned, the funnier and more brilliant I found it, and still do.

Frances Hodgson Burnett, *The Secret Garden*. The first book I read which made me realize the pleasure of story . . . more intense if you read and re-read the story, and know in advance what is to happen. Whole theories of imagination and religion flow from this concept.

The Book of Common Prayer (if possible printed along with the *English Hymnal*). The whole of liturgy, language and music is contained here. At school it was the source of all private pleasures, especially the pleasure of music.

Jane Austen, *Emma*. A lesson in moral sensitivity; and containing Mr Knightley, my second great love (the first being Jo's Professor in *Little Women*).

David Hume, *The Treatise of Human Nature*. The nicest, most sensible and endearing, as well as profound, sceptical philosopher. My first and continued favourite of all philosophers.

J. L. Austin, *Sense and Sensibilia*. Alas, posthumously published. A supreme example of how not to make heavy weather. Deep philosophical insights made funny.

∿

When you read a classic you do not see in the book more than you did before. You see in you more than there was before.
Clifton Fadiman,
Any Number Can Play, 1957

∿

The Most Popular Fiction in Britain 1578–1930

By way of preface to the list of popular reading she compiled for her study *Fiction and the Reading Public* (Chatto and Windus, revised edition 1965) and reprinted below, Q. D. Leavis writes:

> No attempt is made here to record *all* popular successes or even all popular novelists. Each novel is chosen as representative of the popular fiction of its time, and if a gap in years is left it may be assumed that the same kind of fiction was being read in the interval. In general the first successful novel only of a steady bestseller is recorded. Translations that affected popular fiction and taste are asterisked.

1578	*Euphues: The Anatomy of Wit*	John Lyly	
1580	*Euphues and his England*	John Lyly	Reprinted with *Euphues*, and only stopped 1636
1590	*Arcadia*	Sidney	6th ed. 1622
1594	*The Unfortunate Traveller*	Nashe	
1597	*Jack of Newbury*	Deloney	
Pre-1598	*Ornatus and Artesia*	Emanuel Forde	8th impression 1683
1598	*The Gentle Craft*, I	Deloney	Till 18th century
1598	*Parismus*	Emanuel Forde	7th ed. 1724
Pre-1600	*Thomas of Reading*	Deloney	
*1612	*Don Quixote*, I	Cervantes, trans. Shelton	Immensely popular, and other translations
*1637	*Exemplary Novels*	Cervantes	Very popular
*1652	*Cassandra* and *Cleopatra*	Calprenede	Many editions, and several translations
1655	*Parthenissa. A Romance. In Six Tomes*	Roger Boyle	Continued to be issued in parts; reissue of whole 1676
*1655+		Mlle de Scudéry	
1660	*Bentivolio and Urania*	Nathaniel Ingelo	4th ed. 1682
*c. 1660		Scarron	
1655	*The English Rogue*	Richard Head	7th ed. 1723
*1677	*Happy Slave*	Bremond	5 eds by 1729
1678	*Pilgrim's Progress*, I	Bunyan	25th ed. 1738
1680	*Life and Death of Mr Badman*	Bunyan	5 eds by 1724
1682	*The Holy War*	Bunyan	9 eds by 1738
1683	*The Travels of True Godliness*	Benjamin Keach	9th ed. 1726

1683	*The London Jilt*	Alexander Oldys	2nd ed. 1684
1684	*Pilgrim's Progress*, II	Bunyan	15th ed. 1732
1684	*The Progress of Sin . . . in an apt and Pleasant Allegory*	B. Keach	4th ed. 1707
1684	*The Adventures of the Black Lady*	Aphra Behn	
re-1685	*The Unfortunate Lady: a True History*	Aphra Behn	
1687	*Cynthia*		8th ed. 1726
1688	*Oroonoko, The Fair Jilt*, etc.	Aphra Behn	
1692	*Incognita: or, Love and Duty Reconcil'd*	Congreve	34th ed. 1713
*1692	*Ingenious and Diverting Letters of the Lady*	Marie Catherine La Mothe	10th ed. 1735
1696	Collected novels	Aphra Behn	6th ed. 1718, 8th ed. 1735
*1708	*Arabian Nights*		Innumerable editions
1709	*The New Atlantis*, I and II	Mrs Manley	
1710	*The New Atlantis*, III and IV	Mrs Manley	
1719	*Robinson Crusoe*	Defoe	7th ed. 1726
1719	*Love in Excess*, I and II	Mrs Haywood	
1720	*Love in Excess*, III	Mrs Haywood	Also reprinted entire (6th ed. 1725)
1720	*Captain Singleton*	Defoe	2nd ed. 1722
1720	*The Power of Love in Seven Novels*	Mrs Manley	
1721	*Moll Flanders*	Defoe	3rd ed. 1722
1722	*Secret History of Cleomira*	Mrs Haywood	5th ed. 1732
1726	*Gulliver's Travels*	Swift	10 separate eds by 1727
1740	*Pamela*	Richardson	5th eds this year
1742	*Joseph Andrews*	Fielding	
1748	*Clarissa*	Richardson	
1748	*Roderick Random*	Smollett	
1749	*Tom Jones*	Fielding	
1751	*Peregrine Pickle*	Smollett	
1751	*History of Miss Betsy Thoughtless*	Mrs Haywood	4th ed. 1768
1754	*Sir Charles Grandison: A Good Man*	Richardson	
1759	*Tristram Shandy*, I	Sterne	And so on
1761	*Memoirs of Miss Sidney Biddulph*	Frances Sheridan	
1765	*The Castle of Otranto*	Walpole	
1766	*The Vicar of Wakefield*	Goldsmith	

1766	*The Fool of Quality*	Richard Cumberland	
1771	*The Man of Feeling*	Henry Mackenzie	And so on till 1810+
*1773	*Tears of Sensibility*	Baculard d'Arnaud	
1775	*The Correspondents*	Minerva Press	Reprinted 1775, 1776, 1784
1777	*The Old English Baron*	Clara Reeve	
1778	*Evelina*	Fanny Burney	4 eds by 1778
1789	*A Sicilian Romance*	Ann Radcliffe	4th ed. 1809
1790	*Ethelinda*	Charlotte Smith	
1791	*The Romance of the Forest*	Ann Radcliffe	4th ed. 1795
1791	*A Simple Story*	Mrs Inchbald	
1795	*The Monk*	Gregory Lewis	4th ed. 1798
1795	*Henry*	Richard Cumberland	3rd ed. 1798
1798	*The Children of the Abbey*	Regina Maria Roche	10th ed. 1825
1803	*Thaddeus of Warsaw*	Jane Porter	Passed through several eds straightaway
1803	*Belinda*	Maria Edgeworth	
1806	*The Wild Irish Girl*	Lady Morgan	7 eds in less than 2 years
1806	*A Winter in London; or, Sketches of Fashion*	T. S. Surr	
1814	*Waverley*	Scott	Sold 12,000 copies rapidly, considered remarkable
1821	*Life in London, or the Adventures of Tom and Jerry*	Pierce Egan	
1823	*Theresa Marchmont, or the Maid of Honour*	Mrs Gore	
1825	*Tremaine, or The Man of Refinement*	Robert Plumer Ward	
1826-9	*Sayings and Doings*	Theodore Hook	
1828	*Pelham*	Lytton	
1829	*Richelieu*	G. P. R. James	
1831	*Mothers and Daughters*	Mrs Gore	
1832	*Eugene Aram*	Lytton	
1834	*The Last Days of Pompeii*	Lytton	
1837	*Pickwick Papers*	Dickens	
1838	*Oliver Twist*	Dickens	
1841	*Ten Thousand a Year*	Samuel Warren	
1841	*Charles O'Malley, the Irish Dragoon*	Charles Lever	
1844	*Coningsby*	Disraeli	
1847	*Jane Eyre*	Charlotte Brontë	
1848	*Vanity Fair*	Thackeray	

1852	*Uncle Tom's Cabin*	Harriet Beecher Stowe	1 million sold in England this year
1853	*The Heir of Redclyffe*	Charlotte Yonge	
1854	*Westward Ho!*	Charles Kingsley	
1855	*Paul Ferroll*	Mrs Archer Clive	
1856	*John Halifax, Gentleman*	Mrs Craik	
1856	*'It is never too late to mend'*	Charles Reade	
1857	*Guy Livingstone, or Thorough*	George A. Lawrence	
1857	*Tom Brown's Schooldays*	Thomas Hughes	
1858	*Adam Bede*	George Eliot	7th ed. 1859, 10th ed. 1862
1860	*The Woman in White*	Wilkie Collins	
1861	*East Lynne*	Mrs Henry Wood	
1861	*The Cloister and the Hearth*	Reade	
1861	*Framley Parsonage*	Trollope	
1862	*Lady Audley's Secret*	M. E. Braddon	3 eds of 500 copies each sold out in 10 days
1863	*Held in Bondage*	Ouida	
1864	*Lost Sir Massingberd*	James Payn	
1867	*'Cometh up as a Flower'*	Rhoda Broughton	Enormous sales till end of century
1869	*Lorna Doone*	R. D. Blackmore	
1871	*A Daughter of Heth*	W. Black	
1874	*Far from the Madding Crowd*	Hardy	
1875	*'Comin' Thro' the Rye'*	Helen Mathers	
1876	*The Golden Butterfly*	Besant and Rice	
1880	*John Inglesant*	Shorthouse	9 eds in 12 months
1880+		Silas Hocking	Till 1900+ sells average 1000 copies a week to his Methodist public
1886		Rider Haggard	Begins
1886		Hall Caine	Begins
1886		Marie Corelli	Begins
1888	*Robert Elsmere*	Mrs Humphry Ward	
1888	*Plain Tales from the Hills*	Kipling	
1889	*Three Men in a Boat*	Jerome K. Jerome	
1889	*The Master of Ballantrae*	R. L. Stevenson	4 eds in 1889
1891	*The Little Minister*	J. M. Barrie	
1893	*Ships that Pass in the Night*	Beatrice Harraden	
1893	*A Gentleman of France*	Stanley Weyman	
1894	*The Prisoner of Zenda*	A. Hope	
1895	*Trilby*	George du Maurier	

1900	*The Life and Death of Richard Yea-and-Nay*	Maurice Hewlett	
1905	*The Scarlet Pimpernel*	Baroness Orczy	
1905	*The Morals of Marcus Ordeyne*	W. J. Locke	
1905	*The Hill*	H. A. Vachell	
1905	*The Garden of Allah*	Robert Hichens	
1908	*The Blue Lagoon*	H. de Vere Stacpoole	
1909		Wells	Becomes popular as a propagandist in fiction
1909	*The Rosary*	Florence Barclay	
1910	*The Broad Highway*	Jeffery Farnol	
1912	*The Way of an Eagle*	Ethel M. Dell	
1914	*Tarzan of the Apes*	Edgar Rice Burroughs	
1919	*Peter Jackson, Cigar Merchant*	Gilbert Frankau	
1921	*If Winter Comes*	A. S. M. Hutchinson	
1922	*The Forsyte Saga*	Galsworthy	3 reprints in 1922
1923	*The Middle of the Road*	Philip Gibbs	
1924	*The Green Hat*	Michael Arlen	
1924	*Beau Geste*	P. C. Wren	
1925	*The Constant Nymph*	Margaret Kennedy	
1925	*Sorrell and Son*	Warwick Deeping	
1926	*Gentlemen Prefer Blondes*	Anita Loos	
*1927	*Jew Süss*	Feuchtwanger	
1928	*The Bridge of San Luis Rey*	Thornton Wilder	
1930	*The Good Companions*	J. B. Priestley	
1930	*Vile Bodies*	Evelyn Waugh	

~

It took me fifteen years to discover I had no talent for writing, but I couldn't give it up because by that time I was famous.

Robert Benchley

~

UK Bestsellers 1974–84

1974

Paperbacks

1	*Watership Down*	Richard Adams	Puffin	£0.40
2 {	*The Great Gatsby*	Scott Fitzgerald	Penguin	£0.35
	Papillon	Henri Charrière	Panther	£0.60
4	*The Odessa File*	Frederick Forsyth	Corgi	£0.50
5	*The Exorcist*	William Peter Blatty	Corgi	£0.40
6	*The Gulag Archipelago*	Alexander Solzhenitsyn	Fontana	£0.80

Fiction

1	*Breakheart Pass*	Alistair MacLean	Collins	£2.00
2	*Tinker, Tailor, Soldier, Spy*	John Le Carré	Hodder	£2.95
3	*Spy Story*	Len Deighton	Cape	£2.25
4	*Cashelmara*	Susan Howatch	H. Hamilton	£3.40
5 {	*Jaws*	Peter Benchley	Deutsch	£1.95
	Thunder at Sunset	John Masters	M. Joseph	£2.75

Non-fiction

1	*The Ascent of Man*	Jacob Bronowski	BBC	£5.00
2	*The Wild Flowers of Britain and Northern Europe*	R. and A. Fitter and M. Blamey	Collins	£1.60
3	*America*	Alistair Cooke	BBC	£5.00
4	*A Field Guide to the Trees of Britain and Northern Europe*	Alan Mitchell	Collins	£2.95
5	*The World at War*	Mark Arnold Forster	Collins	£3.00
6	*In Search of Ancient Gods*	Erich von Däniken	Souvenir	£2.95

1975

Paperbacks

1	*Let Sleeping Vets Lie*	James Herriot	Pan	£0.45
2	*Watership Down*	Richard Adams	Penguin	£0.60
3	*If Only They Could Talk*	James Herriot	Pan	£0.30
4	*It Shouldn't Happen to a Vet*	James Herriot	Pan	£0.30
5	*Jaws*	Peter Benchley	Pan	£0.60
6	*Banco*	Henri Charrière	Panther	£0.60

Fiction

1 {	*The Dogs of War*	Frederick Forsyth	Hutchinson	£2.00
	Shardik	Richard Adams	Collins/Allen Lane	£3.95

3	Circus	Alistair MacLean	Collins	£2.95
4 {	The Moneychangers	Arthur Hailey	M. Joseph	£3.60
	The Snow Tiger	Desmond Bagley	Collins	£2.75
6	North Star	Hammond Innes	Collins	£2.75

Non-fiction

1	The Ascent of Man	Jacob Bronowski	BBC	£5.50
2	America	Alistair Cooke	BBC	£5.00
3	The Wild Flowers of Britain and Northern Europe	R. and A. Fitter and M. Blamey	Collins	£1.60
4 {	The Bermuda Triangle	Charles Berlitz	Souvenir	£3.25
	The Good Food Guide 1975	Christopher Driver (ed.)	Hodder	£2.95
6	The Guinness Book of Records	Norris McWhirter (ed.)	Guinness	£1.70

1976

Paperbacks

1	Vet in Harness	James Herriot	Pan	£0.60
2	Some of Me Poetry	Pam Ayres	Galaxy	£1.00
3	It Shouldn't Happen to a Vet	James Herriot	Pan	£0.50
4	Let Sleeping Vets Lie	James Herriot	Pan	£0.50
5	If Only They Could Talk	James Herriot	Pan	£0.50
6	One Flew Over the Cuckoo's Nest	Ken Kesey	Picador	£0.75

Fiction

1	Touch Not the Cat	Mary Stewart	Hodder	£3.50
2	Curtain/Poirot's Last Case	Agatha Christie	Collins	£2.95
3	The Golden Gate	Alistair MacLean	Collins	£3.50
4	The Shepherd	Frederick Forsyth	Hutchinson	£1.50
5 {	Ragtime	E. L. Doctorow	Macmillan	£3.50
	Passage to Mutiny	Alexander Kent	Hutchinson	£3.45

Non-fiction

1 {	The Ascent of Man	Jacob Bronowski	BBC	£5.50
	America	Alistair Cooke	BBC	£6.00
3	MCC: The Autobiography of a Cricketer	Colin Cowdrey	Hodder	£4.95
4 {	The Greatest	Muhammad Ali	Hart-Davis	£3.95
	Your Kitchen Garden	G. Seddon and H. Radecka	M. Beazley	£5.95
6	Vets Might Fly	James Herriot	M. Joseph	£3.50

1977

Paperbacks

1	The Eagle Has Landed	Jack Higgins	Pan	£0.80
2	The Queen's Silver Jubilee	Olwen Hedley	Pitkin	£0.95
3	Bring On the Empty Horses	David Niven	Coronet	£0.95
4	Superwoman	Shirley Conran	Penguin	£0.80
5 {	The Moneychangers	Arthur Hailey	Pan	£0.95
	The Lonely Lady	Harold Robbins	NEL	£1.25

Fiction

1	Oliver's Story	Erich Segal	Hart-Davis	£2.95
2 {	Seawitch	Alistair MacLean	Collins	£3.50
	The Honourable Schoolboy	John Le Carré	Hodder	£4.95
4 {	The Silmarillion	J. R. R. Tolkien	Allen & Unwin	£4.95
	The Rich Are Different	Susan Howatch	H. Hamilton	£4.95
6	The Plague Dogs	Richard Adams	Allen Lane/ R. Collings	£3.95

Non-fiction

1	Country Life Book of the Royal Silver Jubilee	Patrick Montague-Smith	Hamlyn/ C. Life	£4.95
2	Majesty: Elizabeth II and the House of Windsor	Robert Lacey	Hutchinson	£5.45
3	The Country Diary of an Edwardian Lady	Edith Holden	Webb & Bower/ M. Joseph	£5.50
4	Old Wives' Lore For Gardeners	M. and B. Boland	Bodley Head	£1.95
5 {	George, Don't Do That	Joyce Grenfell	Macmillan	£1.95
	The Oxford Literary Guide to the British Isles	D. Eagle and H. Carnell	OUP	£3.95

1978

Paperbacks

1 {	Vets Might Fly	James Herriot	Pan	£0.70
	The Plague Dogs	Richard Adams	Penguin	£0.95
3 {	Star Wars	George Lucas	Sphere	£0.95
	A Sparrow Falls	Wilbur Smith	Pan	£1.25
	Emma and I	Sheila Hocken	Sphere	£0.85
6	Sleeping Murder	Agatha Christie	Fontana	£0.75

Fiction

| 1 | The Silmarillion | J. R. R. Tolkien | Allen & Unwin | £4.95 |
| 2 | The Human Factor | Graham Greene | Bodley Head | £4.50 |

3	*Hungry as the Sea*	Wilbur Smith	Heinemann	£5.50
4	*The Plague Dogs*	Richard Adams	Allen Lane/	£4.95
			R. Collings	
5	*SS-GB*	Len Deighton	Cape	£4.95
6	*The Honourable Schoolboy*	John Le Carré	Hodder	£4.95

Non-fiction

1	*The Country Diary of an Edwardian Lady*	Edith Holden	Webb & Bower/ M. Joseph	£5.50
2	*Royal Heritage*	Huw Weldon and J. H. Plumb	BBC	£10.00
3	*Dear Me*	Peter Ustinov	Heinemann	£5.90
	The New Oxford Book of Light Verse	Kingsley Amis (ed.)	OUP	£4.25
4	*The Country Life Book of Queen Elizabeth the Queen Mother*	Godfrey Talbot	Hamlyn	£6.50
6	*Most Secret War*	Prof. R. V. Jones	H. Hamilton	£6.95

1979

Paperbacks

1	*The Thorn Birds*	Colleen McCullough	Futura	£1.50
2	*Alien*	Alan Dean Foster	Futura	£0.95
3	*The Women's Room*	Marilyn French	Sphere	£1.50
	The Far Pavilions	M. M. Kaye	Penguin	£2.50
5	*The Honourable Schoolboy*	John Le Carré	Pan	£1.25
6	*Tinker, Tailor, Soldier, Spy*	John Le Carré	Pan	£1.25

Fiction

1	*Wild Justice*	Wilbur Smith	Heinemann	£5.50
2	*Proteus*	Morris West	Collins	£4.95
3	*Good as Gold*	Joesph Heller	Cape	£4.95
	The Last Enchantment	Mary Stewart	Hodder	£5.95
5	*Now God Be Thanked*	John Masters	M. Joseph	£5.95
6	*War and Remembrance*	Herman Wouk	Collins	£8.50

Non-fiction

1	*The Country Diary of an Edwardian Lady*	Edith Holden	Webb & Bower/ M. Joseph	£4.95
2	*Life on Earth*	David Attenborough	Collins/ BBC	£7.95
3	*Einstein's Universe*	Nigel Calder	BBC	£6.25
	By Myself	Lauren Bacall	Cape	£5.95
4	*Clementine Churchill*	Mary Soames	Cassell	£7.95
	Mountbatten: 80 Years in Pictures		Macmillan	£8.95

1980

Paperbacks

1	*Cookery Course Part II*	Delia Smith	BBC	£3.75
2	*The Hitchhiker's Guide to the Galaxy*	Douglas Adams	Pan	£0.80
3 {	*Testament of Youth*	Vera Brittain	Fontana	£1.75
	The Throw Back	Tom Sharpe	Pan	£0.95
5	*Traveller's France*	Arthur Eperon	Pan	£1.75
6	*The Human Factor*	Graham Greene	Penguin	£1.25

Fiction

1	*The Devil's Alternative*	Frederick Forsyth	Hutchinson	£5.95
2	*Smiley's People*	John Le Carré	Hodder	£5.95
3	*Solo*	Jack Higgins	Collins	£5.95
4	*Sins of the Fathers*	Susan Howatch	H. Hamilton	£6.50
5	*Whip Hand*	Dick Francis	M. Joseph	£5.25
6	*Flowers of the Field*	Sarah Harrison	Macdonald	£5.95

Non-fiction

1 {	*James Herriot's Yorkshire*	J. Herriot and D. Brabbs	M. Joseph	£6.50
	The Country Diary of an Edwardian Lady	Edith Holden	Webb & Bower/ M. Joseph	£6.95
3	*Life on Earth*	David Attenborough	Collins/ BBC	£7.95
4	*The Henry Root Letters*	Henry Root	Weidenfeld	£4.50
5 {	*Life On Earth*, enlarged ed.	David Attenborough	Collins/ Reader's Digest	£12.95
	The Book of Heroic Failures	Stephen Pile	Routledge	£4.95

1981

Paperbacks

1	*The Hitchhiker's Guide to the Galaxy*	Douglas Adams	Pan	£0.80
2 {	*Cookery Course Part II*	Delia Smith	BBC	£4.25
	Not! The 9 O'Clock News	The Not! Team	BBC	£1.95
	The Restaurant at the End of the Universe	Douglas Adams	Pan	£0.95
5	*Kane and Abel*	Jeffrey Archer	Coronet	£1.95
6	*Not! 1982*	The Not! Team	Faber	£2.99

Fiction

1	*Noble House*	James Clavell	Hodder	£8.95

2	*Men of Men*	Wilbur Smith	Heinemann	£7.95
3	*Rites of Passage*	William Golding	Faber	£5.95
4	*Earthly Powers*	Anthony Burgess	Hutchinson	£6.95
5	*Unfinished Tales*	J. R. R. Tolkien	Allen & Unwin	£7.50
6	*XPD*	Len Deighton	Hutchinson	£6.95

Non-fiction

1	*James Herriot's Yorkshire*	J. Herriot and D. Brabbs	M. Joseph	£7.50
2	*Cosmos*	Carl Sagan	Macdonald	£12.50
3	*Invitation to a Royal Wedding*	Brenda Ralph Lewis	Purnell	£2.50
4 {	*The Lord God Made Them All*	James Herriot	M. Joseph	£6.95
	Ireland: A History	Robert Kee	Weidenfeld	£9.95
6	*Debrett's Book of the Royal Wedding*	Hugo Vickers	Debrett	£8.95

1982

Paperbacks

1	*The F-Plan Diet*	Audrey Eyton	Penguin	£1.50
2 {	*Gorky Park*	Martin Cruz Smith	Pan	£1.95
	Ancestral Vices	Tom Sharpe	Pan	£1.50
4	*Midnight's Children*	Salman Rushdie	Picador	£2.95
5	*Life, the Universe and Everything*	Douglas Adams	Pan	£1.50
6	*The White Hotel*	D. M. Thomas	Penguin	£2.25

Fiction

1	*The Prodigal Daughter*	Jeffrey Archer	Hodder	£7.95
2	*No Comebacks*	Frederick Forsyth	Hutchinson	£6.95
3	*Midnight's Children*	Salman Rushdie	Cape	£6.95
4	*The Angels Weep*	Wilbur Smith	Heinemann	£8.50
5	*The Parsifal Mosaic*	Robert Ludlum	Granada	£7.95
6	*Flashman and the Redskins*	George MacDonald Fraser	Collins	£7.95

Non-fiction

1	*Roget's Thesaurus*		Longman	£7.95
2	*The Concise Oxford Dictionary*, 7th ed.		OUP	£7.95
3	*Michelin Guide to France 1982*		Michelin	£5.85
4 {	*Princess*	Robert Lacey	Hutchinson	£7.50
	Better Than New	A. Jackson and D. Day	BBC	£4.75
6	*Weekend Wardrobe*	Ann Ladbury	BBC	£4.95

1983

Paperbacks

1	*The F-Plan Diet*	Audrey Eyton	Penguin	£1.25
2	*The Prodigal Daughter*	Jeffrey Archer	Coronet	£2.50
3	*Vintage Stuff*	Tom Sharpe	Pan	£1.75
	The Lord God Made Them All	James Herriot	Pan	£1.95
5	*Lace*	Shirley Conran	Penguin	£2.50
6	*Kane and Abel*	Jeffrey Archer	Coronet	£2.50

Fiction

1	*The Little Drummer Girl*	John Le Carré	Hodder	£8.95
2	*The Valley of the Horses*	Jean Auel	Hodder	£8.95
3	*White Gold Wielder*	Stephen Donaldson	Collins	£8.95
4	*Schindler's Ark*	Thomas Keneally	Hodder	£7.95
	Shame	Salman Rushdie	Cape	£7.95
6	*Exocet*	Jack Higgins	Collins	£7.95

Non-fiction

1	*The Official Sloane Ranger Handbook*	Ann Barr and Peter York	Ebury	£4.95
2	*Indian Cookery*	Madhur Jaffrey	BBC	£4.25
3	*Delia Smith's Complete Cookery Course*	Delia Smith	BBC	£10.95
4	*Jane Fonda's Workout Book*	Jane Fonda	Allen Lane	£8.95
5	*Concise Oxford Dictionary, 7th ed.*		OUP	£9.50/ £7.75
6	*The Illustrated Lark Rise to Candleford*	Flora Thompson	Century	£12.50

1984

Paperbacks

1	*The Secret Diary of Adrian Mole, Aged 13¾*	Sue Townsend	Methuen	£1.50
2	*Hollywood Wives*	Jackie Collins	Pan	£2.50
3	*The Jewel in the Crown*	Paul Scott	Granada	£2.50
4	*The Seeds of Yesterday*	Virginia Andrews	Fontana	£1.95
	Vegetarian Kitchen	Sarah Brown	BBC	£4.50
6	*The Little Drummer Girl*	John Le Carré	Pan	£2.50

Fiction

1	*The Raj Quartet, complete ed.*	Paul Scott	Heinemann	£12.95
2	*The Leopard Hunts in Darkness*	Wilbur Smith	Heinemann	£8.95
3	*First Among Equals*	Jeffrey Archer	Hodder	£8.95

4	*The Name of the Rose*	Umberto Eco	Secker	£8.95
	The Aquitaine Progression	Robert Ludlum	Granada	£8.95
6	*The Growing Pains of Adrian Mole*	Sue Townsend	Methuen	£4.95

Non-fiction

1	*The Living Planet*	David Attenborough	BBC/ Collins	£12.00
2	*The Country Diary of an Edwardian Lady*	Edith Holden	Sphere	£4.50
3	*The Brotherhood*	Stephen Knight	Granada	£8.95
4	*To Be a Pilgrim*	Cardinal Basil Hume	St Paul	£7.50
5	*The Making of 'The Jewel in the Crown'*		Granada	£5.95
6	*Fellwalking with Wainwright*	A. Wainwright and Derry Brabbs	M. Joseph	£12.95

The lists above were compiled by Bookwatch for the editor.

Six of the Best

JEFFREY ARCHER

My choice of six books that have had the most influence on me is:
Charles Dickens, *A Tale of Two Cities*
George Eliot, *Middlemarch*
Evelyn Waugh, *Sword of Honour*
Scott Fitzgerald, *Tender Is the Night*
Saki (H. H. Munro), short stories
Fred Ullman, *Reunion*

∿

The principle of procrastinated rape is said to be the ruling one in all the great bestsellers.

V. S. Pritchett,
The Living Novel and Later Appreciations

∿

Bedtime Reading

MILES KINGTON

Books I Have Re-read Most Often in Bed
Arthur Conan Doyle, *Adventures of Gerard*
H. L. Mencken, *Selected Prejudices*
Charles Macomb Flandrau, *Viva Mexico!*
Alex Atkinson and Ronald Searle, *By Rocking-chair Across America*
Raymond Chandler, *The High Window*
Quentin Crisp, *How to Have a Life-style*

Books I Have Had Longest by My Bedside Without Reading
E. C. Bentley, *Complete Clerihews* (six months)
Mrs Oliphant, *Laurence Oliphant* (a year)
The Penguin Money Book (eighteen months)
Howard Teichmann, *Smart Aleck — The Wit, World and Life of Alexander Woolcott* (three years)
A Pictorial Record of Great Western Architecture (four or five years)
Pick of Punch 1959 (twenty-five years)

Books I Would Like to Read in Bed
The Real Reason Why Your Flowers Are Dying
How to Make Your Own Whisky for as Little as 50p a Bottle
Rupert Murdoch, *Collected Poems*
Selected Addresses of Men Who Will Come and Mend Your Hi-Fi, Cheaply, Cheerfully and Often
The Bible in Franglais
Jeffrey Archer, *My Last Novel*

The first two lists, naturally, are all genuine. I've been through three copies of the Mencken book.

~

One always tends to overpraise a long book because one has got through it.

E. M. Forster

~

Some All-time Bestsellers by Category

Religion   If figures were available the Bible would probably come out on top if only by virtue of its multiple translations. It has been rendered into some 1735 languages, in many of which various alternative translations exist.

Politics   During the 1965–8 Cultural Revolution in China Maoist doctrine was vigorously reasserted and the great man's writings embodied in a *Little Red Book* of aphoristic instruction. It is said to have reached 800 million people, but since its possession was hardly voluntary it cannot really be counted as the all-time political bestseller.

In 1953 it was announced in the USSR that 672,058,000 copies of the works of Stalin had been sold 'or distributed', and translations made into 101 languages.

The sales of Hitler's *Mein Kampf* were boosted by similarly dubious means. Every newly married couple in Nazi Germany was supposed to be presented with a copy of the Führer's great work.

Reference Books   *The Guinness Book of Records* features in its own lists of record breakers as the bestselling book of all – over 45 million copies by the end of 1982, and selling some 500,000 copies a year. The original inspiration for this, the ultimate in argument settlers, came from saloon-bar speculation about the highest, biggest, fastest etc. phenomena in the world.

Textbooks   How many schoolboys struggling through Kennedy's *Latin Primer* have cursed the author and his subject – unjustly so, for Kennedy replaced Lily's *Grammar*, an unbearably dry and cluttered text. In the mid-1970s the *Primer* was still selling 4000 copies a year.

Ronald Ridout's *First English Workbook* has sold some 5 million copies, and between 1948 and 1982 he published 445 titles with sales of 77,530,000. Louis Alexander, the guru of ELT (English Language Teaching), has also sold well over 5 million books. E. F. Candlin's *Present Day English for Foreign Students* sold more than 2½ million between 1962 and 1973.

Romance   Barbara Cartland's global sales are around the 300 million mark for over 350 titles in seventeen languages.

Crime Agatha Christie's eighty-seven novels have sold over 300 million in 103 languages. Erle Stanley Gardner has sold more than 315 million copies of his books in thirty-seven languages.

Pulp Fiction Jacqueline Susann's *Valley of the Dolls*, published in March 1966, had sold by the mid-eighties some 26 million copies.

Romantic Novels When publisher Harold S. Latham of Macmillan was on a book-finding tour of the USA, he was visited in Atlanta by a local (unpublished) lady writer named Peggy Marsh. She left him a manuscript that filled a large suitcase, had no first chapter but variant versions of others; chunks were missing. The heroine was called Pansy and the title was *Tomorrow Is Another Day*. After a lot of work and with a good deal of courage on the part of the publisher it was brought out in 1936 as *Gone with the Wind*. It sold a million in six months and as many as 50,000 in a single day. By the 1960s its sales were in excess of 10 million and it is still in print. The film rights went for what was at the time a record $50,000 and in 1974 NBC paid $5 million for a single broadcast of the work.

'Women's Fiction' The silliest of all novels in this genre was Elinor Glyn's *Three Weeks* (1907), which had sold 5 million copies by the early thirties. The plot, if such it can be called, concerns an Englishman who meets an astoundingly beautiful woman in Switzerland and goes to bed with her (in effect) for three weeks.

The lady turns out to be a Ruritanian princess and is using the adulterous relationship to produce an heir to her country's throne, something her drunken, brutish and infertile husband is unable to do. In the end she is murdered by the last-named and our hero is able to witness his little son being crowned king of his country.

According to Elinor Glyn, this farrago of nonsense was read with delight by 'crowned heads, Australian bushmen, bishops, Klondyke miners, mothers and priests of the church' — a typical cross-section of the reading public, in fact.

A later book, *Six Days* (1924), concerns a couple touring the World War I battlefields. As they are being shown round a dugout by a priest, it collapses on top of them. The priest just has time to marry them before he expires, and they then embark on married life entombed in the dugout, with plenty of time for fervid love-making before they are rescued.

Elinor Glyn coined the word 'it' for sexual magnetism and set herself up as an authority on love; it is a sad irony that she was unable to translate theory into fact. Her marriage started promisingly, however, and during the honeymoon her husband hired the public baths in Brighton for two days so that he could watch her swimming up and down naked. She had a 'passionate friendship' with Lord Curzon – unfortunately brought to a halt by his second marriage – and spent a while in Hollywood, where she gave Rudolf Valentino lessons in screen love-making.

Children's Books   As far as numbers go, Dr Seuss's phenomenal *Green Eggs and Ham* must be a candidate for twentieth-century bestseller amongst the juveniles. By 1975 it had sold some 2 million copies, and still sells some 100,000 a year.

Other bestselling authors include that apostle of imperialism and clean living, G. A. Henty; Enid Blyton, best known for her Noddy and Famous Five series; Beatrix Potter, creator of Peter Rabbit; and Anna Sewell, author of the most famous of all animal classics, *Black Beauty*.

Diet Books   This miserable genre is not as recent as some suppose – the bestselling book in 1924 and 1925 in America was *Diet and Health* by Lulu Hunt Peters. Since then an avalanche of more or less didactic or faddist books has poured from the presses; the latest million-seller success is Audrey Eyton's *F-Plan Diet*, which sings the praises of fibre in our food.

Westerns   Zane Gray began his career as a dentist in New York. In 1904 he published, at his own expense, a historical novel called *Betty Zane* which no publisher would touch. Then he turned to westerns and became the leading writer in the genre. His third, *Riders of the Purple Sage* (1912), sold nearly 2 million copies. The estimated sales of his fifty-plus books are in excess of 20 million. Between 1917 and 1925 Grey was continuously on the bestseller list.

Baby Care   Benjamin Spock's *Common Sense Book of Baby and Child Care* was first published in 1946 and since then has sold about a million copies a year. A pathfinding book in that it advocated a so-called 'permissive' attitude to child-rearing, it was also one of the first popular medical books in which acknowledged experts wrote for a general audience. Spock also espoused liberal causes in politics and was accused by President Nixon – himself a shining example of the results of a non-permissive upbringing – of having corrupted a whole generation of American youth by his advocacy of patience and common sense.

Humour   The great humorous classics stay in print, selling steadily as new generations discover them. They also acquire a huge audience who know the characters but haven't read the books – everyone has heard of Mr Pooter, Bertie Wooster and Jeeves. A remarkable irruption that looks like breaking previous records is Sue Townsend's *The Secret Diary of Adrian Mole, Aged 13¾*, published in 1982. As in *The Diary of a Nobody*, it is the author's uncanny ear for dialogue, and the pathos that lies behind the aspirations and failures in a circumscribed world, that snares the reader, if not into sympathy, at least into horrified fascination with the hero. By Christmas 1984 the Mole Diary had sold some 86,500 in hardback and an astonishing 1⅓ million in paperback. The sequel, which records with no less angst-ridden gloom *The Growing Pains of Adrian Mole*, was heading purposefully towards sales of 250,000 in hardback. Many foreign editions have appeared. The author, a divorced ex-social worker who left school at fifteen, is estimated to have received royalties in excess of £250,000.

Pre-publication Success   Victor Hugo's *Les Misérables* was published in April 1862 and had been translated into nine languages before publication; it appeared in the bookshops on the same day in Paris, London, Berlin, Madrid, Brussels, St Petersburg, Turin and New York. Unfortunately, the adulation that Hugo received went to his head: he believed, for instance, that Paris should be renamed 'Hugo' in his honour.

Biography   Hard though it is for the modern reader to understand the mixture of affection and awe in which the great statesmen of the nineteenth century were held, at the turn of the century this was still a factor on which a shrewd publisher could count. *The Life of Gladstone* by John Morley appeared in three volumes in 1903 and demand for it swamped the publisher. Incredible scenes were reported of crowds at the Macmillan offices, of huge piles of the book stacked in the front room, of collectors fighting over the bulky packages at the trade counter, and so forth; 25,041 copies were sold in the first year. Morley was an ambitious man whose trademark was high-principled rectitude. Perhaps this made him the ideal biographer of Gladstone; but there were those who saw through him. Shaw remarked that he was 'the worst of all political scoundrels – the conscientious high-principled scoundrel'.

Cookery The financial crash of 1866 ruined an enterprising young man who had already made a name as a go-ahead publisher. Samuel Orchart Beeton woke up one morning to find himself a 'licensee in bankruptcy' of Ward, Lock and Tyler (as it then was). As if this was not enough, two years before, Beeton had lost his delightful and intelligent wife Isabella, who had compiled her famous *Book of Household Management* and *Dictionary of Cookery* before dying of puerperal fever aged twenty-eight.

Beeton became an editor for Ward Lock, but broke the terms of his contract. Ward Lock were then left in possession of some exceedingly hot properties in the form of the Beeton books, still in print in various forms to this day.

The Mrs Beeton of America is Fannie Farmer's *Boston Cooking School Cook Book*, first published in 1896, by Little, Brown in a modest edition of 3000 copies. By 1963 the book had gone through eleven editions and was still in print. Like Mrs Beeton, Fannie Farmer catered for an un-calorie-conscious age, her breakfasts consisting of beef, bacon, eggs, potatoes, bread, cream, coffee, cheese and pie.

Coffee Table Books This is a pejorative term, implying books that are to be looked at rather than read, and perhaps not even looked at much, but left in an eye-catching position to impress the casual visitor with one's erudition and taste. Coffee table books are also 'gift books' – a more neutral term, and the one usually applied to the most extraordinarily successful book in this category ever published. By March 1981 *The Country Diary of an Edwardian Lady*, Edith Holden's 1906 naturalist's diary, had been on the bestseller list of the *Bookseller* 145 times since publication, which was easily a record. It was on the *Sunday Times* bestseller list continuously for a total of fifty-nine weeks until a strike at Times Newspapers interrupted its run. The total first printing was 148,000 copies, so great was the cumulative interest in Britain and America. This, of course, was just the beginning of a fabulous sales record that embraced spin-offs featuring calendars, stationery, fabrics, and even a range of crockery exclusive to a big London store.

Spy Stories According to Lietta Tornabuoni in *The Bond Affair* (Macdonald, 1966), in the twelve years between sitting down to write the first Bond book in 1952 and his death in 1964 Ian Fleming had seen 25 million copies sold of thirteen Bond adventures. They had been translated into eighteen languages, including Turkish and Catalan, and reached 50 million readers. With the enormous popularity of the Bond films sales took off all over again, and a Bond cult overtook Europe and America.

Naturally Bond has made enemies in the literary as well as the spy world. Alberto Moravia, the Italian novelist, wrote of *Goldfinger*: 'From the literary point of view Fleming's book does not exist and would not be worth the trouble of discussing. The only way of considering Fleming's books is in their psychological or sociological sense.' But it is only psychologists and sociologists who wish to 'explain' the Bond appeal; readers enjoy a gratification of fantasies expertly served.

Thrillers   Probably the most successful offering of pulp violence ever penned was the work of a modest man called René Raymond who worked in the book wholesalers Simpkin, Marshall. In this capacity he read a number of American efforts in the genre and, with the time-honoured optimism of literary innocents, decided he could do better. *No Orchids for Miss Blandish* (1939) was taken on by the somewhat puritanical firm of Hutchinson, then presided over by the half-mad 'Mr Walter' Hutchinson. As a minimum of two favourable reader's reports was required to get the chairman's endorsement, and as it was not the sort of manuscript to get such reports, the book's editor, Jim Reynolds, forged them. An advance for £30 was sent to Raymond, who as James Hadley Chase embarked on a long and profitable career writing sadistic trash. The book had sold some half a million copies five years after publication.

Some Individual Bestsellers

Thor Heyerdahl, *Kon-Tiki*   At one time Allen and Unwin had 50,000 copies of this mighty seller in production, and these were in excess of what appeared to be the requirements for the next five or six months. Three printers and four binders worked simultaneously and in competition with each other over delivery dates; Stanley Unwin found himself able to dictate that there would be no book club edition for two years (one year was usual) and managed to sell more copies the second Christmas than he had the first.

To the sneer of one competitor that any house could show profits if it had a *Kon-Tiki*, Unwin responded with typical aplomb. He had a set of accounts prepared excluding the bestseller, which demonstrated that for the year in question, 1950, profits were within a few hundred pounds of the previous year's.

The Green Hat   This novel by the Armenian Michael Arlen, who sensibly changed his name from Dikran Kouyoumdjian, was published in 1924 and instantly became one of the phenomena of the age. Mayfairish cynical sex farces are not the sort of book normally associated with Collins, yet this was one of their historic successes, selling 200,000 copies in three years and all told about half a million. A story is told in David Keir's *The House of Collins* (Collins, 1952) of Sir Godfrey Collins contesting the Greenock constituency in the election of that year; his agent reported enthusiastically on the polling, but Sir Godfrey was elsewhere. 'Think of it,' he murmured. 'Seventy thousand copies! Never been known before! What a winner!' It was Alexander Woollcott who wittily said of Arlen that he was 'every other inch a gentleman'.

~

A little squib that might amuse you when it comes out. . . .
George Orwell on *Animal Farm*

~

George Orwell's *Animal Farm*   This novel, which in 1945 was considered politically too hot to handle by several publishers in England, and by even more in the USA, must have over-earned its advance more than most. Secker and Warburg give the following figures for sales up to 1971. USA: hardback 150,000. Book of the Month Club 460,000 between 1946 and 1949. Paperback in New American Library 5 million. Over 6 million copies all told, and in the early 1970s still selling 350,000 copies a year, mostly paperback. England: 70,000 hardback. Penguin 2½ million. Educational edition 430,000 copies. A total of over 3 million copies, and in the early 1970s still selling some 140,000 paperback copies a year. Many foreign editions appeared, including illegal ones for Russia and the Ukraine.

Both *Animal Farm* and *1984* are unusual in that they tend to sell better as the years go by. School curricula may assist, but it must be partially due to an increasing perception of the books' relevance and insight, though *1984* was a warning rather than a prophecy.

King Solomon's Mines   One of the great adventure stories of all time, Rider Haggard's book was the result of a boast to his brother that he could write a better book than Stevenson's *Treasure Island*, then enjoying a huge success. Cassell offered him a royalty or £100 for the copyright. With two lengthy failed novels behind him Haggard was not in a bargaining mood, and was inclined to accept the £100. However, while the editor was fetching the agreement a clerk whispered to Haggard that he would be better off accepting the royalty; when the editor came back Haggard told him he had changed his mind, and thus saved himself from a great financial loss. By Christmas, after an autumn publication, the book had sold 6000, and by the following Christmas 31,000. In a decade it had sold over 100,000 and the first printing for the cheap edition was another 100,000.

Six of the Best

CLARE FRANCIS

Six books that continue to give me most pleasure are:
  F. Scott Fitzgerald, *Tender Is the Night*
  Palinurus, *The Unquiet Grave*
  The Times Atlas of World History
  The Complete Works of Plato and Aristotle
  Arthur Ransome, *Winter Holiday*
  Erskine Childers, *The Riddle of the Sands*

Longest Individual Works

The *Guinness Book of Records* states that the longest novel ever written is Jules Romains's twenty-seven-volume *oeuvre*, *Les Hommes de Bonne Volonté* (1932–47). The English version comes in the handy fourteen-volume pack (*Men of Good Will*, 1933–47).

I am again indebted to Guinness for the information that *Tokuga-Wa-Ieyasu* by Sohachi Tamaoka has been pushing gently ahead in newspaper serialization in Japan for some twenty years. This is for those who can't wait for the projected forty-volume hardback.

Novelists don't have it all their own way: the poet of the Kirghiz folk epic *Manas* managed 500,000 lines (so far no English translation); and in England John Fitchett (1766–1830) wrote a poem about King Alfred of 129,807 lines which occupied him for forty years – though actually the last 2585 lines were added by his editor.

Paperbacks

∿

I would be the first to admit that there is no fortune in this series for anyone concerned. . . .
Allen Lane, writing in the Bookseller
prior to the launch of Penguin Books in 1935

∿

The ancestors of the modern paperback are distinguished. They include Aldine editions of classical texts, printed in Venice in 1501; Constable's Miscellany series in the 1830s; and John Murray's Family Library. The latter two reduced the price of a book by 80 per cent by printing on the new machine-made wood pulp paper and binding the books with paper boards.

Penguin Allen Lane's new publishing venture in the mid-thirties meant that a middle-aged bank clerk could buy a Penguin for what he would be paid for about twenty minutes' work.

The first ten Penguins published in 1935 at 6d each were:

Agatha Christie, *The Mysterious Affair at Styles* (in place of *Murder on the Links*, which was postponed)

André Maurois, *Ariel*

Compton Mackenzie, *Carnival* (subsequently withdrawn due to copyright difficulties)

Ernest Hemingway, *A Farewell to Arms*

Eric Linklater, *Poet's Pub*

Susan Ertz, *Madame Claire*

Beverley Nichols, *Twenty-five*

E. H. Young, *William*

Mary Webb, *Gone to Earth*

Dorothy L. Sayers, *The Unpleasantness at the Bellona Club*

American Pocket Books   The ancestors of American paperbacks lie with institutions such as the Boston Society for the Diffusion of Useful Knowledge, whose paper-bound book series began in 1831, and magazines such as *Brother Jonathan* and *New World*. In the early 1840s these magazines printed as supplements whole novels, a practice not attempted in England until 1984 when the *Mail on Sunday* ran the latest Jeffrey Archer over three issues.

A paperback war broke out, with publishers undercutting each other; in the 1860s dime novels and 10 cent romances were hugely successful. By the seventies rotary presses had brought down prices yet again and the *New York Tribune* was by 1875 issuing a new 'novel' in its Lakeside Library every week. The logical conclusion was a new title every day — a feat achieved by the Seaside Library in the late seventies. Only the international copyright law of 1891 put an end to the frenetic rate of production.

Robert Fair Degraff started Pocket Books in 1939, and it remains the best known and probably the most consistently successful modern American paperback house. Its list includes what is claimed as the all-time paperback bestseller, Dr Spock's *Pocket Book of Baby and Child Care*.

The first ten Pocket Book titles published in 1939 (figures are for sales up to June 1957) were:

James Hilton, *Lost Horizon:* 1,759,000
Dorothea Brande, *Wake Up and Live!:* 420,000
William Shakespeare, *Five Great Tragedies:* 2,101,000
Thorne Smith, *Topper:* 1,564,000
Agatha Christie, *The Murder of Roger Ackroyd:* 653,000
Dorothy Parker, *Enough Rope:* 210,000
Emily Brontë, *Wuthering Heights:* 1,176,000
Samuel Butler, *The Way of All Flesh:* 210,000
Thornton Wilder, *The Bridge of San Luis Rey:* 431,000
Felix Salten, *Bambi:* 298,000

~

What harm can a book do that costs a hundred crowns? Twenty volumes folio will never cause a revolution; it is the little port-able volumes of thirty sons that are to be feared.
                                                                 Voltaire

~

The Most Implausible Book Titles

In the 1970s the Diagram Group decided to enliven the proceedings of that dismal publishers' *suk*, the Frankfurt Book Fair, by awarding a magnum of champagne to the person who submitted the name of the most improbable title on offer. The results were published in the *Bookseller*, the self-confessed 'Organ of the Book Trade'.

The 1978 winner was *Proceedings of the Second International Workshop on Nude Mice* (University of Tokyo Press). Runners up included *Ethics of Bureaucrats*; *Fight Acne and Win*; and *Macramé Gnomes*; also *100 Years of British Rail Catering*, which did for nostalgia what the Boston strangler did for door-to-door salesmen.

In 1979 the winner was *The Madam as Entrepreneur: Career Management in House Prostitution* (Transaction Press). In 1980 the accolade went to *The Joy of Chickens* (Prentice Hall), described as 'a history and celebration of the chicken'. Also well up in the running came *Do It Yourself Brain Surgery and Other Home Skills*; *Entertaining with Insects: The Original Guide to Insect Cookery*; and a manual for parents who have second thoughts: *Where Do Babies Come From and How to Keep Them There*.

In 1981 the prize was won by the somewhat sick-sounding *Last Chance at Love — Terminal Romances* (Pinnacle Books), while the runners up included *Biochemist Songbook*; *New Guinea Tapeworms and Jewish Grandmothers*; and the intriguing *Seven Years of 'Manifold': 1968–1980 (sic)*. An academic publishing house had the foresight to put out a book entitled *The Coming Penal Crisis* written by A. E. Bottoms, and not to be confused with an Indian work: *The Water of Life — A Treatise on Urine Therapy*.

The 1982 award was shared between *Population and Other Problems* (China National Publications), Minority Report; and *Braces Owners' Manual: A Guide to the Wearing and Care of Braces* (Patient Information Library). Runners up included *Sex after Death*, a title unrelated to *The Sacred and the Feminine: Towards a Theology of Housework* (perhaps inspired by the well-known lines of George Herbert: 'Who sweeps a room, as for thy laws,/Makes that and th' action fine'). Whilst on religious themes, the judges were understandably attracted by *The Creation* (revised edition).

Surely the most alarming book of black humour in that or any year was the cheerfully entitled *Nuclear War Fun Book*, something to keep the children from becoming fretful after the big bang has disrupted normal telly-watching. This could fit nicely on the shelf next to the other sure-fire winner of 1982: *Tourists' Guide to Lebanon*.

In 1983 the winner was *The Theory of Lengthwise Rolling* (MIR — a Soviet publishing house). Among the runners up were *Nasal Maintenance: Nursing Your Nose through Troubled Times*; *The Care and Feeding of Stuffed Animals*; *Living with Antiques in New Zealand*; and *Wife Battering: A Systems Theory Approach*.

The 1984 prize was awarded to *The Book of Marmalade: Its Antecedents, Its History and Its Role in the World Today*. Strong contenders included *Napoleon's Glands and other Ventures in Biohistory*; *Big and Very Big Hole Drilling* (this from the Technical Publishing House in Bucharest); and *Shoes and Shit: Stories for Pedestrians* — heavy going perhaps, but a book about which proud owners are bound to feel anally retentive.

Of course, odd titles are hardly new — the sixteenth century, that most vivid period of writing and bookmaking, was full of them. Two of the most appealing are *A Quip for an Upstart Courtier; or a Quaint Dispute between Velvet Breeches and Cloth Breeches & etc.* (1592), and *A Check or Reproof of Mr Howlet's Untimely Screeching in Her Majesty's Ear* (1581). They don't make them like that any more.

~

An order emanating from Palestine for T. E. Lawrence's master work, Seven Pillars of Wisdom, *produced a happy error in transmission. The requested title became* Seven Kilos of Wisdom.

~

Six of the Best

JOANNA LUMLEY

Here's my desert island list:
    Stella Gibbons, *Cold Comfort Farm*
    Anthony Powell, *A Dance to the Music of Time*
    Jane Austen, *Pride and Prejudice*
    Saki (H. H. Munro), *The Clovis Chronicles*
    V. S. Naipaul, *A House for Mr Biswas*
    Walter De La Mare, *Come Hither*

Rules for Converting a Gothic Novel into an Ordinary One

How to turn a gothic into an ordinary novel and vice versa: a witty set of instructions produced by C. J. Pitt in 1810 and quoted in H. R. F. Keating's *Whodunit? A Guide to Crime, Suspense and Spy Fiction* (Windward/WHS Distributors, 1982).

Where you find:	*Put:*
A castle	An house
A cavern	A bower
A groan	A sigh
A giant	A father
A bloodstained dagger	A fan
A knight	A gentleman without whiskers
A lady who is the heroine	Need not be changed, being versatile
Assassins	Telling glances
A monk	An old steward
Skeletons, skulls etc.	Compliments, sentiments etc.
A gliding ghost	A usurer, or an attorney
A midnight murder	A marriage

Do's and Don'ts for Detective Writers Dealing with Sex in the 1930s

~

Murder is a crime. Describing murder is not. Sex is not a crime. Describing sex is.

Gershon Legman

~

The following requirements were laid down by the editors of *Spicy Detective* and are quoted by Colin Watson in his *Snobbery with Violence*.

1   In describing breasts of a female character, avoid anatomical descriptions.

2   If it is necessary for the story to have the girl give herself to a man, or be taken by him, do not go too carefully into details. . . .

3   Whenever possible, avoid complete nudity of the female characters. You can have a girl strip to her underwear or transparent negligee or nightgown, or the thin torn shred of her garments, but while the girl is alive and in contact with a man, we do not want complete nudity.

4   A nude female corpse is allowable, of course.

5   Also a girl undressing in the privacy of her own room, but when men are in the action try to keep at least a shred of something on the girls.

6   Do not have men in underwear in scenes with women, and no nude men at all.

The idea is to have a very strong sex element in these stories without anything that might be interpreted as being vulgar or obscene.

Six of the Best

DICK FRANCIS

Six books which, if I was going to be stranded on a desert island, I would like to have with me to help pass away the time:

Charles Lindbergh, *The Spirit of St Louis*. As a matter of fact I did once appear with the late Roy Plomley on his *Desert Island Discs* radio programme, and even in those days I chose the No. 1 in this list. It's terrific reading, and whenever I got to the end of Lindbergh's story I'd be quite happy to go back to the beginning and start again. That says a lot for any book, don't you think?

Snow Tiger was written by a great friend, Desmond Bagley, and is one of my favourite adventure/thriller stories. Sadly Desmond (Simon, as we all knew him) died recently and we miss him (and his work) a lot.

Bomber Command is a different type of thriller, but being an ex-RAF pilot myself I found Max Hastings's description of Bomber Command both exciting and very true to life – unfortunately in many cases 'true to death' too.

Whereas *The Spirit of St Louis*, *Snow Tiger* and *Bomber Command* all had their dark moments, I don't recall one page which wasn't full of fun in David Niven's *The Moon's a Balloon*. Its only trouble was that one got to the end too soon. It was terrific, and is easily my No. 4.

My remaining two are those closest to my own life; that of horses. John Welcome's *Fred Archer — His Life and Times* is a truly remarkable biography of one of the greatest jockeys of all times. All I can say is that if the book I am now writing about Lester Piggott is half as good as Welcome's story about Archer then I shall be a happy man.

Finally we come to one of the 'greats' of equestrian literature. *Handley Cross (Mr Jorrock's Hunt)* is a must in every household which knows that a horse has a head, a tail and four legs. I'm afraid it is some time since I've read it, but we have it on our bookshelves and I'm determined to read it again one of these days.

Ronald Knox's 'Decalogue' for the Construction of a Detective Novel

This list by that versatile cleric Ronald Knox is taken from H. R. F. Keating's *Whodunit?*

I   The criminal must be someone mentioned in the early part of the story, but must not be anyone whose thoughts the reader has been allowed to follow.

II   All supernatural or preternatural agencies are ruled out as a matter of course.

III   Not more than one secret room or passage is allowable.

IV   No hitherto undiscovered poisons may be used, nor any appliance which will need a long scientific explanation at the end.

V   No Chinaman must figure in the story.

VI   No accident must ever help the detective, nor must he ever have an unaccountable intuition which proves to be right.

VII   The detective must not himself commit the crime.

VIII   The detective must not light on any clues which are not instantly produced for the inspection of the reader.

IX   The stupid friend of the detective, the Watson, must not conceal any thoughts which pass through his mind; his intelligence must be slightly, but very slightly, below that of the average reader.

X   Twin brothers, and doubles generally, must not appear unless we have duly prepared for them.

Raymond Chandler's Ten
Commandments for the Detective Novel

1 It must be credibly motivated, both as to the original situation and the dénouement.

2 It must be technically sound as to the methods of murder and detection.

3 It must be realistic in character, setting, and atmosphere. It must be about real people in a real world.

4 It must have a sound story value apart from the mystery element; i.e., the investigation itself must be an adventure worth reading.

5 It must have enough essential simplicity to be explained easily when the time comes.

6 It must baffle a reasonably intelligent reader.

7 The solution must seem inevitable once revealed.

8 It must not try to do everything at once. If it is a puzzle story operating in a rather cool, reasonable atmosphere, it cannot also be a violent adventure or a passionate romance.

9 It must punish the criminal in one way or another, not necessarily by operation of the law. . . . If the detective fails to resolve the consequences of the crime, the story is an unresolved chord and leaves irritation behind it.

10 It must be honest with the reader.

∿

You get it in the sonnet, you get it in the detective story, you get it in the blurb.

C. Day-Lewis,
on the strictness of form
that endeared him to detective fiction

∿

My Choice of the Six Greatest Mystery Books

H. R. F. KEATING

Agatha Christie, *The Murder of Roger Ackroyd*
Dorothy L. Sayers, *The Documents in the Case*
Edmund Crispin, *The Moving Toyshop*
Nicholas Blake, *The Private Wound*
Julian Symons, *The Man Who Killed Himself*
Peter Dickenson, *The Poison Oracle*

Hoaxes

Doris Lessing/Jane Somers   The well-known author Doris Lessing wrote two novels under the pseudonym Jane Somers, who was described on the jackets as a 'well-known woman journalist' when writing under her real name. These books were received with almost total critical indifference, and turned down by the writer's usual publishers (but accepted by the ones who had published her most famous work, *The Golden Notebook*). In the novelist's eyes this all proved what many people, especially writers, had suspected all along: that a writer's name mattered more to a commercial publishing industry than did the content of the book; a similar attitude was to be expected from a sheep-like corps of critics and a conditioned public. By the same token, work submitted was judged by several criteria of commercial acceptability, but seldom on its purely literary merits. The problem with this theory is that it has to assume that the two 'Jane Somers' books were at least nearly as good as works by 'Doris Lessing'. In due course the deception was made plain and Lessing's usual publisher, Tom Maschler of Cape, wrote a somewhat injured article in the *Sunday Times* analyzing his author's act of solidarity with her fellow writers and concluding: 'The crucial question remains what has the advent of Jane Somers contributed to improving the lot of the unknown writer? The short answer in my opinion is: nothing.'

Too Many Lamas in Tibet   In his memoirs, *All Authors Are*

Equal, publisher Frederic Warburg gives a hilarious account of how his company, Secker and Warburg, were successfully hoaxed – by no means to their financial disadvantage – by a man who wrote under the name of T. Lobsang Rampa. His official name, he said, was Dr Kuan-suo and he wished to sell his autobiography, a remarkable work which described how he had grown up in a Tibetan lamasery since the age of seven. Having attained the requisite higher knowledge, he had been operated on to open a 'third eye' by boring a hole in his forehead. (Of this, a tiresomely unimaginative reader had commented: 'The operation could only have resulted in death from sepsis'.) *The Third Eye* seemed an appropriate title for the doctor's memoirs and Warburg grew increasingly enthusiastic about the project. True, it gradually emerged that other publishers had turned him down from lack of faith in his veracity. Warburg himself was a little shaken, when he met the doctor for lunch, by the mystic's determination to order fish and chips.

After *The Third Eye* had notched up 45,000 sales and been translated into five languages (not, apparently, Tibetan), the *Daily Mail* discovered the truth about Lobsang Rampa. He was the son of a Devon plumber and his real, if more prosaic, name was Cyril Henry Hoskins. The exposure had been masterminded by Heinrich Harrer, who had himself written a bestseller entitled *Seven Years in Tibet*.

When the story broke, Hoskins/Kuan/Rampa was holed up in a Dublin hotel, but said he could explain everything. He was, he said, actually an Englishman whose body was inhabited by a Tibetan lama. This bodily possession had occurred one day after he fell out of a tree while trying to photograph an owl. As he lay stunned on the ground a lama in blue and saffron robes floated towards him and then, so to speak, entered into him.

George Psalmanazar – Geographer One of the most engaging hoaxers in history was the self-styled George Psalmanazar, who arrived in England in 1703 with an affecting tale of his origins and adventures. He was, he said, a native of Formosa, this distant land perhaps being chosen since the average Englishman would never have heard of it. Psalmanazar had, he said, been snatched away from his homeland by unscrupulous Jesuits who shipped him to France and tortured him into becoming a Catholic. He had escaped these desperadoes and gone to Germany where he met William Innes, the chaplain to a Scottish regiment, under whose influence he became an Anglican. Supported by a letter of recommendation from Innes, the exotic traveller arrived at the Bishop of London's palace. Then began his career in fashionable society under the auspices of the Bishop and clergy. Psalmanazar presented the Bishop with a translation of the catechism in the Formosan language, whose bizarre script was designed to be read from right to left.

Transplanted to Oxford, Psalmanazar instructed aspirant missionaries in the Formosan tongue and the mysteries of the Formosan way of life. These included, he assured them, human sacrifice — which may have dampened the ardour of some students. (According to Psalmanazar, the fastidious natives ate only raw meat, including the flesh of executed criminals, and 'annually offered a sacrifice to the Gods of 18,000 hearts cut from the breasts of boys under the age of nine'.) To expound his knowledge more fully, he published in 1704 his *Historical and Geographical Description of Formosa*, based in part on a Dutch account of Japan, but principally on his own imagination. It was pleasantly illustrated with pictures of natives who seemed to favour fur shawls over a nude body made decent by an enlarged cowboy belt round the middle. These pictures were helpfully labelled with such nomenclature as 'A Country Bumpkin'.

Psalmanazar's reputation declined after his Oxford triumph and his patrons distanced themselves. An exception was Dr Johnson, who delighted in Psalmanazar's company and regarded him as a sort of saint. Certainly Psalmanazar seems to have been good company and a talented linguist. His languages included French 'with a Gascoin accent' and English 'with a cockney accent', not to mention Latin, in which tongue he loved to chatter to the great lexicographer.

Psalmanazar's accomplice in deception had been the Rev. William Innes, who thought up the idea. In 1728 Psalmanazar publicly confessed to his deception. The way of a deceiver is a stony one, however, for almost as many refused to believe his confession as had believed in the wonderful world of Formosan savages.

The Bathtub in America On 28 December 1917, feeling that the drab war years needed brightening up a little, H. L. Mencken wrote his account of the bathtub in America under the title 'A Neglected Anniversary'. It appeared in the *New York Evening Mail*. According to Mencken, this was the seventy-fifth anniversary of the introduction of the bathtub to America, and its progress towards acceptance by the American people had been a slow and often stormy one. It had been denounced as dangerous to health in winter, for using too much water, and even for 'softening the moral fibre of the Republic'. However, after it had been vindicated by the medical profession and even Presidents began having tubs installed, it won the day.

This fantasy was accepted at face value and eagerly copied into reference books. According to Curtis Macdougall's book *Hoaxes* (1954), fifty-five references drawing on Mencken's article could eventually be found, including a mention in a speech by a Harvard professor of medicine, and another in a speech by President Truman. As Mencken ruefully observed after he tried (and failed) to expose his own hoax: 'As far as I know, I am the first person to actually question these facts in print.' As a result he would be roundly condemned by all the people with an interest, commercial or academic, in bathtubs; and that included the Cincinnati publicists who had been boasting that the bathtub industry began there — as was stated in the article; also the medical men who 'having swallowed my quackery, will denounce me as a quack for exposing them. In the end, no doubt the thing will simmer down to a general feeling that I have commited some vague and sinister crime against the United States, and there will be a renewal of the demand that I be deported to Russia.'

My Uncle Joe   A peculiar hagiography appeared under the inno-cent-sounding title of *My Uncle Joe*, supposedly written by Stalin's nephew, Budu Svanidze, and published in 1952. The curious thing about this hoax is that, although it was fabricated by a White Russian in exile, it is not hostile to the great butcher, unless some massive irony was intended that would surely have been lost on the majority of its readers. In his book *The Pleasures of Deception* (Chatto and Windus, 1977) Norman Moss captures the romantic flavour of the book when he writes: 'Here is Stalin cooking his native Georgian dishes for other members of the politbureau; raising his strong, firm, kindly hand to stop the excesses of the 1930s' purges; learning that the Germans had invaded Russia when he was out fishing with Svanidze . . .' and so forth. It was obviously a book of charm and considerable, if unintentional, satire. The reviewers wrote about it with due solemnity and the *Sunday Dispatch* serialized it.

Naked Came the Stranger   Reeling from the impact of an interview with Harold Robbins, who had just been paid a $2 million advance for a novel solely on the strength of its title, Mike McGrady of *News-day* magazine conceived the project of cooking up the worst sex novel ever commited to paper. As he put it in a note to the members of the syndicate who were to write it: 'There will be an unremitting empha-sis on sex. Also true excellence in writing will be blue-pencilled into oblivion.' The syndicate came up with the goods, although some con-tributions had to be rejected as being either too well written or not dirty enough, or both. In the big promotional campaign the part of the supposed authoress, Penelope Ashe, was taken by McGrady's glamorous sister-in-law, who was a genuine admirer of the work of Robbins and Jacqueline Susann. She put across the appealing idea that the exotic sexual behaviour of the suburban Americans featured in the book which, as McGrady said, 'would have overstated the situation in Sodom', was really nothing but the norm.

Even after the hoax was revealed the book continued to sell, presumably on its erotic content. It chalked up an astonishing 100,000 copies in hardback, perhaps because masturbators could always claim that they were buying it for the joke, which would make it socially legitimate, whereas straight erotica had to be purchased furtively. McGrady wrote an account of the hoax entitled *Stranger Than Naked, or How to Write Dirty Books for Fun and Profit*.

~

A bestseller is the gilded tomb of a mediocre talent.
Logan Pearsall Smith

~

The Ripoff with Class – the Howard Hughes Hoax McGraw Hill's new release on 7 December 1971 immediately exploded into a big affair – the eccentric and reclusive billionaire Howard Hughes was about to reveal his life story. The author, Clifford Irving, was supposed to have been paid $300,000. Although the deception was only sustained for sixty-seven days, it was one of the most spectacular publishing frauds ever; its motive was obviously financial.

Hughes was such a recluse that nobody really knew if the denials of the authenticity of the 'autobiography' were themselves genuine or not. Irving worked busily on background material, ransacking files from the Atomic Energy Commission to *Time-Life*. He managed to forge Hughes's signature so well that the handwriting experts were taken in. The money intended for Hughes was put into a Swiss bank account by Irving's wife, who invented the persona of Helga R. Hughes for the purpose. This required considerable skullduggery, a forged passport and an elaborate disguise complete with wig. The case was enlivened by a walk-on cast of colourful eccentrics, fast-talking lawyers, shifty public relations men and glamorous women, among them the singer Nina van Pallandt. Her manager later remarked cheerfully: 'The publicity was worth five hit records and an Academy Award.' As for Irving, after the trial he wrote his version of the affair, which sold very nicely.

Six of the Best

SIR HUGH CASSON

I read voraciously and omnivorously: books if possible but also, if pushed, old newspapers lining sock-drawers, insurance forms or labels on medicine bottles (when the journalist Antony Grey was a prisoner of the Chinese in Peking he kept an Eno's fruit salts bottle label to read on Christmas Day, and so would I). I have no idea what books have influenced me — only those that I have enjoyed, and for a desert island I would choose books for thickness rather than literary merit — e.g. Ruskin or Dickens or the *Oxford Book of English Verse* or Banister Fletcher's *History of Architecture*.

Of those books enjoyed I particularly remember:

as a child Kenneth Grahame, *The Wind in the Willows*
as a student Kenneth Clark, *The Gothic Revival*
as a young man Harold Nicolson, *Some People*
as a middle-aged man Evelyn Waugh, *The War Trilogy*
as an elderly man John Ruskin, *Praeterita*
as an old man John Betjeman, *Summoned by Bells*

Forgeries

Where there is literature there is forgery. Even the most careful librarians, let alone gullible and/or greedy collectors, can be taken in. The Ptolemies' library at Alexandria contained splendid manuscripts by Themistocles, Aristotle, Euripides and others, all of them fakes. When Petrarch was at the height of his fame, there were as many forged works of Petrarch about as there were Keatings in a later age. Certain writers were bound to attract the fakers — of whom the most obvious example was Byron, whose exotic exploits and scandalous reputation invited commercial gain and character assassination in about equal quantities. Other forgeries, such as the unpleasant *Protocols of the Elders of Zion*, have a transparently political motive.

William Lauder, a One-legged Scottish Forger   d. 1771   'Some of the most sinister forgeries in modern times have been perpetrated by Scotchmen,' remarks Isaac D'Israeli provocatively in his *Curiosities of Literature*; and indeed it has to be admitted that the Scots have provided their fair share of mountebanks. William Lauder had a pathological aversion to Milton which rivals that of the Baconians for Shakespeare. In 1750 he published *An Essay on Milton's Use and Abuse of the Moderns in his Paradise Lost*, in which he characteristically inserted an advertisement for himself as a Latin teacher. According to Lauder, Milton had plagiarized some all but unknown earlier authors, and in exposing parallel passages between these authors and his hated Milton he hoped to prove his point. However a Milton enthusiast, the Rev. John Douglas, became suspicious and with great labour unearthed the obscure Staphorstius, Taubmann etc. In nearly every instance he found that Lauder had tampered with the text and 'impudently inserted several lines of a translation of the *Paradise Lost* by William Hogg, and others of his own manufacture'.

Johnson was drawn into the dispute as he had written a preface and postscript to Lauder's work – he frequently wrote prefaces for works which he had neither the time nor the inclination to read. He forced Lauder to confess to the deception, which he did, very ungraciously. The booksellers put an announcement in the press to the effect that they disowned their disreputable author; however, being anxious not to lose money, they added: '. . . we shall for the future sell his book ONLY as a masterpiece of fraud, which the public may be supplied with at 1s 6d stitched.'

William Henry Ireland   1777–1835   The Stratford Jubilee of 1769, presided over by Garrick, turned Shakespeare into a national monument and set in motion a Shakespeare industry that has continued unabated to this day. Suddenly relics of all kinds began to appear – the Bard's inkstands, his chair, his shoehorn, his seal-ring, two pairs of his gloves – even a dog which was indubitably descended from Shakespeare's coach dog.

In this atmosphere of bardolatry William Henry Ireland grew up. He began modestly enough by forging a dedicatory epistle to Queen Elizabeth I, and then with his father's connivance Shakespeariana began to appear. Most of these forgeries were crude, for Ireland, though a passable copier of style, could not be bothered with Elizabethan orthography or chronological accuracy. On the other hand, he was fascinated by materials, and went to the length of tearing off a strip of ancient tapestry from the walls of the House of Lords to tie up his bundles of cheerful love letters between 'Willy' Shakespeare and 'Anna Hathaway'.

Emboldened by his success, Ireland held an exhibition at his father's house. Visitors were encouraged to sign a *Certificate of Belief* as to the genuineness of the exhibits, and many did, among them Boswell, who made a sentimental speech about being able to die happy after having seen such sights. But others, including the greatest Shakespearian scholar of the day, Edmund Malone, were sceptical. The *Telegraph* solemnly announced that it too had un-covered a cache of Shakespearian relics and quoted a colourful letter from the Bard to his cheesemonger: 'Thee chesesse you sent mee werree tooee sweattie, and tooe rankee inn flauvorre, butte thee redde herringges were addmirabblee.'

Ireland's imposture moved inexorably towards its apotheosis and exposure. A 'new' play by Shakespeare was secured by Sheridan. Two days before the first performance of *Vortigern*, Malone launched his torpedo, a 400-page pamphlet which tore the Ireland forgery to shreds and sold 500 copies in two days.

Thomas Chatterton 1752–70 When Chatterton was a child an earthenware maker is said to have offered him one of his pieces as a present, and to have asked what device he would like painted on it. 'Paint me an angel,' was the reply, 'with wings and a trumpet to trumpet my name over the world.'

In 1789 he entered into a promising correspondence with Horace Walpole, who was at first deceived by a transcript of a manuscript that Chatterton sent, purporting to be by a fifteenth-century monk called Thomas Rowley. Walpole's antiquarian acquisitiveness was aroused and he wrote Chatterton an enthusiastic letter of thanks. The forger then sent Walpole another batch of material which, how-ever, was instantly pronounced by experts to be a forgery. Walpole wrote, not unkindly, suggesting that the young man stick to honest work, a reply that displeased Chatterton, who complained that Wal-pole's own *Castle of Otranto* (1764) was represented in the preface as having been found in the library of an ancient Catholic family in the North of England, and having been printed in Naples in 1529.

In 1770 Chatterton went to London and embarked on a literary career. He made a good start, pouring out satires, stories, political essays and verses. The Lord Mayor took him up — but shortly after-wards died, leaving Chatterton patronless. After weeks of semistarvation Chatterton took arsenic, having proudly refusing an invitation from his landlady to take a meal with her. He was seventeen.

Chatterton is interesting in that he is generally agreed to have had a fine facility for verse, and his bogus medievalism in no way obscures this. To the romantics Chatterton became a cult, both for his evocation of the past and because he died suitably young and in an appropriately dramatic manner – the artist defying the world. Wordsworth eulogized Chatterton as:

> . . . *the marvellous Boy,*
> *The sleepless Soul that perished in his pride.*
> 'Resolution and Independence'

James Macpherson (Ossian) 1736–96 Macpherson is a rare example of a man who became rich and stayed rich as a result of his frauds. His career began when he showed certain Edinburgh scholars some extracts from 'Gaelic poetry', which he claimed to have collected but had in fact written himself. Against the background of the first rumblings of romanticism and the suppressed nationalism of the Scots recently crushed at Culloden, Macpherson's early sagas had immense appeal.

In 1781 Macpherson published the epic poem 'Fingal', followed in 1783 by 'Temora', both works claimed to be by Ossian, a legendary third-century bard and hero. These were a huge success and rapidly appeared in French, German and Italian translations; German scholars ranked the Gaelic bard's work with that of Homer. Not everyone was so enthusiastic, the most notable sceptic being Dr Johnson, who described the ballads as 'impudent forgeries' and was later asked whether he thought any men of a modern age could have written such poems. This enabled him to make the memorable reply: 'Yes, Sir, many men, many women, and many children.'

Nevertheless the influence of the Ossian poems was undeniable; they were admired by Goethe, Schiller, Byron and Coleridge, besides achieving the dubious distinction of being Napoleon's favourite reading. Arrogant to the last, Macpherson paid for himself to be buried in Westminster Abbey – amongst the real poets.

Major George Gordon de Luna Byron This gentleman claimed to be the accidental result of a torrid affair between the poet Byron and an aristocratic Spanish lady, the Countess de Luna. The boy was educated in various European countries and then apparently went into the Indian Army. By the 1840s he had got to America, where the first indications of a motive for his exploitation of the Byron name emerge — he left New York owing considerable debts. His attempts at borrowing from Byron's family and his publisher, John Murray, were unsuccessful.

'Major' Byron came to London, and his first great stroke of fortune was to lodge in the house of a bookseller who had a number of papers and letters relating to Byron and Thomas Moore. On the bookseller's death, he came into possession of some genuine letters and transcripts. This *coup* started him on his life of forgery. His first success was to sell some forged Shelley letters of a private nature to the poet's widow, using a mixture of blandishment and thinly disguised threats. Mary, anxious to protect her husband's reputation, unwisely paid for the letters — which only encouraged the forger to produce more. He also kept copies of those he sold in order to keep the threat of publication dangling over her.

After muddying Shelleyan waters, Byron turned to his supposed father and produced his labour of love, *The Inedited Works of Lord Byron*, an adroit mixture of new material, liftings from other scholars and plain forgery. So effective was he that Byron scholarship was bedevilled with his inventions and distortions for generations.

John Payne Collier   In 1850 Collier was at the height of his reputation. His works on English drama, his edition of Shakespeare, and his remarkable discoveries of early manuscripts and editions had made him one of the greatest scholars of his age. Ten years later his name was universally execrated, and just before his death he feebly scratched the following words into his journal: 'I am bitterly and most sincerely grieved that in every way I am such a despicable offender. I am ashamed of almost every act of my life,' and signed it: 'J. Payne Collier, Nearly Blind.'

Collier was an unscrupulous forger for most of his life, but only discovered as such towards the end of it. The cause of his downfall was his 'discovery' of a copy of the Second Folio of Shakespeare that contained thousands of corrections in what looked to be a nearly contemporary hand. It appeared to supersede all existing Shakespearian textual scholarship, and Collier shrewdly exploited its commercial possibilities. His exposure came about when this 'Perkins Folio' came into the hands of the British Museum, who detected pencil markings inadequately rubbed out, and some of them overinked, all in a modern hand. A furious row broke out, much of it vented in the columns of *The Times*.

One cannot help admiring Collier's extraordinary persistence in his trade. At the age of eighty-six he was still writing imperturbably to a friend: 'I have just discovered a most interesting book — a folio full of Milton's brief notes and references: 1500 of them.' 'Touching as is the old rogue's enthusiasm,' observes Schoenbaum drily in *Shakespeare's Lives*, 'one need not regret that posterity has been spared the Milton Folio.'

Thomas Wise   'I am sure,' cracked the Victorian writer Edmund Gosse, 'that on the Day of Judgement Wise will tell the Good Lord that "Genesis is not the true first edition".' Wise's idea was laughably simple — he printed conveniently small pieces by collected authors, and dated them earlier than any known first editions. Among the forgeries in Wise's famous Ashley Library were fakes of Browning, George Eliot, Kipling, Ruskin, Swinburne, Tennyson and Thackeray. Three years before his death John Carter and Graham Pollard produced their painstaking *Enquiry into the Nature of Certain 19th Century Pamphlets*, which demonstrated from analysis of the printing types and paper used that many of Wise's Ashley Library items could not have been printed at the dates claimed. Wise was unable to answer this devastating exhibition of his deception and died, generally unlamented, in 1937.

Protocols of the Elders of Zion   The most powerful and most vicious of historical forgeries was the so-called *Protocols of the Elders of Zion*, which first appeared in a St Petersburg newspaper of 1903 and graphically related the conspiracy of Judaism to take over the world by stealth. The methods advocated included weakening human bodies by injections of microbes, fomenting international hatred and concentrating gold into the hands of the Jews. This document appears to have been the handiwork of Tsar Nicholas II's secret police — though the Tsar later prohibited its propaganda use — and was remarkably successful because it expressed what many people wanted to believe. Some of the ideas in the *Protocols* seem to have been lifted from a novel entitled *Biarritz*, published in 1868 and written by Hermann Goedsche, pen-name Sir John Redcliffe. Much of the rest came from a French satire called *Dialogue aux Enfers entre Montesquieu et Machiavel*. Machiavelli's cynical ideas on how to obtain and retain power, as expressed in the satire, were adapted by the Russians to fit the Elders.

By the time Hitler came to power in 1933 there were several German translations. Since 1921, when Philip Graves, the *Times* correspondent in Constantinople, first exposed them, they have been repeatedly re-exposed – and definitively so by a judicial inquiry held in Berne in 1934–5. Revivals of Nazism or fascism stimulate the demand for the *Protocols*, and unscrupulous politicians take advantage of their deeply appealing and unpleasant power. According to *Time* magazine, the late King Faisal of Saudi Arabia had free copies distributed to visiting Western tourists with an assiduousness of which the Gideons would have been proud.

Gerd Heidemann and the Hitler Diaries The most recent, and in some ways the most spectacular, of forgeries was announced for serialization by the West German photo-weekly *Stern* on 22 April 1983. A journalist on *Stern* named Gerd Heidemann had obtained Hitler's diaries, miraculously saved from an air crash near Dresden on 21 April 1945 – all sixty-two volumes of them nicely bound in imitation leather covers and folio-sized for easier perusal. *Stern* set about marketing the diaries with a zeal that far exceeded their efforts to establish if they were genuine. *Paris-Match* and Italy's *Panorama* hastened to sign contracts and the *Sunday Times* began boasting of its exclusive as soon as the ink was dry on a $400,000 contract between News International and *Stern*.

On the board of Times Newspapers was the historian Lord Dacre, formerly Hugh Trevor-Roper and the author of *The Last Days of Hitler*. After examining the 'Hitler Diaries' in a Swiss bank he pronounced them authentic, as did several other scholars. The right-wing historian David Irving, who had originally interrupted a *Stern* press conference to denounce the diaries, was the only 'scholar' to change his mind in the wrong direction just as the exposure broke.

Stern might profitably have checked out their ace reporter. At his wedding the two official witnesses were former Nazi generals. He had once berated the historian Werner Maser for writing that Hitler had been fully aware of the mass extermination of the Jews and in fact wanted it speeded up. This, according to Heidemann, was smearing the Führer's good name. As for Dacre and Irving, their capacity to believe in such material, shown to them in such unsatisfactory circumstances, can only be ascribed to their great expertise in the field – as George Orwell once remarked, 'You have to be an intellectual to believe that sort of thing; no ordinary person would be so stupid.'

In the subsequent trial Heidemann was revealed as a 'Third Reich junkie' (as the *Financial Times* called him) who had conspired with a former nightclub owner and Nazi memorabilia dealer who actually wrote the forgeries.

III
Publishers

Publishers are like wives; everyone wants somebody else's — but when you have them where's the difference?

Norman Douglas

~

Now Barabbas was a publisher . . .
Attributed to both Byron and Thomas Campbell

~

Gentlemen, I agree with you that Napoleon is a tyrant, a monster, the sworn foe of our nation. But, gentlemen — he once shot a publisher!

Thomas Campbell

~

Gustave Doré's illustrations for the Bible were launched as a part-work in the 1860s by his ultra-conservative English publishers, Cassell. One of the original sketches was hastily withdrawn as it depicted God and was therefore considered irreverent.

'What was the matter, Doré? Wasn't it thought like? Not a good portrait, eh?' asked a friend.

'No,' he replied. 'It resembled neither of my chief English or French publishers. . . .'

~

First Publisher

In 1534 Cambridge University Press received the Royal Charter. Since 1584 it has been 'printing and publishing continuously'. According to Cambridge University Press's most recent historian, M. H. Black, in *Cambridge University Press 1584–1974* (CUP, 1984), this makes it the oldest printing and publishing house in the English-speaking world and, as far as is known, in the entire world. (Oxford University Press received a charter only in 1632, though it had been in the business of printing and publishing since 1585.) However, the 'publishing' part of Cambridge University Press's activities remained extremely modest until the nineteenth century.

Six of the Best

DENIS HEALEY

Here is a list of the six books which have influenced me most as a public figure – only the first two are among my six favourite books:

William Butler Yeats, *Collected Poems*. Though Yeats wrote about politics with bitter insight, his poems about his own predicament as a 'makar' have more to tell a public figure, particularly his insistence on preserving the integrity of private and personal values.

Fyodor Dostoevsky, *The Brothers Karamazov*. A stupendous parable about the id, the ego and the super-ego, written with Dickensian gusto – the greatest of all philosophical novels. Ivan's dream about the Grand Inquisitor tells you all you need to know about Andropov or Jaruzelski.

Heinrich Woelfflin, *Principles of Art History*. Though primarily a book about style in the visual arts, the categories by which Woelfflin defines the difference between the classical and the romantic apply as much to music and writing – and to politics, witness Gaitskell and Bevan.

These three are all books which I first read in my schooldays. Since World War II, when I have been actively engaged in politics, I have found the following three books most illuminating:

Nicolas Berdyaev, *Slavery and Freedom*. I read the Russian

mystics, Shestov and Ouspensky, at Balliol, but later found Berdyaev's Christian Orthodox exploration of the fundamental human and political dilemmas most penetrating, and a necessary corrective to the Blue Book strain of English socialism. Reinhold Niebuhr provides another corrective with his Protestant pessimism.

Joseph Schumpeter, *Capitalism, Socialism and Democracy*. One of the very few useful books about economics because it takes full account of the political context – perhaps because the author had failed as a conservative finance minister in Austria. Written in 1940, it accurately predicts and explains the 'stagflation' of the modern world. Asser Lindbeck's *The Political Economy of the New Left* brings the story up to date.

Karl Popper, *The Poverty of Historicism*. Another Austrian empiricist exposes the falsity of all 'inexorable laws of historical destiny'. Its attack on dogma is as relevant to some types of socialist and conservative thinking as to the Communist and Fascist doctrines which are its main targets.

Six 'Reasons' for a Publisher Deciding to Take On a Book

This list is taken from publisher John Baker's own book *The Book Business* (1971). 'All are good reasons for publishing in certain circumstances,' writes Baker, and adds: 'providing they are accepted with eyes open.'

1   Because the author's books have been previously published by the firm.

2   As a matter of 'policy' and in line with 'the character of the firm's list'.

3   'As a service to scholarship or literature' (often serving the personal interests of the managing director).

4   Because the author is 'a nice chap' (a friend).

5   Because 'if we don't, someone else will'.

6   Because we must get a list together for next year, and because it will help to 'cover the overheads'.

Some Misguided Rejections

E. E. Cummings 1894–1962 In 1935 the poet published *No Thanks*, dedicated to fourteen publishers who had rejected the manuscript, and to his mother who paid for it to be printed.

Robert Graves b. 1895 In 1948 T. S. Eliot decided that Faber should publish *The White Goddess* by Robert Graves. And just as well, one might think. Of the previous two publishers who turned it down, the first died of a heart attack a month later and the second, who remarked that the book would be of no interest to anyone, subsequently hanged himself on a tree. When they cut him down he was found to be wearing a woman's bra and panties.

John Creasey 1908–73 He is said to have received 743 rejection slips before a publisher accepted one of his mystery novels in 1932. This (unaudited) figure may be open to doubt, but the figures for his productivity are not (see p. 19).

James Joyce 1882–1941 *Dubliners* was rejected by twenty-two (but some say forty) publishers before Grant Richards very gingerly took it on. In a reversal of the role all too frequently adopted by other authors' wives Mrs Joyce is said to have rescued the 60,000-word first draft fragment of *A Portrait of the Artist as a Young Man*, known as *Stephen Hero*, from the flames — after the twentieth publisher's rejection had arrived, Joyce had thrown the manuscript into the fire.

Publicity Coups

Tobias Smollett – Spreading the Word In order to publicize his *Complete History of England* (issued in instalments, 1755–8 and 1760–1), Smollett bribed parish clerks to place prospectuses for the book in church pews.

Dead President Gives Kiss of Life to Book *From Log Cabin to White House*, an extremely dull biography of the undistinguished American President James Garfield, was written in the pious and eulogistic Victorian manner by the Rev. William Thayer. Its sales were negligible until the President was shot by a disappointed office seeker on 2 July 1881. While Garfield lingered on the threshold of death there was just time to add a hasty final chapter, and the presidential demise, on 19 September, proved to be in good time for the Christmas market. As the only book available, Thayer's turgid eulogy took off; by the end of the year it had sold 79,000 copies. By 1887 it was in its twenty-seventh printing and had sold 161,000 copies. It had reached a fourth edition by 1893, before being consigned to that respectable cemetery for inspirational and worthy books, Routledge's school prize list.

Knickerbocker's *History of New York*   Diedrich Knickerbocker was the pseudonym of Washington Irving, and in order to promote his subsequently famous book before its publication on 6 December 1809 a series of fake news items was inserted in the newspapers. First it was reported that Knickerbocker was missing from his lodgings, then that a curious book had been left in his room, and would have to be disposed of to pay his outstanding bills if he didn't reappear. The work was then announced for publication in order to 'discharge Knickerbocker's debts'.

It was a success – Irving earned $2000 from it in a year – which all began from an innocent paragraph headed 'DISTRESSING' in the *New York Evening Post* of 27 October 1809:

> Left his lodgings some time since, and has not yet been heard of, a small elderly gentleman, dressed in an old black coat and cocked hat, by the name of Knickerbocker. . . .

John Newbery   1713–67   One of the earliest publishers of books for children, Newbery was remarkably successful. The stream of titles that came out under his imprint included a number of books thinly disguised to sugar an educational pill – he being the first to assess correctly the commercial possibilities of combining instruction with pleasure; probably the most famous of the fiction titles he issued was *Goody Two-Shoes*.

Newbery died a rich man – but not solely because of his publishing activities. In London he had bought the rights to a famous medicine of the day, Dr James's Fever Powder, and the publisher adroitly mixed a little of the remedy into his fiction, as a sort of subliminal advertising. When the characters resorted to it, an instant and gratifying cure for their ailments was effected; but Goody Two-Shoes's father was unfortunately 'seized with a violent fever in a place where

Dr James' Powder was not to be had'. The tragic consequences were all too predictable. He died.

Newbery's powder, which was sufficiently versatile to cure distemper in cattle as well as rescuing humans, remained in production until World War II; it only vanished from the scene because the secret formula was destroyed in the Blitz.

Newbery was also an early exponent of what John Rowe Townsend, in *Written for Children* (Kestrel, 1983), calls 'The Amazing Free Offer'. At the beginning of 1755 he advertised New Year gift books – 'for every little boy who would become a great Man and ride upon a fine Horse; and to every little Girl who would become a great Woman and ride in a Lord Mayor's gilt coach' – absolutely free to anyone who called at the Bible and Sun in St Paul's Churchyard. There was a small charge, of course – twopence per book to cover the cost of binding. This provoked *The World* to announce satirically that it would offer three volumes of that journal 'gratis, at every bookseller's shop in town, to all sorts of persons, they paying only nine shillings for the bindings'.

Another idea of Newbery's was to introduce his books as having a distinguished, though fake, pedigree. Thus *Goody Two-Shoes* was rendered from 'an original Manuscript in the Vatican at Rome', the blurb claimed, illustrated by none other than Michelangelo.

Definitely Not for Feminists A beguiling ad. for a 1951 Dell paperback entitled *What a Body!* explained in a logical, point-by-point comparison (with pictures of the two items in question, helpfully labelled 'book' and 'woman') why it was relatively unrewarding and expensive to curl up with a good woman.

Book		*Woman*
49%	← Texture →	100%
100%	← Availability →	2–100% (depending on competition)
60,000	← Number of words →	11
97%	← Laughter production →	3% average
0%	← Miserability (capacity to make you feel terrible) →	73%
80%	← Insomniability (ability to keep you up all night, one way or another) →	79%
100%	← Overcoatability (ease of placing in overcoat pocket) →	11%
25c	← Cost →	$45 for dinner (wine and cabs not included)

Fastest Book Production

The eccentric Thomas Tegg was an early entrepreneur who managed one of the fastest-produced topical books ever. Immediately following the Battle of Trafalgar, he rushed through the press in a few hours *The Whole Life of Nelson*, and over the subsequent days sold 50,000 copies at sixpence each. Tegg was a shrewd exploiter of the folly of others, and thus treated as something of a pariah by the trade and by authors — Carlyle especially hated him. When the great financial crash came in 1825, he picked up many of Scott's novels for fourpence apiece from struggling booksellers and later resold them at at large profits. As he remarked in his autobiography, he was 'the broom that swept the booksellers' warehouses' — an early incarnation of that agent of retribution known to publishers as the mortician: that is, the remainder merchant. (By an unhappy quirk of language the word 'undertaker' once used to carry the meaning of 'publisher'. We must be glad that this occasionally apposite meaning is now obsolete.) Tegg also held nightly auctions in Cheapside which became one of the spectacles of the city, and sold reprints on the 'pile 'em high, sell 'em cheap' principle.

T. P. O'Connor's *Life of Parnell* was written, set up in type and published within five days of the Irish leader's death in 1891 — one of the greatest feats of instant biography ever. Ward Lock were the publishers.

In 1877 the Oxford University Press held a celebration to mark the four hundredth anniversary of the first book (as it is thought) to have been printed in England: William Caxton's *The Dictes or Sayengis of the Philosophres*. In twelve hours they managed to print, bind and deliver the 1052-page *Caxton Memorial Bible* — a limited edition for presentation purposes only.

On Monday, 6 June 1927 Appleton in the USA received the manuscript of *The Life of Charles Lindbergh*, who had just made his nonstop solo flight from New York to Paris. By Thursday noon of the same week they had received bound copies of the work — 40,000 words, 24 illustrations, making 250 pages, the whole clothbound and complete with colour jacket.

Franklin D. Roosevelt seems to have stimulated American publishers to remarkable achievements of speed and efficiency. Alfred E. Smith's biography of 1929 was delivered at 11.30 a.m. on a Tuesday and was at the printers by 2 p.m. By 5 p.m. it had been set, proofread and plated. By 10 a.m. on Thursday it was printed, and bound copies were ready by 4 p.m. When Roosevelt died, on 12 April 1945, Pocket Books immediately put in hand *Franklin Delano Roosevelt − A Memorial*, which must have been standing ready like a *Times* obituary, awaiting only the date and manner of death − and by 18 April 300,000 copies were on sale.

Other presidential quickies include *The End of the Presidency* (1974), which was on sale four days after Nixon left the White House, and the *Warren Commission Report* on the assassination of Kennedy (1964), which was in the stores only eighty hours after being officially released to the public.

In 1967 William Stevenson conceived, wrote and had published by Bantam an account of the Arab-Israeli War called *Strike Zion*. Between the first finger on the typewriter to the first book being on sale, a period of just twenty days elapsed.

Between 1.30 p.m. on 4 October 1965 and 8 a.m. on the 7th fifty-seven writers and editors of the *New York Times* (which happened to be on strike) wrote, and Bantam produced, 160 pages of *The Pope's Journey to the United States*. This was the fastest known production of a book − 66½ hours − up to that time.

The record for fast book production, as claimed in *The Guinness Book of Records*, seems to be a work celebrating the American Olympic Gold Medal team, which was again published by Bantam and again written by journalists on the *New York Times*. *Miracle on Ice* took 46½ hours from receipt of manuscript to finished copies over 27, 28 and 29 February 1980. No doubt public interest in such a work scarcely endured for a period longer than that of production.

Authors more accustomed to waiting months − or even years − before seeing their manuscripts turned into books will no doubt view the above examples with mixed feelings.

Slowest Book Production

Nearly the slowest gestation of all − happily the sales were more brisk − was that of the *Grimms' Deutsches Wörterbuch*, begun in 1854 and published in its entire and final form in 1971. *The Oxford English Dictionary* (1884−1928) was, by comparison, a rush job. But not even the *Deutsches Wörterbuch* can compare for leisurely progress with Jean Bolland's *Acta Sanctorum*, which he began compiling in

1643. The *Acta* are carefully arranged according to saints' days, and by 1925 the publication had reached the month of November. However, the publishers very sensibly decided that the last lap should not be approached at reckless speed, and by 1940 an introduction to the month of December had appeared. It is indeed fortunate that hagiology is one of the less ephemeral branches of publishing.

One of the longest gestations was described by Philip Howard in an article in *The Times* in 1985 to celebrate the appearance of the definitive edition of the Latin poet Ennius. This project, triumphantly completed in 848 pages of painstaking scholarship, was apparently first discussed within Oxford University Press in 1935. In 1943 they decided to take the plunge, and a scholar named Otto Skutsch set to work on the *Annals of Quintus Ennius* (600 lines from eighteen books of verse on the history of Rome). He was to have included fragments from the twenty Tragedies as well, but there really wasn't enough space – perhaps they will appear in a companion volume. The ideal dedicatory motto to preface this forty-two-year-long labour of love is, as it happens, provided by Ennius himself in Book 9 of his *Annals*: 'No sooner said than done – so acts the man of worth.'

Calamities of Publishers

Difficult Authoress   If one is inclined to think that calamities only affect authors, or, if they do not, that only authors deserve sympathy in the face of them, the *Letters to Macmillan* edited by Simon Nowell Smith (Macmillan, 1967) would surely alter the most prejudiced mind. Poor Edward Freeman was responsible for editing Macmillan's *Historical Course for Schools* and had to deal with a most troublesome authoress in Charlotte M. Yonge, or 'Aunt Charlotte' as he called her. Miss Yonge was a bestselling writer of Victorian fiction, but she was no historian, a fact that did not deter her from writing history books. It took her four years to do her *History of France* in the Macmillan series, and much of the time was spent in rewriting, as Freeman desperately tried to replace fiction with fact, and inaccuracy with accuracy. In November 1877 an exhausted Freeman wrote to Macmillan:

. . . I have sent off the rest of the latter part of Aunt Charlotte. . . . If you think I have changed too much, ask . . . anybody. You would hardly have wished me to keep these propositions:

1st That the last tyrant LNB [Louis-Napoleon Bonaparte] . . . being elected President, called himself First Consul.

2nd That Worth [spelled in some odd way] was the first engagement in 1879.

3rd That Thiers was the son of the beloved Queen of Prussia.

4th That the Duke of Orleans's horses ran away, leaving two infant sons.

The first of these errors I take on myself to denounce: the fourth, which may or may not be an error, I leave to such as be learned in the pedigrees of horses. . . .

And later, in another letter:

. . . And after all I do not venture to say that [the book] is good or accurate, only less shamefully bad and inaccurate than it was aforetime. . . .

What made things especially difficult for Freeman was the air of sweet resignation with which all his suggestions were received, making it difficult, if not impossible, for him to justify losing his temper with her.

Disappearing Cash   Although authors may be the principal source of publishers' woes, they are by no means the only one. Oxford University Press, whose financial control was not quite as strict in the eighteenth century as it now is, failed to profit from their first major popular success. Between 1703 and 1707 Clarendon's *History of the Great Rebellion* was published in three volumes. Although the sales were very substantial, little money seemed to be accruing from them, and the reason was not discovered for some time. The then Vice-Chancellor, William Delaune, had embezzled the profits, although exactly why such a distinguished gentleman should stoop so low was something of a mystery. A clue is provided by Thomas Hearne, who says of him that he was 'a good companion and one who understood Eating and Drinking nicely'; so perhaps he lived beyond his means. Although he was stripped of the Presidency of St John's he was given the Lady Margaret Professorship of Divinity to console him for this loss. He seems to have embezzled £2280 3s 9d.

Rash Offer   According to Sheila Hodges in *Gollancz – the Story of a Publishing House 1928–1978* (Gollancz, 1978), *Lucky Jim* (1954) was slow to get off the ground in England and even slower in America. Kingsley Amis's comic masterpiece of fifties' disillusion- sold so miserably for Doubleday that the gallant publisher offered a 'money back' guarantee to any purchaser who didn't find it uproariously funny. The returned copies 'tumbled into their ware- house in shoals' (to the great amusement of the author, when he was told; the publishers would have been unlikely to see the funny side of it) — proving that it doesn't always pay to put your money where your mouth is. In paperback, however, it sold 1¼ million copies.

Lively Competition   In the days before the first Act regulating copyright, in 1709, it was difficult for a publisher, still less an author, to protect his literary property — especially with men like Edmund Curll around. Among the practices he favoured was that of announcing a 'Life' of any recently deceased man when he had no material at all, but at the same time advertising for any scraps of biographical information, which, on receipt, he subsequently made into the book; John Arbuthnot, friend of Pope and Dryden, des- cribed him as 'one of the new terrors of death'. He used this method in various other ways to choke off rivals and queer the pitch for genuine works on the same subjects. But his most brazen effort was to steal the works of Matthew Prior (1664–1721) from Jacob Tonson, the poet's honourable and painstaking publisher. Curll somehow got hold of Prior's poems, or a good body of them, and announced publication of a comprehensive edition. Tonson advertised that his was the genuine edition (which it was) and Curll's a spurious piracy (which it was); but to no avail — Curll's book was out within a week (an indication of the amount of work that went into its preparation) and Tonson's edition did not appear for nearly two years. Mean- while, Curll published a 'second edition' of Prior, at which the poet protested loudly and publicly.

Curll was several times punished for his rascally behaviour — once being tossed in a blanket and otherwise humiliated by Westminster schoolboys for the unauthorized printing of a funeral ode. He was later brought before the bar of the House of Lords through the intrigues of Alexander Pope, who hoaxed him in the matter of his letters. (Curll was advertised as the publisher of these letters, which were being sent to him anonymously, and supposedly contained some written by peers. It was an offence to publish peers' letters.) The upshot was still good business for Curll. As soon as the case was dismissed, he busily began printing volumes of Pope's letters in competition with the official edition. He issued splendid critical denunciations of the latter — which had indeed been somewhat doctored by the self-conscious and waspish Pope.

A Little Widow Is a Dangerous Thing   Citing this maxim, Sir Stanley Unwin gives an account of a beleaguered colleague, one of whose authors, before he died, had sold rights direct to an American publisher, who had in turn leased UK rights to the British publisher. With 'large unearned advances on all the direct contracts and royalties payable to the American publishers', it was obvious that no money was due from the British licensee. The widow saw it differently, and:

> The morning's post contained long letters from the author's agent [egged on by the widow], a solicitor acting for the widow, and a still longer one from the widow herself. Before [the publisher] had time to read them, all three were on the telephone, and before the day was over, all three had called on [him]. So had the widow's daughter, and a friend of the widow! A film company rang up to say that they understood that [he] owed the widow money and were they safe in advancing some cash on the strength of it, as also did a Government official. The agent admitted at the outset that all was in order and apologised for being troublesome. The solicitor, after examining agreements and correspondence, saw he was wasting his time. Both resigned. . . . But there are plenty of solicitors in London, and the game started afresh. The agreements became worn out with constant examination because as each solicitor reported that everything was in order another was found. One had the temerity to suggest to [the publisher] (at the instigation of the widow) that because the original contract between the author and the American publishers, which naturally were in New York, could not be produced by [him] in London, [he] had no rights, and would it not be much better to pay the widow something to go away. [He] pointed out that if she found it profitable to make herself a nuisance, she would never go away.

It was, in fact, a long time before she did.

Getting On OK?   The following letter was received by Karl Marx from his German publisher:

Dear Herr Doktor,
 You are already 18 months behind time with the manuscript of *Das Kapital* which you have agreed to write for us. If we do not receive the manuscript within six months, we shall be obliged to commission another author to do the work.

A Troublesome Father – Mr Micawber Comes to Call   While history is full of instances of sons who run into debt and have to be bailed out, improvident fathers are less of a cliché. Unbeknown to the son, Charles Dickens's father was quick to take advantage of the young writer's success and started turning up regularly at his publishers, Chapman and Hall, asking for what he delicately called 'accommodation'. It comes as no surprise to learn that John Dickens was in part the inspiration for Wilkins Micawber, the lovable optimist of *David Copperfield*, whose attitude to domestic economy was so memorably summoned up in the following words: 'Annual income twenty pounds, annual expenditure nineteen nineteen and six, result happiness. Annual income twenty pounds, annual expenditure twenty pounds ought and six, result misery.' Like Micawber, John Dickens had been in the Marshalsea prison for debt, and like him was possessed of a quaint charm that successfully unloosed the purse strings of most of those to whom he explained his circumstances.

His letters to Chapman and Hall, says Arthur Waugh in his 1930 history of the firm, were 'in themselves enough to open the till-drawer of the stiffest stickler for convention'. 'The want of £15', he would write, 'places me in a situation of the most particular difficulty – as regards home affairs; if it was any matter less urgent than the question of rent, nothing would induce me to intrude my affairs on your notice.' But – 'the subject is one of settlement by two o' clock, and unless I so arrange it, I am lost'. The publishers paid up and tactfully refrained from telling Dickens. As is the way, one payment led to an application for another; and still another. Quietly, Chapman and Hall subsidized the charming but unregenerate father of their hottest publishing property, no doubt resignedly attributing the outward flow of cash to 'overheads'.

Mr Shaw's Will Be Done   Those few persons who are inclined to feel sorry for publishers would surely have sympathized with Messrs Chapman and Hall when they took on *The Table Talk of George Bernard Shaw*. Not only did he refuse to give the usual indemnity that the author gives the publisher against libel (inevitably there subsequently *was* a libel action and Shaw magnanimously paid up), but he wrote into the agreement a clause to the effect that if, within two years of publication, the book had not sold 2000 copies, the publishers should pay him royalty on the figure just the same. The appalled publishers protested – vainly – that they had never before been asked to include such a clause. To this Shaw replied with irrefutable logic that no book bearing his name had ever sold fewer than 2000 copies. If the publishers failed to sell that number they would merely be demonstrating their total incompetence in the performance of their business. This was no fault of the author. Indeed he was the wronged party. Accordingly, the least they should do was to compensate him for their inefficiency – and pay up. Chapman and Hall's desire to have the book overcame their outrage at Shaw's Mephistophelean line in argument, and they signed.

Collapse of Constable in 1826 'One day', wrote Thomas Carlyle, 'the Constable mountain, which seemed to stand strong like the other rock mountains, gave suddenly, as the icebergs do, a loud-sounding crack; suddenly, with huge clangor shivered itself into ice-dust; and sank, carrying much along with it.' He is describing the most spectacular collapse in publishing history, that not only ruined the proprietors of two prominent Scottish firms, Constable (publisher) and Ballantyne (printer and bookseller), but beggared one of the most popular writers of that or any other age – Sir Walter Scott. The various transactions that resulted in this house of cards effect were tangled indeed, and neither Scott nor the Ballantynes appeared to have been remotely aware of the imminent danger. Indeed, John Ballantyne had died before the crash, unaware that he was bankrupt and bequeathing in his will a non-existent £2000 towards the completion of the new library at Scott's house, Abbotsford. Scott had the major interest in Ballantyne, a firm which had long been ill managed and a drain on his resources – even when he was earning £15,000 a year from the Waverley novels. Constable went down for £250,000. The Ballantyne liability was £130,000 – and Scott, as senior partner, accepted the responsibility of paying off the debts, which he was well on the way to doing by the time of his death in 1832. The suddenness and dramatic nature of the crash was due not only to the financial unwisdom of the principals but also to the financial crash of that year that followed a period of wild speculation not unlike the South Sea Bubble.

~

If Faber continue to publish this sort of book as a lead-title it will not be long before the portrait of T. S. Eliot should be taken from the boardroom and hung in the servants' lavatory.
Christopher Hawtrey in the *Spectator*,
reviewing *The Burning Book* by Maggie Gee

~

Law Suits

Harriette Wilson 1786–1855 Biographers describe Harriette Wilson, *née* Dubochet, as a *'demi-mondaine'*, and she was the mistress of a number of aristocrats in the early nineteenth century; they included the Earl of Craven, the Duke of Argyll, the Marquess of Worcester and, most famously, the Duke of Wellington. In 1825 she published what was threatened as merely the opening chapter in a series of volumes describing her adventures in high society. Entitled *Memoirs of Herself and Others*, it was preceded by a barrage of menacing publicity intended to frighten potential victims into paying the authoress to keep their names out of subsequent volumes; this seems to have worked very well with some of her previous clients, but the victor of Waterloo met her threats with characteristic *sangfroid*, telling her to 'publish and be damned'.

The book was put out by a shady publisher called J. Stockdale, who himself 'edited' the works he published under the pseudonym of Thomas Little. This Thomas Little added a postscript to Harriette's effort, remarking that the publication 'would not fail to produce the greatest moral effect on the present and future generations'. An effect it certainly had, and panic-stricken meetings were held at White's, Brooks's and the United Service Clubs in order to decide what counter-measures should be taken. A group of Harriette's ex-lovers are thought to have financed the action taken in the courts by a Piccadilly stonemason named Blore, whose clumsy advances had been sarcastically described by the object of them in her book. He was awarded £300 for libel and another plaintiff extracted even more; but by then the book had been such a success – as each serial part was announced, the publisher had been obliged to keep eager customers at bay by erecting a barricade round his premises – that Harriette seems to have considered she had milked her ex-clients sufficiently to live agreeably in Paris, whither she had wisely retired before publication. Indeed, the fines must have been a drop in the ocean compared to the proceeds of thirty editions of the *Memoirs* that appeared in a year in England, and the eight-volume edition that was published in France; not to mention the hush money paid by those anxious not to appear in future instalments of the work.

All this disagreeable worry for the fornicating aristocracy might have been avoided if the Duke of Beaufort had kept his word and paid Harriette an annuity of £500, as agreed, instead of the £1200 lump sum dictated by his meanness.

Elinor Glyn 1864–1943 Her novel *Three Weeks* (1907) eventually sold over 5 million copies — see p. 93 for the somewhat banal plot — but without the efforts of press agent Harry Reichenbach in the USA it might have gone totally unnoticed. He drew to the attention of the US Post Office Department the pages on which strategically placed asterisks seemed to hint at something lurid and — yes — obscene. The Post Office promptly banned it, and the ban was immediately challenged and lifted (the book was quite innocuous — even to a prurient bureaucrat). Thus the novel that invented the pregnant expression 'it' for sex appeal became a bestseller. (*Three Weeks* was followed later by *Six Days*, an indication perhaps, as one critic unkindly pointed out, that the hero and heroine's sexual powers were waning.)

Three Weeks came before the courts again because a movie company made a film of it and omitted to ask the author's permission to do so. She therefore sued them for breach of copyright and the case was heard by a High Court Judge, Mr Justice Younger. He ruled that the episode that the author claimed had been pirated was so 'grossly immoral in its essence, its treatment and its tendency' that 'no protection will be extended by a Court of equity'. In other words, as C. H. Rolph puts it in *Books in the Dock* (André Deutsch, 1969): 'What he said amounted to a decision that if a single judge, sitting in a Chancery court, took the view that a book was obscene, its author had no copyright in it.' In the gratuitous comments of British judges ignorance and prejudice are all too often dressed up in the language of Solomon, but Mr Younger's contempt for justice was considered remarkable, even by the standards of his fellows.

~

> . . . *in seven days she fellates her father, takes on board her two regular lovers, sleeps with her ex-husband, is half-raped by a homosexual, has her anus enlarged by an adroit French restaurateur, sleeps chastely with a lesbian ex-lover, picks up a buffet-car attendant, and is back for more.*
>   Times Literary Supplement
>   summary of the plot of *Love All*, by Molly Parkin

~

Working for the BOSS An interesting instance of multiple libel was still rumbling on in 1984; Penguin Books described Gordon Winter's *Inside BOSS*, which purported to reveal the secrets of the South African Bureau of State Security, as 'the most problematic book we have ever published'. It gradually emerged that Winter's role as author was decidedly equivocal, resembling that of an *agent provocateur* more than that of a whistle blower. One person libelled in the book, a South African photojournalist named Stanley Winer, accused Winter of being simply an agent working for BOSS. Three people received substantial damages – Winer, Harold Soref (the former Tory MP) and Mr Nana Mahomo (a founder of the Pan Africanist Congress of South Africa). Other aggrieved parties were said to be still negotiating with the publisher's solicitors. The water-muddying tactics of the book may be seen from the accusation, which was untrue, that Nana Mahomo had taken part in a CIA campaign to discredit another Pan Africanist leader. If the grisly and Nazistic BOSS were indeed behind the whole venture, they must have been well pleased with their work.

Plagiarism and Bluster In his *Memoirs of a Journalist/Publisher* (W. H. Allen, 1978) publisher Mark Goulden tells the remarkable story of Norman Mailer's Marilyn Monroe book, which Goulden originally hoped to assess with a view to publishing it. At the last moment he was mysteriously denied a chance to see the manuscript and the contract went to Hodder and Stoughton. Goulden soon discovered why: when his lawyers examined the text of the Mailer book side by side with two previous books on Monroe that Goulden's firm had published, they found remarkable similarities – almost a quarter of one of the books reappeared very thinly disguised in the new work. Legal action was then taken on behalf of the two W. H. Allen authors, who had innocently given permission for a few quotes to appear in Mailer's work; the permission was withdrawn and a substantial copyright fee demanded. A battle of words was waged through the intermediary of the press, Mailer blusteringly threatening (it was reported) to fly over to England and beat up Goulden, and Goulden retorting that he would take on Mailer in any sport 'except prose-lifting'. A high point of hilarity was reached when a soapy American publisher rang Goulden and suggested that a thousand dollars should see him right on the copyright fees; Goulden refused. Matters continued in similar vein for some time, with the unfortunate Hodder caught in the crossfire, having an enormous first edition under wraps and an unrecoverable outlay of £30,000 for the British rights. In the end they came to an amicable agreement with W. H. Allen, a fee was paid with costs and a statement of settlement terms published – all rather bad luck on Hodder, who were in no way knowingly to blame.

A Hiding to Nothing – Chapman versus Northcliffe   The power of newspaper barons is legendary and indeed has induced something approaching megalomania in not a few of them. Lord Northcliffe demonstrated one way of wielding it in his decision to put publishers Chapman and Hall in their place in 1913. They had published a work about the Northcliffes, *Lord London*, by a former employee of the magnate, Keble Howard; the book, which was indifferently written, appeared to be as sycophantic as the circumstances and Britain's wonderful libel laws required.

After it appeared, Chapman and Hall became aware that reviews of their publications in Northcliffe papers had mysteriously dried up. Soon they were not even mentioned in the 'New Books' column. Finally, all advertisements for the publisher's books were refused without explanation. Through the intervention of William Heinemann, Chapman and Hall were able to confirm what they had immediately suspected – the book had given offence to his lordship, who held that it depicted his father as a foolish old fellow who spent his time playing the violin in an upstairs room. As long as the book was in circulation, the name Chapman and Hall would not appear in his newspapers. As these by then included *The Times*, the *Evening News*, the *Daily Mail* and the *Daily Mirror*, besides a host of weekly publications and provincial newspapers, this was an embargo that was difficult for any publisher to laugh off.

The passage complained of was innocuous in the eyes of most readers, but the book had been out seven months and ceased to sell, and other authors were suffering because of it. So Chapman and Hall decided to withdraw it, only to be met with a writ from the author who accused them of breaching their contract by not keeping the book on sale. Moreover, although Northcliffe agreed to the book being reissued provided the offending passages were cut out, the author refused to have a single word deleted. The publishers were caught in a cleft stick; counsel's opinion was that they were clearly in breach of contract. In the end they had to pay off the author in an out of court settlement, besides making a considerable loss on the book, as they had to credit the booksellers for returned copies.

All this must have been but water off a duck's back to Northcliffe, whose attitude to people and power is well summed up in an early remark of his, recorded by the journalist Hannen Swaffer: 'When I want a peerage I shall buy one like an honest man.'

A Bon Mot   Not all law suits with their legal jargon, self-serving claims and counter-claims succeed in provoking *bon mots*. One that did, however, was the Rev. Mr Mason's suit against publisher John Murray, for publishing some fifty lines of Gray's poems in which Mason claimed exclusive property under the statute of Queen Anne. Murray had not intended any infringement of Mason's rights (the lines were, anyway, widely reprinted elsewhere without permission), but when he heard that Mason was starting legal proceedings he hastened to go to him, explained the situation, and offered such settlement as Mason might think reasonable. Mason vindictively pursued the case, however, and obtained an injunction to stop the sale of the book. This was reported to Dr Johnson in company, and he commented that he was not surprised since Mason was a Whig.

Mrs Knowles (not hearing distinctly): 'What! A prig, Sir?'

Johnson: 'Worse, Madam; a Whig! But he is both.'

The *Exodus* Case   Leon Uris's bestselling novel *Exodus* (William Kimber, 1959) was the subject of one of the most bizarre and unpleasant legal cases in publishing history. In the course of the book, which dealt with the oppression and suppression of Jews in twentieth-century Europe and the Middle East, there was an account of operations performed to sterilize Jews in Auschwitz, which named four doctors involved in these evil and racist tasks, mis-spelling one of them. Most of the people responsible had either been tried for their crimes, or made themselves scarce; and certainly it hardly seemed credible that any of them should court publicity by suing for libel. This, however, is exactly what Dr Dehring, or Dering, by that date a North London practitioner, decided to do when he discovered he was named in the book. Dr Dering had barely escaped extradition to Poland in 1947 after successfully enduring an identity parade in front of ex-Auschwitz inmates. Both the French and Czech governments had also been interested in capturing him.

Uris had taken his information from a book by Joseph Tenenbaum, but this author was now dead, so Dering's past had to be laboriously traced from scratch. In due course a formidable array of defence witnesses confronted the doctor, of whom the most impressive was Dr Adelaine Hautval, who had been sent to Auschwitz for protesting to the Gestapo about the treatment of Jews in France.

Although moral questions loomed large in the trial, for Dr Dering claimed that he had had to carry out the operations or risk death, and that, in any case, if he had not performed them someone else (possibly unskilled) would have done so, the outcome was decided on the facts. It appeared, for instance, that the figure of 17,000 experimental operations which the book suggested were performed by Dering was grossly in excess of the true figure. Suggestions that he had not used anaesthetic were also wide of the mark. It seemed to the jury that the remarks made in the book were defamatory and could not be proven on the evidence given, though what was revealed of Dr Dering was so damning that one wonders why he should ever have contemplated legal action. He was awarded precisely one halfpenny damages and ordered to pay defence costs of £20,000; when he died the following year £17,000 of this was still outstanding. William Kimber had also lost money because of their legal bill and the vast commercial loss incurred by withdrawing the book for the duration of the trial. The publishers calculated that it would have cost about a tenth of what they had lost if they had settled out of court.

A Glossary of Curious Terms

Thud and Blunder   Thriller writer John Gardner coined this useful term for the school of complicated spy novels where periods of intense obscurity in which nobody, including the reader, has the faintest idea what is going on, are interspersed with sudden and horrific bouts of violence.

Faction   Novels based on the accumulation of documentary fact, for example Arthur Hailey's *The Final Diagnosis*, are regarded as faction. In Sheila Hailey's *I Married a Best Seller* (Michael Joseph, 1978) she recalls his research for this novel: 'He watched open heart surgery, listened to radiologists, pathologists, anaesthetists, talked with nurses, interns, hospital directors.' In other words, never mind the quality – feel the width. A compliment of a kind has been paid to Hailey's work, though not exactly a literary one: in certain institutions for trainee caterers in the United States his novel *Hotel* is on the required reading list.

Blurb   This word describes the more or less truthful description of a book's contents printed on a flap of the jacket or on the cover. So many reviewers go no further with a book than the blurb that in 1923 an American house sent out its review copies in plain wrappers giving only the author, date of publication and price. (This practice eventually had to be discontinued because of the indignation of reviewers.) The invention of the name is credited to Gelett Burgess, editor of a small review called *The Lark*. 'A blurb,' he said, 'is a check drawn on Fame, and is seldom honoured.'

Burgess's book *Are You a Bromide?* was presented to booksellers at their trade association's annual dinner. For these special copies, Burgess designed a jacket featuring the simpering lady from a toothpaste advertisement, in parody of the anaemic damsels almost indiscriminately portrayed on the jackets of novels at that time; his description of the text referred to this lady as 'Miss Belinda Blurb'.

Annie Carrie Nina According to Frederic Warburg, the trade counter at Routledge, where he started work in the 1920s, had developed a curious *argot* by which titles could be recognized. The 'reps' from the London book trade ('aged men carrying huge sacks') read out their orders 'in a monotonous voice and a system of pronunciation as mysterious as Tibetan'. Tolstoy's well-known novel became 'Annie Carrie Nina'. Unfortunately the 'collectors', as they were known, often had difficulty in reading their own writing and it was not always easy to identify the title required. According to Warburg, these collectors were cheerful, if unlettered, individuals who resented only one thing in life, and that was a bestseller. 'It made their sacks uncomfortably heavy.'

Grangerize This verb originated with the Rev. James Granger (1726–76), who removed thousands of illustrations from other books intending to use them in his *Biographical History of England*. In later editions of his work he obligingly provided blank pages on which people could stick the fruits of their own grangerizing. Since Granger himself had amassed some 14,000 illustrations, and since his readers made up sets of Granger with as many as 3000, the havoc wreaked in libraries may be easily imagined. The process reached its apotheosis in the mid-nineteenth century when a Granger was sold that ran to nineteen volumes.

The Nipple Cover In the 1940s, when nipples had vanished completely from book covers in America, a paperback was issued that startled everybody by its candid portrayal of this by now only rumoured part of the female anatomy. Promisingly titled *The Private Life of Helen of Troy*, the book was therefore not only a triumph of research, but a breaker of taboos. As Piet Schreuder observes in his *History of the Paperback*, an exception was probably made in the case of Helen's nipples 'because of her respected position in classical antiquity'.

Bowdlerize The appearance of Dr Bowdler's cleaned up text of Shakespeare (ten volumes, 1818) gave the world four new items of book terminology — 'bowdlerize', 'bowdlerization', 'bowdlerizer' and 'bowdlerism'. To 'bowdlerize' a text was to remove from it, often silently and absurdly, everything that might offend delicate eyes and ears; in other words, to take out the dirty, contentious and blasphemous bits. As a result of the mania for mutilation that began with Bowdler, three or four generations in England and America grew up with inaccurate and misleading texts of many literary classics. The expurgators were by no means only the usual small-minded and vindictive type of person who stock the censors' offices of the world, but high-minded men of letters such as Noah Webster, William Cullen Bryant, John Masefield, Palgrave, Lewis Carroll, and others. Bowdlerization, unlike censorship, is a voluntary procedure, not imposed by authority.

There are other analogous and picturesque terms for the bowdlerizer's craft: editions were said to have been 'gelded', as they were in France, where the problem was at its most acute in the seventeenth and eighteenth centuries and such books were known as *livres châtrés*. As hypocrisy increased so did the gentility of language: books were later described as 'purged', 'pruned' and 'chastened'. By 1850 there were seven expurgated editions of Shakespeare on the market; by 1900 the number had risen to nearly fifty. Bowdlerization was a highly profitable activity. Shakespeare was also said to have been 'lambed' after the publication of Charles and Mary Lamb's *Tales from Shakespeare*.

~

> . . . *Against this sham virginity of a prostituted age I shall always offend, as long as I can hold a pen, therefore I shall never be popular. So our fashionable ladies, taking their manners from men about town, their talk from livery stables, their air, hair and dress from kept women. Yet one of them would faint if my hero blows his nose. How can you fail to see the rottenness of such refinement?*
>
> Mrs Gaskell, in a letter to her publishers,
> Macmillan, 27 January 1866

~

The Books in Hell Names which are given to collections of erotica in libraries are 'an index of the discomfort and terror with which they [the libraries] handle such materials', writes Ralph Ginzberg in *An Unhurried View of Erotica* (Secker and Warburg, 1959). At the

Bibliothèque Nationale in Paris it is called *L'Enfer* collection; at the British Museum, Arcana. The Armed Forces Medical Library in Washington refers to the Cherry Case, Harvard to the Hell Hole and the Library of Congress, eruditely, to the Delta collection, after the Greek symbol for the female sex organ. Brooklyn Public Library keeps erotica in the Treasure Room, while at New York it is confined to the Cage, according to Ralph Ginzburg 'a fenced off portion of the stacks whose key is entrusted only to the more senescent members of the staff'.

When erotic books come up for auction they are described by such discreetly suggestive terms as Amatory, Curiosa, Deliciae, Esoteric, Facetiae, Occult or simply Varia. In the USA the most exotic name for erotic — usually straight pornographic — literature used to be Tijuana Bibles, because Tijuana in Mexico was the porn Mecca for those unable to obtain such material at home.

Pasquinade The origin of this expression, meaning a lampoon, is interesting. After the death of Pasquino, a fifteenth-century Roman tailor noted for his caustic wit, somebody dug up a mutilated statue and placed it opposite his house near the Piazza Navona. From this happy coincidence the anonymous statue came to be called 'Pasquin', and the custom grew of affixing unflattering literature regarding the Pope and other figures of authority to it. It thus acquired a dubious institutional status somewhat akin to *Private Eye* in our own times. Retaliation to the pasquinades was traditionally hung on Marforio, an ancient statue of Mars at the other end of the city.

Acroidal This term describes a murder mystery in which the author supposedly cheats on the reader by disobeying some of the rules of detective stories that were considered sacrosanct until Agatha Christie disobeyed them in *The Murder of Roger Ackroyd* (1926).

Bodice Rippers (or Sweet and Savages or Hot Ones) The difference between these three similar genres of steamy romance lies chiefly in the degree of sexiness permitted, and to what extent an undertow of bondage, rape, flagellation etc. becomes, so to speak, an overtow. The genres are of course able to parody themselves, either intentionally or unintentionally, and occasionally to break their own rules; thus Jilly Cooper's cheerful romps were aptly described by one critic as 'Barbara Cartland without the iron knickers'.

Trasky   In 1965 writer Betty Trask made a will leaving her substantial fortune to the Society of Authors, who were to use it to
establish an annual literary prize. The award was to be made to any
author below the age of thirty-five for a 'romantic novel', or at any
rate a novel of 'traditional' rather than 'experimental' nature. When
Miss Trask, herself an undistinguished novelist, died in 1983 a panel
of judges was set up to award her prize; it was worth £12,500 to the
winner and £1100 each for five runners up (rather more than the
Booker Prize). From the judges' almost impossible deliberations (how
were such words as 'romantic' and 'traditional' to be interpreted?)
was born the word 'trasky'. But what kind of fiction actually was
trasky? Some thought it implied a story without four-letter words, not
sexually explicit and with a healthy leitmotiv of cheerfulness, or at
least nothing dreary or depressing. Others thought traskiness implied
romance, preferably of the slushier variety. After a lot of heart-
searching, the judges came to some sort of a conclusion – but the first
winner, a book about a child travelling across Europe in the back of a
car, listening to his parents quarrelling, didn't seem to give many
clues as to the essence of traskiness. Nor did it seem very 'romantic',
although the theme of a married couple who hate each others' guts
might, at a pinch, be considered 'traditional'. 'Traskiness' has therefore yet to be successfully defined – which won't prevent many people
from knowing exactly what it means.

~

*We all have nothings. We need rackfillers to elbow out the com-
petition.*

A member of the book trade,
discussing a book that sold 25,000 in paperback;
quoted by Alex Hamilton in the *Guardian*

~

Six of the Best

QUENTIN CRISP

Books are for writing – not for reading. . . . On a desert island, I should require the following:

A manual on how to build a seaworthy boat; preferably by the gentleman who wrote *Kon-Tiki*.

A manual on how to navigate a small craft in high seas: preferably by Mr Chichester.

A handbook on how to attract the attention of rescue teams.

A cook book containing recipes requiring no food and no stove, by Mrs Cradock.

A tailoring manual demonstrating the way to make clothes from palm leaves, preferably by Mr Cardin.

A long playing record saying, 'Help'.

Four Memorable Moments in a Publisher's Career

ANTHONY CHEETHAM

Greatest Publishing Scoop   Although it does not include heady sums of money this remains *84 Charing Cross Road* by Helene Hanff, for which I bravely risked £250 for the paperback rights after the book had been on André Deutsch's backlist for some years. The first paperback printing was 15,000 copies, but in the next five years it went on to sell well over 300,000 copies and in 1984 was still going strong on the Futura list – very gratifying for a slim volume of correspondence between an anglophile New Yorker and a London secondhand bookseller.

Greatest Commercial Disaster   The original novel of *King Kong* was supposed to be the movie tie-in of the decade, rushed out to coincide with the Dino de Laurentiis film. We paid a vast advance, sold 150,000 copies − and got over 100,000 back in returns.

Largest Advance Ever (and the Best Seller, Luckily) I paid $266,000 for Colleen McCullough's *The Thorn Birds*. The auction went on until one o'clock in the morning, by which time my chairman and all my colleagues had long gone to bed. I exceeded my limit by over £100,000 and had a lot of explaining to do over the next week. But *The Thorn Birds* did sell a good 1.5 million copies before the TV series. It must have sold a lot more since.

Worst Legal Entanglement As this one never came to court perhaps it does not really qualify, but I remember buying from United Artists the right to commission a series of novels based on the classic western, *The Magnificent Seven*. The contract from United Artists' legal department came to more than 100 pages of close type, substantially longer than the first of our novels. I had to call the deal off simply to spare ourselves the pain of reading through the contracts.

A Publisher's Dreams and Successes

TOM ROSENTHAL

The Six Books I Would Most Like to Have Published

Tristram Shandy, by Lawrence Sterne, partly because of its literary merits, which are too obvious to labour here, but partly because one of my most treasured possessions is a first edition of the book which took nine volumes, several years and no fewer than three different printer/publishers before the great man could bring it to fruition; it is good to know that, as long ago as 1760−7, even the greatest of writers had difficulty finding the right publisher.

The *Dictionary of National Biography* and the *Oxford English Dictionary*, because I really only read fiction for pleasure; these two massive publications in their complete form are the only non-fiction that can completely ensnare my mind and make me forget present problems, and once I look up one entry I tend to be completely hooked for at least two hours, reading many others at random.

Nostromo, by Joseph Conrad, because I have an abiding interest in politics as well as literature. *Nostromo* is not only a masterpiece as a novel but also a masterpiece of that deadly political perception possessed by only the greatest of writers, who always see with much further and deeper vision than their political masters.

David Copperfield, because it was the first 'major English novel' I ever read. Since my parents came to England as refugees from Hitler's Germany, their *Complete Dickens* was the only available English literature in a house full of books in German and a multitude of the oriental languages of which my father was, and is, a scholar. It therefore made an ineradicable impression upon me and gives me just as intense a pleasure when I re-read it as when I read it first some forty years ago.

James Joyce's *Ulysses*, because every time I pick it up and open it at random I am instantly sucked into a world which is totally alien and at the same time absolutely familiar. A few pages of Joyce at his best is worth a stroll round Dublin and many a pint of Guinness at Davy Byrne's or any other Dublin watering hole.

The Three Books Which I Am Most Proud of Having Published
The Throwback, by Tom Sharpe, simply happens to be my favourite among the eleven Tom Sharpe novels I have published. *Terra Nostra*, by Carlos Fuentes, is in my view a virtually unclassifiable work of genius, bearing out the author's philosophy, which I happen passionately to agree with, that the only reality is fiction. Lastly, simply because it is the only piece of original Orwell I have had the honour to publish, the facsimile of the manuscript of *1984*.

Since the guilty must be protected with the innocent, I shall not name any book which I now regret having published.

～

> We had considerable stock of an art book in two volumes which was incredibly good value at £3 3s 0d the set, but booksellers would not buy it at £2 2s 0d nor the public at £3 3s 0d. We charged the price on the jacket to £3 3s 0d per volume, i.e. £6 6s 0d per set; told the booksellers that they could sell it at half price and pay us £2 2s 0d. The stock just melted away. There was no change in the price either to the booksellers or the public.
>
> Sir Stanley Unwin,
> *The Truth about a Publisher*

～

A Young Publisher's Scoop

A modest man, J. R. R. Tolkien did not anticipate the huge success of his Middle Earth books. Little did he know that by the 1970s Americans would be wearing buttons with the slogan: 'Tolkien is hobbit-forming.' The simplicity of the basic struggle between light and darkness was perhaps the reason for its cult appeal. In a letter to me Rayner Unwin, chairman of Allen and Unwin, says that his greatest publishing scoop ever was to write 'at the age of ten, a favourable report on J. R. R. Tolkien's book *The Hobbit*, for which I was paid £5'. He adds that : 'the most unlikely commercial success I can recall is *The Lord of the Rings*, which was at least three times as long as any normal work of fiction and fell into no recognizable category that trade buyers would respond to. I reckoned that it would lose £1000, which would not have constituted a great commercial disaster, but would have been uncomfortable. . . .' Tolkien remains the firm's bestselling author.

IV
Readers
and
Reviewers

If you understood everything you have read in your life, you would already know what you are looking for now.
P. D. Ouspensky, *In Search of the Miraculous*

~

A book unsurpassed in readability and human interest.
Dictionary of National Biography,
on Moulton and Milligan's
Vocabulary of the Greek New Testament, 1914

~

I never read a book before reviewing it; it prejudices a man so.
Sydney Smith

~

As for you, little envious Prigs, snarling bastard puny criticks, you'll soon have snarled your last: Go hang yourselves.
François Rabelais

~

Samuel Taylor Coleridge's
Four Classes of Book Reader

Sponges, who absorb all they read and return it nearly in the same state, only a little dirtied.

Sand-glasses, who retain nothing, and are content to get through a book for the sake of getting through the time.

Strain-bags, who retain merely the dregs of what they read.

Mogul diamonds, equally rare and valuable, who profit by what they read, and enable others to profit by it also.

Endorsements

C. Day-Lewis 1904–72 In his autobiography *The Buried Day* (1960), the poet records the startling effect that endorsements can sometimes have. A gossip column reported in 1934 that Winston Churchill had been told by T. E. Lawrence that Day-Lewis was the most important of the younger poets. At the Hogarth Press all hell was let loose as soon as the paper came out:

> Leonard and Virginia Woolf, having sold the usual small number of each of my three books they had so far published, had covered the stack of unsold copies with chintz . . . and were using it as a settee. The orders now pouring in for these books caused Leonard and Virginia to subside until, within a few hours, they were sitting on the floor.

Mary Webb 1881–1927 A famous endorsement, the results of which the authoress was unable to enjoy as she died shortly before it was delivered, was provided by Stanley Baldwin for Mary Webb's fifth novel, *Precious Bane*, first published in 1924. Hamish Hamilton, Webb's publisher, sang her praises at a dinner party at which the deputy secretary of the cabinet was present; he thought it might interest Baldwin as it was set in Shropshire, from where the Baldwin family hailed. Baldwin read it and later, in a speech, remarked that both James Barrie and John Buchan had told him that Mary Webb was one of the best living British writers, but that the public was indifferent to her. The results were electrifying. Baldwin himself wrote an introduction to one of *five* reprints called for in that year (1928). It was then reprinted in 1929 (three times), 1930 (twice), 1931, 1932 (three times), 1933 (three times), 1934, 1935 (twice), 1937, 1938, 1939 (twice), 1941, 1942, 1943, 1945, 1947, 1949, 1953, 1956, 1957, 1963 and 1967. Perhaps the ultimate accolade was delivered by Stella Gibbons, who made it the model for her irresistible send-up, *Cold Comfort Farm* (1932).

Elkanah Settle 1648–1724 Trying to secure endorsements in the seventeenth century could be a shabby business. Settle was one of the great time-servers of literary history, immortalized not for anything he wrote – his works generally being considered abysmal – but for provoking Dryden and Pope to undertake some of their wittiest demolition jobs:

> Doeg, *though without knowing how or why*
> *Made still a blundering kind of Melody;*
> *Spurred boldly on, and Dash'd through Thick and Thin*
> *Through Sense and Non-sense never out nor in.*
> > Dryden, 'Absalom and Achitophel'

His method of obtaining patronage was appallingly simple, as described by Isaac D'Israeli in *Calamities of Authors*:

When Elkanah Settle published any *party poem*, he sent copies round to the chiefs of the party, accompanied with addresses, to extort pecuniary presents. He had latterly one standard *Elegy* and *Epithalamium* printed off with blanks, which, by the ingenious contrivance of filling up with the names of any considerable person who died or was married, no one who was going out of life or entering it *could pass scot-free* from the *tax levied by his hackneyed muse*. The following letter accompanied his presentation copy to the Duke of Somerset, of a poem in Latin and English, on the Hanover succession, when Elkanah wrote for the Whigs, as he had for the Tories:
Sir, – Nothing but the greatness of the subject could encourage my presumption in laying the enclosed Essay at your Grace's feet, being, with all profound humility, your Grace's most dutiful servant,
> > E. Settle

Marie Corelli 1855–1924 Endorsed by the great, spurned by the critics, Marie Corelli is one of those writers whose entries in reference books provide the perverse kind of pleasure to be derived from watching an angry literary historian trying to explain an undeserved success. 'In the perfervid prose of her novels she conducted a crusade against the sins of society, concerning which she was totally uninformed . . .' (*Longman Companion to 20th Century Literature*) is typical, as is: 'the pretentious treatment of lofty themes by the illiterate for the illiterate . . .' (*Concise Cambridge History of English Literature*).

These glowing endorsements of her work are replicated by the remarks made by the critics at the time her books appeared, who so incurred her displeasure that she eventually refused to have her books sent out for notice. In any case she could dispense with the literary scorpions, for the great and the good hastened to sing her praises. The Dean of Westminster read from *Barabbas* (1893) from the pulpit of Westminster Abbey on Easter Sunday. A Church of England clergyman was saved from suicide by *A Romance of Two Worlds* (1886), her first book, in which it is revealed that God is electricity — electric light was at that time coming into general use. Queen Victoria and the Empress of Austria were devoted to her works, as were Tennyson, Gladstone, Dean Farrar and Ella Wheeler Wilcox.

The appeal of Marie Corelli's books for all these distinguished people, as for many thousands of others, was her reconciliation of science with orthodox religion, something she achieved by combining misinformation about both. All her books sold like hot cakes; *Sorrows of Satan*, one of the most successful, was in its sixty-third edition by 1918. And she is still paid the compliment of critical abuse to this day, a vivid demonstration that the endorsement of the humble reader has more staying power than the venom of the literati.

Sir Henry Newbolt 1862–1938 For generations of schoolchildren, almost the first English poem of which they became aware was Newbolt's rumbustious 'Drake's Drum' (1896), the first in a number of patriotic poems with a seafaring theme. That one evocative lyric should have done so much to catapult a poet of very minor talent to such a pinnacle of fame is now difficult to explain or understand. The greatest men of the day hastened to endorse his patriotic verses. At the Albert Hall in 1917 a setting by Stanford of Newbolt's 'Farewell' deeply moved A. J. Balfour, who was reported to have laid down his wordsheet 'with a kind of sigh'. Robert Bridges said of 'Drake's Drum': 'It isn't given to a man to write anything better than that.' Even Newbolt's novels, now unread, attracted plaudits from such unlikely sources as H. G. Wells and Gertrude Bell, and Newbolt received honorary degrees from Oxbridge and elsewhere. Fame and honours were heaped upon him.

Newbolt is not, in fact, quite as bad as the endorsements of politicians might lead one to suppose; and his poetry benefits considerably from being set to music — it is easier to sing what is hard to swallow. And 'Drake's Drum' is still marvellous, a parody of its own genre that succeeds far better than any possible original.

Arnold Bennett's Choice of the Twelve Finest Novels in the World

According to Arnold Bennett, writing in the *Evening Standard* of 17 March 1927, the twelve best novels ever written are all Russian; perhaps he was being mildly provoking, but his list is an interesting one:

1   *The Brothers Karamazov*
2   *The Idiot*
3   *The House of the Dead* ('the most celestial restorative of damaged faith in human nature that any artist ever produced'.)
4   *Crime and Punishment*
5   *Anna Karenina*
6   *War and Peace*
7   *Resurrection*

Of numbers 5, 6 and 7 he says: 'Everybody who has read them remembers them and admits their sway; and those who haven't read them must either pretend they have, or submit to being thrown out of the argument with contumely.

8   *Torrents of Spring*
9   *Virgin Soil*
10   *On the Eve*
11   *Fathers and Children*

Of numbers 8, 9, 10 and 11 he says: 'All these books are classics. They do not take you by the neck. They steal around you, envelop you; they impregnate you.'

12   *Dead Souls* ('a rollicking and murderous satire, and must have directly or indirectly influenced all later novelists who have castigated their country because they loved it'.)

Leo Tolstoy's List of Books That Made the Most Impression on Him

Sent in response to a request from a St Petersburg publisher, this list is taken from R. F. Christian (ed.), *Tolstoy's Letters* (Athlone Press, 1978).

This letter which I am now copying out I wrote about three weeks ago, and at the same time I began to compile a list of books which had made a strong impression on me, defining the extent of the impression by four [*sic*] degrees which I denoted by the words 'enormous', 'very great' and 'great'. I subdivided the list according to ages, thus: (1) childhood to fourteen, (2) fourteen to twenty, (3) twenty to thirty-five, (4) thirty-five to fifty and (5) fifty to sixty-three. I partly compiled this list, in which I recalled up to fifty various works which had made a strong impression on me, but I saw that it was very incomplete since I couldn't recall everything, and I was recalling and inserting things one at a time. The conclusion from all this is as follows: I can't fulfil your wish to compile a list of a hundred books, and I'm very sorry about it; but I'll try to supplement the list of books I am writing about which made an impression on me, and send it to you.

Lev Tolstoy

I am sending the list I began, but didn't finish, for your consideration, but not for publication, since it is still far from complete.

Works Which Made an Impression
Childhood to the Age of Fourteen or So

The story of Joseph from the Bible	Enormous
Tales from The Thousand and One Nights: the Forty Thieves, Prince Qamr-al-Zamán	Great
The Little Black Hen by Pogoreslsky	V. great
Russian *Byliny: Dobrynya Nikitich, Ilya Muromets, Alyosha Popovich*. Folk Tales	Enormous
Pushkin's poems: *Napoleon*	Great

Age Fourteen to Twenty

Matthew's Gospel: Sermon on the Mount	Enormous
Sterne's *Sentimental Journey*	V. great
Rousseau *Confession* [*sic*]	Enormous
Emile	Enormous
Nouvelle Héloïse	V. great
Pushkin's *Yevgeny Onegin*	V. great
Schiller's *Die Räuber*	V. great

Gogol's *Overcoat; The Two Ivans; Nevsky Prospect*	Great
Viy	Enormous
Dead Souls	V. great
Turgenev's *A Sportsman's Sketches*	V. great
Druzhinin's *Polinka Sachs*	V. great
Grigorovich's *The Hapless Anton*	V. great
Dickens' *David Copperfield*	Enormous
Lermontov's *A Hero of Our Time; Taman*	V. great
Prescott's *Conquest of Mexico*	Great

Age Twenty to Thirty-five

Goethe *Hermann und Dorothea*	V. great
Victor Hugo *Notre Dame de Paris*	V. great
Tyutchev's poems	Great
Koltsov's poems	Great
The Odyssey and *The Iliad* (read in Russian)	Great
Fet's poems	Great
Plato's *Phaedo* and *Symposium* (in Cousin's translation)	Great

Age Thirty-five to Fifty

The Odyssey and *The Iliad* (in Greek)	V. great
The *Bylíny*	V. great
Xenophon's *Anabasis*	V. great
Victor Hugo, *Les Misérables*	Enormous
Mrs Wood, Novels	Great
George Eliot, Novels	Great
Trollope, Novels	Great

Age Fifty to Sixty-three

All the Gospels in Greek	Enormous
Book of Genesis (in Hebrew)	V. great
Henry George, *Progress and Poverty*	V. great
Parker, Discourse on religious subject	Great
Robertson's sermons	Great
Feuerbach (I forget the title; work on Christianity)	Great
Pascal's *Pensées*	Enormous
Epictetus	Enormous
Confucius and Mencius	V. great
On the Buddha. Well-known Frenchman (I forget)	Enormous
Lao-Tzu, Julien	Enormous

The Parker discourse was *A Discourse of Matters Pertaining to Religion* (1852) by Theodore Parker, an American renegade Unitarian minister and emancipationist. Robertson's sermons were published as *Sermons Preached at Trinity Chapel, Brighton* in 1855 by Frederick William Robertson. The Feuerbach title which Tolstoy had forgotten was *Das Wesen des Christentums* (1841). The work on the Buddha by a 'well-known Frenchman' was *Lalita Vistara*, translated by Philippe-Edouard Foucaux. 'Lao-Tzu, Julien' was S. Julien's *Lao Tseu . . . Le Livre de la Voie et de la Vertu* (Paris, 1841).

Six (and More) of the Best

BERNARD CRICK

Here are some of the books that have had the most influence on me personally.

Really quite a bad book first made me see political thought as the lynch-pin of our civilization — Harold Laski's *Reflections on the Revolution of Our Time*. I would like to say that it was Tawney, but it was Laski; I heard his lectures and would have been his doctoral student, but he died the year I graduated, 1950.

My second choice was found by chance in a secondhand bookshop, but a teacher must have mentioned it; why else should I pick up Florio's translation of Montaigne's *Essays*? I love the very thought of him.

My first girlfriend gave me Eliot's *Collected Poems*: the 'world-view' of which I disliked intensely but loved the language, imagery and closeness of thought. It opened up modern poetry for me — so I was quite ready for Orwell's calm acceptance that people could be good writers but bad men.

If life is tragic, it is also comic — and I don't know which has influenced me more, the comedy of mind and words of Sterne's *Tristram Shandy* or the comedy of events and institutions of Hasek's *The Good Soldier Schweik* (I still prefer the language of the less complete first Penguin translation).

I was lifted out of the narrow world of British politics at Harvard in my mid-twenties by reading Hannah Arendt's *The Origins of Totalitarianism*, though fortunately I had already read Karl Popper's *The Origins of Totalitarianism*, especially the footnotes to volume 2, as well as hearing his lectures, so the recent enterprise of trying to find common ground between phenomenology and British empiricism has, if rare and difficult, never struck me as absurd.

I cannot remember when I first read it, but long after *The Prince*; yet I keep on re-reading Machiavelli's *Discourses*, the great vindication of both the possibility and desirability of republican government by what J. S. Mill would have called 'a free spirit'.

The Hundred Books That Most Influenced Henry Miller

At the end of his characteristically spirited and rambling work *The Books in My Life* Henry Miller appends his choice of the hundred books or authors that influenced him most, originally prepared for a Gallimard compilation entitled *Pour Une Bibliothèque Idéale* (1951). Here is his selection, printed exactly as it appeared.

Ancient Greek Dramatists	
Arabian Nights Entertainment (for children)	
Elizabethan Playwrights (excepting Shakespeare)	
European Playwrights of the Nineteenth Century, including Russian and Irish	
Greek Myths and Legends	
Knights of King Arthur's Court	
Abélard, Pierre	*The Story of My Misfortunes*
Alain-Fournier	*The Wanderer*
Andersen, Hans Christian	*Fairy Tales*
Anonymous	*Diary of a Lost One*
Balzac, Honoré de	*Seraphita, Louis Lambert*
Bellamy, Edward	*Looking Backward*
Belloc, Hilaire	*The Path to Rome*
Blavatsky, Mme H. P.	*The Secret Doctrine*
Boccaccio, Giovanni	*The Decameron*
Breton, André	*Nadja*
Brontë, Emily	*Wuthering Heights*
Bulwyer-Lytton, Edward	*The Last Days of Pompeii*
Carroll, Lewis	*Alice in Wonderland*
Céline, Louis-Ferdinand	*Journey to the End of the Night*
Cellini, Benvenuto	*Autobiography*
Cendrars, Blaise	Virtually the complete works
Chesterton, G. K.	*St Francis of Assisi*
Conrad, Joseph	His works in general
Cooper, James Fenimore	*The Leatherstocking Tales*
Defoe, Daniel	*Robinson Crusoe*
De Nerval, Gérard	His works in general
Dostoievsky, Feodor	His works in general
Dreiser, Theodore	His works in general
Duhamel, Georges	*Salavin* Series
Du Maurier, George	*Trilby*
Dumas, Alexandre	*The Three Musketeers*
Eckermann, Johann Peter	*Conversations with Goethe*
Eltzbacher, Paul	*Anarchism*
Emerson, Ralph Waldo	*Representative Men*
Fabre, Henri	His works in general

~

It is my ambition to say in ten sentences what everyone else says in a whole book — what everyone does not *say in a whole book.*

Friedrich Nietzsche

~

Cyril Connolly's Hundred Key Books of the Modern Movement

Connolly was an inveterate listmaker, not only of books but of all sorts of trivia, besides dozens of New Year resolutions (or indeed any resolutions) which he solemnly wrote down before failing to keep them. In 1965 he published *The Modern Movement, 100 Key Books from England, France and America, 1880–1950* (André Deutsch/ Hamish Hamilton), a choice of those works that in his opinion best illustrated the spirit of the modern movement, which 'dawned with Flaubert and Baudelaire, reached its zenith early in the century, and only became past history in the fifties – if it has become past history'. The list is limited to French, English and American literature because, as Connolly candidly informs the reader, 'without knowing German or Russian, I cannot absolutely judge a book from a translation, however perfect, and because the dates at which translations appear confuse the time-scale'. His list is as follows:

1	*Portrait of a Lady*	Henry James	1881
2	*Bouvard et Pecuchet*	Gustave Flaubert	1880
3	*Contes Cruels*	Villiers De L'Isle-Adam	1883
4	*A Rebours*	J. K. Huysmans	1884
5	*Oeuvres Posthumes*	Charles Baudelaire	1887
6	*Les Illuminations*	Arthur Rimbaud	1886
7	*Poésies*	Stéphane Mallarmé	1887
8	*Bel Ami*	Guy de Maupassant	1885
9	*Journal*	Edmond and Jules de Goncourt	1887–96
10	*Là-Bas*	J. K. Huysmans	1891
11	*Ubu Roi*	Alfred Jarry	1896
12	*The Awkward Age*	Henry James	1899
13	*L'Immoraliste*	André Gide	1902
14	*Youth*	Joseph Conrad	1902
15	*The Secret Agent*	Joseph Conrad	1907
16	*The Ambassadors*	Henry James	1903
17	*Memoirs of My Dead Life*	George Moore	1906
18	*The Playboy of the Western World*	J. M. Synge	1907
19	*The Longest Journey*	E. M. Forster	1907
20	*Siren Land*	Norman Douglas	1911
21	*Sons and Lovers*	D. H. Lawrence	1913
22	*Alcools*	Guillaume Apollinaire	1913
23	*Du Côté de Chez Swann*	Marcel Proust	1913
24	*Responsibilities*	W. B. Yeats	1914

25	*Satires of Circumstance*	Thomas Hardy	1914
26	*Portrait of an Artist as a Young Man*	James Joyce	1916
27	*The Good Soldier*	Ford Madox Ford	1915
28	*South Wind*	Norman Douglas	1917
29	*Tarr*	Percy Wyndham Lewis	1918
30	*Prufrock and Other Observations*	T. S. Eliot	1917
	The Waste Land	T. S. Eliot	1922
31	*Le Jeune Parque*	Paul Valéry	1917
	Charmes	Paul Valéry	1922
32	*Calligrammes*	Guillaume Apollinaire	1918
33	*Poems*	Gerard Manley Hopkins	1918
34	*One Hundred and Seventy Chinese Poems*	Arthur Waley	1918
35	*Lustra*	Ezra Pound	1916
	Mauberley	Ezra Pound	1920
36	*Poems*	Wilfred Owen	1920
37	*Eminent Victorians*	Lytton Strachey	1918
38	*Sea and Sardinia*	D. H. Lawrence	1921
39	*Crome Yellow*	Aldous Huxley	1921
40	*The Garden Party*	Katherine Mansfield	1922
41	*Later Poems*	W. B. Yeats	1922
42	*Ulysses*	James Joyce	1922
43	*Le Diable au Corps*	Raymond Radiguet	1923
44	*The Flower beneath the Foot*	Ronald Firbank	1923
45	*A Passage to India*	E. M. Forster	1924
46	*Harmonium*	Wallace Stevens	1923
47	*Tulips and Chimneys*	E. E. Cummings	1923
	Is 5	E. E. Cummings	1926
48	*The Great Gatsby*	F. Scott Fitzgerald	1925
49	*In Our Time*	Ernest Hemingway	1924
50	*The Sun Also Rises*	Ernest Hemingway	1926
51	*Si le Grain Ne Meurt*	André Gide	1926
52	*Turbott Wolfe*	William Plomer	1926
53	*The Casuarina Tree*	W. Somerset Maugham	1926
54	*To the Lighthouse*	Virginia Woolf	1927
55	*Nadja*	André Breton	1928
56	*The Tower*	W. B. Yeats	1928
	The Winding Stair	W. B. Yeats	1929
57	*Lady Chatterley's Lover*	D. H. Lawrence	1928
58	*Decline and Fall*	Evelyn Waugh	1928
59	*Living*	Henry Green	1929
60	*A Farewell to Arms*	Ernest Hemingway	1929
61	*Goodbye to All That*	Robert Graves	1929
62	*Les Enfants Terribles*	Jean Cocteau	1929
63	*Brothers and Sisters*	Ivy Compton Burnett	1929
64	*The Bridge*	Hart Crane	1930
65	*Ash Wednesday*	T. S. Eliot	1929
66	*Thirty Cantos*	Ezra Pound	1930
67	*Collected Poems*	Edith Sitwell	1930

68	*Vol de Nuit*	Antoine de Saint Exupéry	1931
69	*Sanctuary*	William Faulkner	1931
70	*The Waves*	Virginia Woolf	1931
71	*Axel's Castle*	Edmund Wilson	1931
72	*Selected Essays*	T. S. Eliot	1932
73	*The Orators*	W. H. Auden	1932
74	*Voyage au Bout de la Nuit*	Luis-Ferdinand Céline	1932
75	*Brave New World*	Aldous Huxley	1932
76	*Miss Lonelyhearts*	Nathaniel West	1933
77	*La Condition Humaine*	André Malraux	1933
78	*Eighteen Poems*	Dylan Thomas	1934
	Twenty-five Poems	Dylan Thomas	1936
79	*Tender Is the Night*	F. Scott Fitzgerald	1934
80	*The Art of the Novel*	Henry James	1934
81	*Selected Poems*	Marianne Moore	1935
82	*Les Jeunes Filles*	Henri de Montherlant	1936–9
83	*Voyage en Grande Garabagne*	Henri Michaux	1936
	Au Pays de la Magie	Henri Michaux	1941
84	*La Nausée*	Jean-Paul Sartre	1938
85	*Autumn Journal*	Louis Macneice	1939
86	*Goodbye to Berlin*	Christopher Isherwood	1939
87	*Finnegan's Wake*	James Joyce	1939
88	*The Power and the Glory*	Graham Greene	1940
89	*Darkness at Noon*	Arthur Koestler	1940
90	*Another Time*	W. H. Auden	1940
91	*Ruins and Visions*	Stephen Spender	1942
92	*Four Quartets*	T. S. Eliot	1943–4
93	*Animal Farm*	George Orwell	1945
94	*L'Etranger*	Albert Camus	1941
95	*La Peste*	Albert Camus	1947
96	*Deaths and Entrances*	Dylan Thomas	1946
97	*Selected Poems*	John Betjeman	1948
98	*The Pisan Cantos*	Ezra Pound	1948
99	*1984*	George Orwell	1949
100	*Patterson 1, 2, 3, 4*	William Carlos Williams	1946–51

Frederic Raphael and Kenneth McLeish's Choice

Frederic Raphael is no stranger to the art of compiling literary lists.
In 1975 he published a collection under the title *Bookmarks* in which
twenty-eight writers discussed their reading – childhood favourites,
influences and inspirations.

More recently Frederic Raphael and Kenneth McLeish have compiled the beguiling *List of Books* (Mitchell Beazley, 1981), 'a recommended library of over 3000 works'. At the beginning of the book are four lists described as the 'cream of the crop'.

Books of the Decade, 1970–80

British Choice

Attenborough, D.	*Life on Earth*	1979
Berger, J.	*Ways of Seeing*	1972
Berryman, J.	*Selected Poems*	1972
Boston Women's Collective	*Our Bodies, Ourselves*	1972
Brown, D.	*Bury My Heart at Wounded Knee*	1972
Clarke, R. and Hindley, G.	*The Challenge of the Primitives*	1975
Davidson, A.	*Mediterranean Seafood*	1972
Gerbi, A.	*The Dispute of the New World*	1973
Greer, G.	*The Female Eunuch*	1970
Halberstam, D.	*The Best and the Brightest*	1972
Harvey, J.	*The Master Builders*	1971
Hill, C.	*The World Turned Upside Down*	1972
Hindley, G. (ed.)	*The Larousse Encyclopaedia of Music*	1971
Johnson, H.	*The World Atlas of Wine*	1971
Koestler, A.	*The Case of the Midwife Toad*	1971
Ladurie, E. le Roy	*Montaillou*	1975
Lovell, B.	*In the Centre of Immensities*	1979
Mendelssohn, K.	*Science and Western Domination*	1976
Morison, S.	*The Great Explorers*	1978
Papanck, V.	*Design for the Real World*	1971
Schumacher, E.	*Small Is Beautiful*	1973
Sendak, M.	*Where the Wild Things Are*	1970
Skinner, B. F.	*Beyond Freedom and Dignity*	1971
Solzhenitsyn, A.	*The Gulag Archipelago*	1974
Steadman, R.	*America*	1974
Thorne, C.	*Allies of a Kind*	1978
Ward, B.	*The Home of Man*	1976
Wilson, C.	*The Occult*	1971
Woodward, B. and Bernstein, C.	*All the President's Men*	1974

American Choice

Bellow, S.	*Mr Sammler's Planet*	1970
Bettelheim, B.	*The Uses of Enchantment*	1977
Boorstin, D. J.	*The Americans: The Democratic Experience*	1973
Boston Women's Collective	*Our Bodies, Ourselves*	1972
Brand, S.	*The Last Whole Earth Catalog*	1975
Brown, D.	*Bury My Heart at Wounded Knee*	1971
Clavell, J.	*Shogun*	1975

Collier, P. and Horowitz, D.	*The Rockefellers: An American Dynasty*	1976
Comfort, A.	*The Joy of Sex*	1972
Cooke, A.	*Alistair Cooke's America*	1973
FitzGerald, F.	*Fire in the Lake*	1972
Halberstam, D.	*The Best and the Brightest*	1972
Haley, A.	*Roots*	1976
Hardwick, E.	*Seduction and Betrayal: Women and Literature*	1974
Hellman, L.	*Pentimento*	1973
Herr, M.	*Dispatches*	1977
Howe, I.	*World of Our Fathers*	1976
Jong, E.	*Fear of Flying*	1973
Kluger, R.	*Simple Justice: The History of Brown v. Board of Education*	1976
Lash, J. P.	*Eleanor and Franklin*	1972
McCullough, D.	*The Path between the Seas: The Creation of the Panama Canal, 1870–1914*	1977
Márquez, G. G.	*One Hundred Years of Solitude*	1970
Milford, N.	*Zelda: A Biography*	1970
Morgan, M.	*The Total Woman*	1973
Pirsig, R. M.	*Zen and the Art of Motorcycle Maintenance*	1974
Singer, I. B.	*Enemies: A Love Story*	1972
Skinner, B. F.	*Beyond Freedom and Dignity*	1971
Terkel, S.	*Working*	1974
Thomas, L.	*The Lives of a Cell*	1974
Toffler, A.	*Future Shock*	1971
Updike, J.	*Rabbit Redux*	1971
Vidal, G.	*Burr: A Novel*	1973
Vonnegut, K.	*Slaughterhouse Five*	1973
Ward, B.	*The Home of Man*	1976
Wolfe, T.	*Radical Chic and Mau-Mauing the Flak Catchers*	1970
Woodward, B. and Bernstein, C.	*All the President's Men*	1974
Woodward, B. and Bernstein, C.	*The Final Days*	1976
Wouk, H.	*The Winds of War*	1971

Editors' Choice

Each editor [Raphael and McLeish] was asked, independently, which twenty-five books he would pack for a desert island holiday. This list is the combined result. Several books were common choices; apart from them, each editor was surprised by several of the books on the other's list.

Aeschylus	*The Oresteia*	Jonson, Ben	*The Alchemist*
Albee, Edward	*Who's Afraid of Virginia Woolf?*	Kafka, Franz	*The Trial*
Attenborough David	*Life on Earth*	McCabe, J. and Kilgore, A.	*Laurel and Hardy*
Aristophanes	*Thesmophoriazusae*	McCarthy, Mary	*The Groves of Academe*
Austen, Jane	*Emma*	Montaigne, Michel de	Essays
Berlioz, Hector	*Memoirs*	Nabokov, Vladimir	*Pale Fire*
Burke, Kenneth	*A Grammar of Motives*		
Byron	*Letters and Journals*	Nietzsche, Friedrich	*Thus Spake Zarathustra*
Cavafy, Constantine	*Collected Poems*	Orwell, George	*Collected Essays*
Dante	*The Divine Comedy*	Pascal, Blaise	*Pensées*
Donne, John	*Poems*	Proust, Marcel	*Remembrance of Things Past*
Dostoyevsky, Fyodor	*The Brothers Karamazov*	Rabelais, François	*Gargantua and Pantagruel*
Durrell, Gerald	*My Family and Other Animals*	Renoir, Jean	*Renoir, My Father*
Durrell, Lawrence	*Reflections on a Marine Venus*	Runciman, Steven	*A History of the Crusades*
Eliot, George	*Middlemarch*	Shakespeare, William	*Collected Works*
Eliot, T. S.	*Four Quartets*		
Flaubert, Gustave	*Madame Bovary*	Singer, Isaac Bashevis	*A Crown of Feathers*
Ford, Ford Madox	*Parade's End*	Stendhal	*The Charterhouse of Parma*
Frazer, Sir James	*The Golden Bough*	Thesiger, W.	*The Marsh Arabs*
Gibbon, Edward	*The Decline and Fall of the Roman Empire*	Thucydides	*The Peloponnesian War*
Heller, Joseph	*Catch-22*	Tolstoy, Leo	*War and Peace*
Hockney, David	*Hockney*	Villon, François	*Poems*
Homer	*The Odyssey*	White, E. W.	*Stravinsky*
Innes, Michael	*Operation Pax*	Wittgenstein, Ludwig	*Philosophical Investigations*
Jarrell, Randall	*Pictures from an Institution*		

Getting to Grips with the Twentieth Century

'If books reflect historical, sociological and cultural growth, the ones recommended here may, we hope [say Raphael and McLeish], help to account for or explain some of the directions human existence has taken in our century. Some of these books are dated, many are infuriating or partial; all are landmarks.'

Acheson, D.	*Present at the Creation*	1967
Anderson, P.	*Considerations on Western Marxism*	1976
Austin, W.	*Music in the 20th Century*	1966
Banham, R.	*Theory and Design in the First Machine Age*	1960
Beauvoir, S. de	*The Second Sex*	1949

Beckett, S.	*Waiting for Godot*	1952
Berry, B. J. L.	*The Human Consequences of Urbanization*	1973
Brittain, V.	*Testament of Youth*	1933
Brownlow, K.	*The Parade's Gone By*	1968
Bruce, L.	*The Essential Lenny Bruce*	1975
Capote, T.	*In Cold Blood*	1966
Carr, E. H.	*The Russian Revolution*	1979
Carson, R.	*Silent Spring*	1962
Cherry-Garrard, A.	*The Worst Journey in the World*	1912
Clark, R. M.	*The Scientific Breakthrough*	1974
Clarke, R. and Hindley, G.	*The Challenge of the Primitives*	1975
Eliot, T. S.	*The Waste Land*	1923
Esslin, M.	*The Theatre of the Absurd*	1961
Fanon, F.	*The Wretched of the Earth*	1961
Friedan, B.	*The Feminine Mystique*	1962
Friedman, M.	*Capitalism and Freedom*	1962
Frith, S.	*The Sociology of Rock*	1978
Graves, R.	*Goodbye to All That*	1929
Halberstam, D.	*The Best and the Brightest*	1972
Harrison, J.	*Marxist Economics for Socialists*	1978
Hebblethwaite, P.	*The Christian-Marxist Dialogue and Beyond*	1976
Ionesco, E.	*The Bald Prima Donna*	1948
Jones, E.	*The Life and Work of Sigmund Freud*	1953
Joyce, J.	*Ulysses*	1921
Kafka, F.	*The Diaries of Franz Kafka*	1948
Kafka, F.	*The Trial*	1937
Keynes, J. M.	*The General Theory of Employment, Interest and Money*	1936
Klee, P.	*On Modern Art*	1943
Kolko, G.	*Main Currents in Modern American History*	1976
Le Corbusier	*Towards an Architecture*	1923
Lichtheim, G.	*Europe in the 20th Century*	1972
Lorenz, K.	*On Aggression*	1963
McAleavy, H.	*The Modern History of China*	1967
Macartney, C. A. and Palmer, A. W.	*Independent Eastern Europe*	1962
McGlashan, A.	*Gravity and Levity*	1976
Mailer, N.	*Marilyn*	1973
Mailer, N.	*The Naked and the Dead*	1948
Malaparte, C.	*Kaput*	1964
Niebuhr, R.	*Moral and Immoral Society*	1932
Orwell, G.	*Animal Farm*	1946
Orwell, G.	*The Road to Wigan Pier*	1937
Papanek, V.	*Design for the Real World*	1971
Pirandello, L.	*Six Characters in Search of an Author*	1929
Piven, F. F. and Cloward, R. A.	*Poor People's Movements*	1977
Reich, W.	*The Sexual Revolution*	1930

Rosen, S.	*Future Facts*	1976
Rosenberg, H.	*The Anxious Object*	1964
Schumacher, E.	*Small Is Beautiful*	1973
Sinclair, A.	*Prohibition: The Era of Excess*	1962
Solzhenitsyn, A. I.	*The Gulag Archipelago*	1974
Stern, J. P.	*The Führer and the People*	1975
Taylor, A. J. P.	*English History, 1914–1945*	1965
Terkel, S.	*Work*	1974
Wing, J. K.	*Reasoning about Madness*	1978

Six for a Desert Island

JOHN JULIUS NORWICH

Edward Gibbon, *The Decline and Fall of the Roman Empire*. An unfailing source of pleasure, first for the fascination of the subject matter, second for those marvellous rolling periods, and third for the jokes. To be read and re-read — it would keep one going for years.

Marcel Proust, *A la Recherche du Temps Perdu*. The only chance I shall probably have to finish it. Besides, it would help keep up my French.

William Shakespeare, *Works*. Or if, as in *Desert Island Discs*, he and the Bible are there already, those of Milton. If he's there too, I'll take Keats.

Hugh Honour and John Fleming, *A World History of Art*. An encyclopaedic work that never ceases to be readable, it would teach me a lot, while the illustrations would be a permanent feast for the eye.

George Eliot, *Middlemarch*. The greatest novel in the English language — how could one be without it?

William Prescott, *The Conquest of Mexico*. (See p. 53.)

~

> *Some books are drenched sands*
> *On which a great soul's wealth lies all in heaps,*
> *Like a wrecked argosy . . .*
> Alexander Smith, 1860–7

~

Anthony Burgess's List of Best Novels

In 1984 Anthony Burgess produced *Ninety-nine Novels* (Allison and Busby), his list of the best novels published in English since 1939, partly as a counterblast to the Book Marketing Council's thirteen 'Best of British' novels which was publicized during the same year. Burgess says in his Introduction that 'all the novelists listed . . . have added something to our knowledge of the human condition (sleeping or waking), have managed language well, have clarified the motivations of action, and have sometimes expanded the bounds of the imagination.' Here is his choice:

1939	*Party Going*	Henry Green
	After Many a Summer	Aldous Huxley
	Finnegans Wake	James Joyce
	At Swim; Two; Birds	Flann O'Brien
1940	*The Power and the Glory*	Graham Greene
	For Whom the Bell Tolls	Ernest Hemingway
	Strangers and Brothers	C. P. Snow (to 1970)
1941	*The Aerodrome*	Rex Warner
1944	*The Horse's Mouth*	Joyce Cary
	The Razor's Edge	W. Somerset Maugham
1943	*Brideshead Revisted*	Evelyn Waugh
1946	*Titus Groan*	Mervyn Peake
1947	*The Victim*	Saul Bellow
	Under the Volcano	Malcolm Lowry
1948	*The Heart of the Matter*	Graham Greene
	Ape and Essence	Aldous Huxley
	The Naked and the Dead	Norman Mailer
	No Highway	Nevil Shute
1949	*The Heat of the Day*	Elizabeth Bowen
	1984	George Orwell
	The Body	William Sansom
1950	*Scenes from Provincial Life*	William Cooper
	The Disenchanted	Bud Schulberg
1951	*A Dance to the Music of Time*	Anthony Powell (to 1975)
	Catcher in the Rye	J. D. Salinger
	A Chronicle of Ancient Sunlight	Henry Williamson (to 1969)
	The Caine Mutiny	Herman Wouk

1952	*Invisible Man*	Ralph Ellison
	The Old Man and the Sea	Ernest Hemingway
	The Groves of Academe	Mary McCarthy
	Wise Blood	Flannery O'Connor
	Sword of Honour	Evelyn Waugh (to 1961)
1953	*The Long Goodbye*	Raymond Chandler
1954	*Lucky Jim*	Kingsley Amis
1957	*Room at the Top*	John Braine
	The Alexandria Quartet	Lawrence Durrell (to 1960)
	The London Novels	Colin MacInnes (to 1960)
	The Assistant	Bernard Malamud
1958	*The Bell*	Iris Murdoch
	Saturday Night and Sunday Morning	Alan Sillitoe
	The Once and Future King	T. H. White
1959	*The Mansion*	William Faulkner
	Goldfinger	Ian Fleming
1960	*Facial Justice*	L. P. Hartley
	The Balkan Trilogy	Olivia Manning (to 1965)
1961	*The Mighty and Their Fall*	Ivy Compton-Burnett
	Catch-22	Joseph Heller
	The Fox in the Attic	Richard Hughes
	Riders in the Chariot	Patrick White
	The Old Men at the Zoo	Angus Wilson
1962	*Another Country*	James Baldwin
	An Error of Judgement	Pamela Hansford Johnson
	Island	Aldous Huxley
	The Golden Notebook	Doris Lessing
	Pale Fire	Vladimir Nabokov
1963	*The Girls of Slender Means*	Muriel Spark
1964	*The Spire*	William Golding
	Heartland	Wilson Harris
	A Single Man	Christopher Isherwood
	The Defence	Vladimir Nabokov
	Late Call	Angus Wilson
1965	*The Lockwood Concern*	John O'Hara
	The Mandelbaum Gate	Muriel Spark
1966	*A Man of the People*	Chinna Achebe
	The Anti-Death League	Kingsley Amis
	Giles Coat-Boy	John Barth
	The Late Bourgeois World	Nadine Gordimer

	The Last Gentleman	Walker Percy
1967	*The Vendor of Sweets*	R. K. Narayan
1968	*The Image Men*	J. B. Priestley
	Cocksure	Mordecai Richler
	Pavane	Keith Roberts
1969	*The French Lieutenant's Woman*	John Fowles
	Portnoy's Complaint	Philip Roth
1970	*Bomber*	Len Deighton
1973	*Sweet Dreams*	Michael Frayn
	Gravity's Rainbow	Thomas Pynchon
1975	*Humboldt's Gift*	Saul Bellow
	The History Man	Malcolm Bradbury
1976	*The Doctor's Wife*	Brian Moore
	Falstaff	Robert Nye
1977	*How to Save Your Own Life*	Erica Jong
	Farewell Companions	James Plunkett
	Staying On	Paul Scott
1978	*The Coup*	John Updike
1979	*The Unlimited Dream Company*	J. G. Ballard
	Dubin's Lives	Bernard Malamud
	A Bend in the River	V. S. Naipaul
	Sophie's Choice	William Styron
1980	*Life in the West*	Brian Aldiss
	Riddley Walker	Russell Hoban
	How Far Can You Go?	David Lodge
	A Confederacy of Dunces	John Kennedy Toole
1981	*Lanark*	Alasdair Gray
	Darconville's Cat	Alexander Theroux
	The Mosquito Coast	Paul Theroux
1982	*The Rebel Angels*	Robertson Davies
1983	*Ancient Evenings*	Norman Mailer

～

All good books have one thing in common — they are truer than if they had really happened.

Ernest Hemingway

～

Critical Gaffes

I should be sorry to think that work so unreal, unhuman and insincere should be found to have any permanent value, nor do I believe that it will be found to have it, any more than Maeterlinck's will be, or Ibsen's, or, in another realm of art, Burne-Jones's or Rossetti's. . . . He has some admirers, I know, but I should judge them to be more noisy than numerous, as is commonly the case with these eccentrics, George Meredith to wit.

Mowbray Morris

Neither rhyme nor reason do I find in one single page . . . these books are to me absolutely empty and void. . . . I do not say it is obscure, or uncouth or barbaric or affected − tho' it is all these evil things; I say it is to me absolute nullity. . . .

John Morley

These are two of Macmillan's reader's reports, quoted in Charles Morgan's *The House of Macmillan*, on *The Wind Among the Reeds* by W. B. Yeats. Because of them Yeats was turned down by the firm in 1900. Within sixteen years Macmillan had changed their minds and became, as they remain, worthy publishers of Yeats.

Yeats on Contemporary Poetry

There is a considerable irony in the fact that Yeats, himself having been the victim of critical myopia, should have measured out the same treatment to another distinguished poet. When he compiled *The New Oxford Book of English Verse* (1936), in succession to Quiller-Couch's respected anthology, he excluded Wilfred Owen altogether. 'I consider him unworthy of the poets' corner of a country newspaper,' he is reported to have said. He also omitted all war poetry ('passing suffering is not a theme for poetry') and under-represented some important poets such as Kipling because the permission fees asked were too high.

Brougham on Byron

We counsel him to forthwith abandon poetry . . . and whatever judgement may be passed on the poems, it seems we must take them as we find them and be content, for they are the last we shall ever have from him. He is at best an intruder in the groves of Parnassus.

So wrote Henry Brougham in *The Edinburgh Review* about *Hours of Idleness* (1807), Byron's first book of poems offered to the public. We must be grateful for Brougham's elephantine remarks, for they called forth the riposte *English Bards and Scotch Reviewers*.

Despite Byron's subsequent fame his notices could still be harsh. *Blackwood's Magazine* said in July 1819 of 'Don Juan':

> It is indeed truly pitiable to think that one of the greatest poets of the age should have written a poem that no respectable bookseller could have published without disgracing himself — but a work so atrocious must not be suffered to pass into oblivion without the infliction of that punishment on its guilty author due to such a wanton outrage on all most dear to human nature.

F. L. Lucas on T. S. Eliot's *The Waste Land*

Unintelligible, the borrowings cheap and the notes useless.

New Statesman and Nation, November 1923

Joseph Conrad on D. H. Lawrence

Filth. Nothing but obscenities.

Wordsworth on Shakespeare

The Sonnets beginning CXXVII to his mistress are worse than a puzzle-peg. They are abominably harsh, obscure and worthless. The others are for the most part much better. . . . Their chief faults — and heavy ones they are — are sameness, tediousness, quaintness, and elaborate obscurity.

Samuel Pepys on Shakespeare

. . . and then to the King's Theatre, where we saw *Midsummer Night's Dream*, which I had never seen before, nor shall ever again, for it is the most insipid ridiculous play that ever I saw in my life. I saw, I confess, some good dancing and some handsome women, which was all my pleasure.

29 September 1662

. . . after dinner to the Duke's house, and there saw *Twelfth Night* acted well, though it be but a silly play, and not related at all to the name or day.

6 January 1663

John Wilson Croker on Keats

On 'Endymion' he wrote in *The Quarterly* in 1818:

> . . . the two first books are, even in his own judgement, unfit to appear, and the 'last two' are, it seems, in the same condition — and as

that is the whole number of books, we have a clear and, we believe, a very just estimate of the entire work.

The protests that Croker's review provoked mostly stressed the mean-spirited party bias of the writer, J. H. Reynolds's remarks reprinted in Leigh Hunt's *Examiner* being not untypical:

. . . no one but a Lottery Commissioner and Government Pensioner (both of which Mr William Gifford, the Editor of the *Quarterly Review*, is) could, with a false and remorseless pen, have striven to frustrate hopes and aims, so youthful and so high as this young Poet nurses.

James Douglas on Aldous Huxley

Reviewing Huxley's novel *Antic Hay* in the *Sunday Express* in 1923 Douglas wrote:

Which is the more despicable — witless smut or witty smut? Which is the more pestiferous — dirty dullness or dirty brilliancy? Which is the more poisonous — stupid indecency or intellectual lubricity? Which is the more dangerous — the swinish dullard or the hog of genius? There can be little doubt about the answer to these questions. Dullness is rarely perilous. It terrifies the sedulous ape. But wit dazzles the young imagination and coruscates in coteries and cenacles. There is pardon for the blockhead who lacks light to sin against. There is no pardon for the artist who bedaubs his own visions and befouls his own dreams. Where much is given, much is required.

Mr Aldous Huxley is beyond question a diabolically clever young man. . . . *Antic Hay* . . . is a witty novel, but its wit compels the reader to hold his nose.

Some Contemporary Reviews of Dickens

On *Hard Times*:

One excessively touching heart-breaking passage, and the rest sullen socialism. The evils which he attacks he caricatures grossly, and with little humour.

Macaulay, *Journal*, 1854

. . . on the whole, the story is stale, flat, and unprofitable; a mere dull melodrama, in which character is caricature, sentiment tinsel, and moral (if any) unsound.

Richard Simpson, *The Rambler*, 1854

It ought to be added that opinions have been sharply divided on *Hard Times* ever since its publication, between those who see it as a clumsy tract and those, like Ruskin and Shaw, who see it as among Dickens's greatest humanitarian fiction.

. . . the general theory of life on which it is based is not only false, but puerile. . . . Fifty years hence most of his wit will be harder to understand than the allusions in the *Dunciad*; and our grandchildren will wonder what their ancestors could have meant by putting Mr Dickens at the head of the novelists of his day.

Saturday Review, perhaps by James Fitzjames Stephen, on
Pickwick Papers, 1858

The *New York Herald* on Shaw

When *Mrs Warren's Profession* was staged in New York on 30 October 1905 the whole cast was arrested on a charge of disorderly conduct. This was because the play dealt with an unmentionable subject — prostitution. This review appeared in the *New York Herald* the next day.

The only way successfully to expurgate *Mrs Warren's Profession* is to cut the whole play out. You cannot have a clean pig stye. The play is an insult to decency because —

It defends immorality
It glories debauchery
It besmirches the sacredness of a clergyman's calling
It pictures children and parents living in calm observance of most unholy relations.

And, worst of all, it countenances the most revolting form of degeneracy, by flippantly discussing the marriage of brother and sister, father and daughter, and makes the one supposedly moral character of the play, a young girl, declare that choice of shame, instead of poverty is eminently right.

Blackwood's Magazine on Shelley

On his poem 'Adonais', written in praise of Keats, the magazine said in 1821:

. . . The subject is indifferent to us, let it be the 'Golden Age' or 'Mother Goose' — 'Waterloo' or the 'Wit of the Watchhouse' — 'Tom Thumb' or 'Thistlewood'. We will undertake to furnish the requisite supply of blue and crimson daisies and dandelions, not with the toilsome and tarty lutulence of the puling master of verbiage in question, but with a burst and torrent that will sweep away all his weedy trophies.

Edmund Wilson on J. R. R. Tolkien

. . . his appeal is to readers with a lifelong appetite for juvenile trash.

Fifty Works of English and American Literature We Could Do Without

BRIGID BROPHY, SIR MICHAEL LEVEY
AND CHARLES OSBORNE

~

Literature is the art of writing something that will be read twice.
Cyril Connolly

~

A choice of over-rated 'classics', first published in 1967; in fact an attack on the whole concept of the schoolroom 'classic' approach to literature. This entertaining piece of iconoclasm is also a plea for individual judgement as against received wisdom and for spontaneous response as against dutiful acceptance. The quotations are taken from the authors' commentary on each title:

Beowulf 'Admiring comment on its poetry is about as relevant as praise for the architecture of Stonehenge.'

The York Mystery Plays '. . . the Bach *St Matthew Passion*, Verdi's *Requiem*, the Karlskirche in Vienna, and the sculpture of Michelangelo are (as religious propaganda) a far cry from the cynically concocted doggerel of a committee of drunken monks at St Mary's Chapel, York in 1350'.

The Faerie Queen, **Edmund Spenser** '. . . the punishing length, utter confusion and unremitting tedium of Spenser's contribution serve not merely to impress uncreative minds, but to illustrate generally that English literature is not an easy option'.

The Alchemist, **Ben Jonson** 'So charmlessly pronounced is its lack of personality that it might have been produced by a computer.'

Hamlet, Prince of Denmark, **William Shakespeare** '. . . the prototype of Western literature's most deplorable and most formless form, autobiographical fiction'.

Pilgrim's Progress, **John Bunyan** '. . . it is impossible to rate his naïve and fevered imagination any higher than that of the gentlemen who walk through the West End of London with sandwich-boards imploring us to flee from the wrath to come'.

Moll Flanders, **Daniel Defoe** 'Defoe—Fielding—Smollett constitute English literature's belt of stockbrokers' Georgian . . . within that belt Defoe represents ribbon development. *Moll Flanders* is the thinnest conceivable trickle of narrative.'

Tom Jones, **Henry Fielding** '[Tom is] a tom cat of remarkable passivity who has to be seduced or flattered into his series of love affairs and finishes as a *jeune premier* in a Doris Day musical, married to the girl next door with full parental blessing.'

'Elegy Written in a Country Churchyard', **Thomas Gray** The penultimate line of Gray's 'Pindaric Ode', according to the authors, 'crystallizes the essential priggishness of the [poet] – 'beyond the limits of vulgar fate' – and 'conveys his perpetual effect of being one who not only writes in mittens but is capable of knitting them for a favourite nephew'. As for the 'Elegy': 'the dignified noise of [the poem] may make it seem to be about something; but the individual lines, when examined, give the lie to such an assumption'.

She Stoops to Conquer, **Oliver Goldsmith** 'For ever dithering about whether to pick up a scalpel or a powderpuff, [Goldsmith] never found the right instrument to carve out a piece of pure art.'

The School for Scandal, **R. B. Sheridan** 'Ultimately there is nothing so offensive in art as the desire not to offend: it is the negation which has eaten away at Sheridan's always tiny talent and left a few piles of sand which were once – briefly – popular plays.'

'I Wandered Lonely as a Cloud' ('The Daffodils'), **William Wordsworth** 'The reason Wordsworth writes of daffodils and clouds as though he had never really set eyes on either of them is that he is an essentially baroque artist, to whom flowers are invisible unless transmuted into precious metals and to whom clouds are merely what sweep apparitions down on to the astounded beholder.'

The Bride of Lammermoor, **Walter Scott** 'According to Scott it is basically a true story, so he need be given no credit for invention. What he has done is run the story under the cold tap of his immature mind, wring it free of anything resembling suspense or passion, and then iron it out with the full starch of his genteel, highfalutin and ever-creaking style.'

The Essays of Elia, **Charles Lamb** '. . . sentimental conservatism'; 'Lamb is one of those people (still richly present among us) who will defend a wrong by appealing to hallowed custom, praising the colourfulness of inequality and ever ready to condemn as "drab" anything that banishes poverty or child labour.'

The Confessions of an English Opium Eater, **Thomas De Quincey** '. . . hollow, glib and pompously written . . .'.

The Dream of Gerontius, **John Henry Newman** 'Aiming at poetry, Newman touched the lowest standard set by *Hymns Ancient and Modern*.'

The Scarlet Letter, **Nathaniel Hawthorne** 'Hawthorne tacitly called up an army of male prejudice, while putting forward a vulgarly romantic idea of woman (or rather, Woman) which probably still remains the American dream.'

'Aurora Leigh', Elizabeth Barrett Browning '"Aurora Leigh" is like a libretto concocted from a George Sand novel . . . the plot . . . is incredible: the worst kind of sentimental Victoriana.'

The Autocrat of the Breakfast Table, **Oliver Wendell Holmes** 'Naturally it was the breakfast table: his facetiousness, his bounce, his sententiousness accost you with precisely the effect of funny stories before 9 a.m.'

Pickwick Papers, **Charles Dickens** '. . . the language . . . is at worst worse than that of a barn-storming trickster, at best that of an anonymous syndicate. This poetaster of cosiness and smug banality has little to offer today.'

The Warden, **Anthony Trollope** '. . . by writing a plainish, porridge-like prose, he *seems* to avoid the crockets of Victorian gothic: but they're there all the same'.

Jane Eyre, **Charlotte Brontë** '. . . blatantly such stuff as daydreams are made on . . . reading *Jane Eyre* is like gobbling a jar full of schoolgirl stickjaw'.

Wuthering Heights, **Emily Brontë** 'Playing more shamelessly than any other work of fiction on the pathetic fallacy, it invites English readers to excuse the lack of psychological coherence and emotional truth in its characters by confusing those characters with elemental forces; and one critic has obediently divided the characters into "children of storm" and "children of calm". . . .'

Moby Dick or *The White Whale*, **Herman Melville** 'Many novelists have tried to anticipate the critic's task by writing both narrative and a commentary alongside it pointing out the deeper beauties, profundities and significances of the narrative. Melville alone has supplied the commentary without supplying the narrative.'

Leaves of Grass, **Walt Whitman** 'Whitman's so-called poetry ranges from a simpleton's idea of Shakespeare and the purpler passages of the Bible to sheer semi-literate sludge.'

Alice's Adventures in Wonderland, **Lewis Carroll** '. . . a nice, wholesome, dull book'.

Tom Brown's Schooldays, **Thomas Hughes** 'The grotesque "character-building" that Dr Arnold and his staff of hypocrites and bullies indulge in is quite blantantly ruinous to character. Yet the entire rigmarole is gushed over and lauded by Hughes.'

The Golden Treasury, **Francis Palgrave** '. . . few vaunted treasures have ever held as much dross as Palgrave managed to pack on board — almost enough to sink the unsinkable vessel of English literature. . . . *The Golden Treasury* is an insult to English literature, not merely emasculated, but misrepresented by Palgrave.'

***Lorna Doone*, R. D. Blackmore**   'Not even the mawkish love passages are funny enough to disturb the deep tedium of the Exmoor landscape . . . the book ends with a great daub of technicolour sentimental cruelty — "I bring her to forgotten sadness, and to me for cure of it." There they stand, huge man and tiny Lorna Doone at his shoulder, with all their money (yes, they're wealthy as well as healthy), ready to take part in any Hollywood historical film that will employ them.'

***The Adventures of Huckleberry Finn*, Mark Twain**   'The adolescent dream goes on, lulling the reader into an immature climate where goodness somehow triumphs and yet every tribute is paid to the abstract concept of boyishness. It is a vision that can be achieved only by that ruthless dishonesty which is the birthright of every sentimentalist.'

***Tess of the D'Urbervilles*, Thomas Hardy**   'We are left standing futilely in the soggy wet fields of novels where the earth is the ravaged, bloodstained scene of dreary crimes and appalling mistakes littered with frostbitten decaying vegetables and plentiful corpses.'

***Poems*, Gerard Manley Hopkins**   '. . . the poetry of a mental cripple'.

***Esther Waters*, George Moore**   'Moore, in trying for the common touch, succeeded only in being commonplace.'

***Collected Poems*, A. E. Housman**   '. . . slovenly calendar-verse'.

'The Hound of Heaven', Francis Thompson   '. . .All the teasing femininity suggested by romantic films, or illustrated by advertisements for high-quality soaps and shampoos, is caught in the lines:

> *With thy young skyey blossoms heap me over*
> *From this tremendous Lover!*
> *Float thy vague veil about me, lest He see.*'

***Peter Pan*, J. M. Barrie**   'An aesthetic massacre of the innocents. . . . *Peter Pan* is by way of being Barrie's *Interpretation of Dreams*'.

***An Habitation Enforced*, Rudyard Kipling**   'Propaganda is a technical failure if it renders its message either unreadable or, once struggled through, preposterous. . . .'

***The History of Mr Polly*, H. G. Wells**   '*The History of Mr Polly* may be Wells' revenge for having had to serve an apprenticeship in a draper's shop.'

The Forsyte Saga, **John Galsworthy** '. . . a thoroughly middle-class substitute for real literature'.

South Wind, **Norman Douglas** 'A good book is not automatically written by composing a Platonic dialogue of un-Platonic length, spicing it with pastiche history and would-be witty hagiography, and assembling a cast of sub-intellectual speakers.'

The Moon and Sixpence, **W. Somerset Maugham** 'One gets from reading this book, not the portrait of a genius but merely a string of theatrically cynical reflections on life and human behaviour, tacked on to an unconvincing story.'

To the Lighthouse, **Virginia Woolf** 'We are all conducting Virginia Woolf novels inside ourselves all day long, thinking how the sunset clouds look like crumbling cheese, wondering why the dinner party guests don't go, puzzling about children growing up, noticing for the first time the colour of a bus ticket. This famed sensitivity is everybody's birthright, and probably Virginia Woolf was applauded first by those who were delighted to find literary expression of their own commonplace sensations. To have those put in a book and called a novel . . . only dots can do justice to their delight.'

Lady Chatterley's Lover, **D. H. Lawrence** '. . . a straightforward novelette, which fabricates a wish-fulfilment love affair . . .'.

1914 Sonnets, **Rupert Brooke** 'Don't go in for flag-waving if you're limp-wristed.'

Collected Poems, **Edith Sitwell** 'Whatever the intention, this is the language not of feeling but of someone who has nothing to communicate and who seeks to conceal the fact behind a barrage of manner.'

Notes on The Waste Land, **T. S. Eliot** 'It is folly to expect a songbird to utter truths about the universe. The folly becomes ludicrous when the songbird himself claims to do so: and shameful when people believe his claim.'

Point Counter Point, **Aldous Huxley** 'He writes in the half clinical, half with-genteel-attention-averted manner of someone obliged to clean the lavatory.'

The Sound and the Fury, **William Faulkner** '. . . a vain and humourless purveyor of turgid Southern tosh'.

The Silver Chair, **C. S. Lewis** 'You cannot fake the ambiguous morality of myths by simply whispering your own prejudices behind your hand.'

A Farewell to Arms, **Ernest Hemingway** '. . . a footnote to the minor art of Gertrude Stein, an appendix to the biography of the great novelist Scott Fitzgerald, and the Ouida of the thirties'.

Looking Back in 1985

BRIGID BROPHY

Since we published *Fifty Works of English Literature We Could Do Without*, I have formed only one regret, and that a qualified one.

'We' in this context stands for Charles Osborne, Michael Levey (to whom I am married) and I. Each of the essays was by an individual, but the choice of the works included was by consensus.

I am not sorry that we included one of Anthony Trollope's Barchester novels. However, the (much misunderstood) purpose of our book was less to jump on bad literature than to call attention to better (in many cases by the same person), and I (and to my knowledge at least one of my colleagues) feel sad that we missed the chance to praise Trollope's political and psychological novels, including *He Knew He Was Right, The Kellys and the O'Kellys* and the magnificent Palliser sequence.

Our trouble was ignorance. Not until some British and US paperback publishers did their belated duty by putting virtually his whole *oeuvre* back into print did I discover Trollope to be one of the very greatest novelists: perhaps less spectacularly gifted than Dickens but a sounder psychologist, especially on the subject of women, whom Trollope knows to be ordinary humans, and a more graceful and architectural designer of fictions; a true heir to Jane Austen (from whom I surmise he learned much) and true precursor of Oscar Wilde's wit; a peer indeed to Thackeray, whom he so greatly and so rightly admired.

Otherwise I am sorry only, and only faintly, that we wrote too early to include any of the works that have been exhumed, with claims of classic status, for no better reason than that they are by women. (My list may be improvised by anyone: pick any six at random.) The reading that would have been imposed on us would have been deeply tedious, but I should have enjoyed expressing a sex-egalitarian's disapproval of the unjustified disesteem of women shown by professional feminists, who are so regularly bowled over on finding that any woman born before 1960 could, even badly, wield a pen or (which is so much rarer) an imagination.

CHARLES OSBORNE

As Brigid Brophy, Michael Levey and I wrote in the preface to our *Fifty Works of English Literature We Could Do Without*, 'The popular distinction between "constructive" and "destructive" criticism is a sentimentality: the mind too weak to perceive in what respects the bad fails is not strong enough to appreciate in what the good succeeds.' If one finds oneself more frequently castigating the bad than praising the good, that may be because there is so much more of the former than of the latter.

Nevertheless, freed now (eighteen years later) of cabinet responsibility for the opinions expressed in *Fifty Works*, I can reveal that I was shocked by the inclusion of two titles in our list. We each of us chose sixteen or seventeen works we could do without, and did not exercise any power of veto over one another's choices. It was not I, but Brigid or Michael, who thought we could do without *Hamlet* and *Wuthering Heights*. I certainly would not want to be without the poetry of the one or the emotional force of the other. But I stand by most of the choices in our volume, and I hope (for I can no longer remember) that it was I who described John Bunyan as a 'seventeenth-century Billy Graham' and complained of A. E. Housman's calendar verse as being 'as rhythmically monotonous as Brahms or Dixieland jazz'.

However, if today I am asked to nominate three works which I consider over-rated and three which I consider under-rated, I think my three over-rated works will have to be that embarrassingly whimsical novelette, *Lady Chatterley's Lover*; that feeble comedy, *She Stoops to Conquer*; and whatever has most recently dropped heavily from the pen of Mr Anthony Burgess (no matter what it was or how it may have been critically received).

As for three under-rated works, they present no problems:

1. Brigid Brophy's *Black Ship to Hell*, an astonishingly erudite and psychologically penetrating survey of our world's self-destructive impulses.

2. Michael Levey's elegantly conceived and written *Life and Death of Mozart*.

3. That critical volume which, on its first appearance, was appreciated only by the tasteful and discerning few, but which is, in due course, destined itself to become a classic: *Fifty Works of English Literature We Could Do Without*.

Michael Levey chose to reverse the original process and compile his list of most under-rated works.

Six of the (Under-rated) Best

SIR MICHAEL LEVEY

My list concentrates on authors under-rated in English literature, and it would be a long one if it could survey the whole area. Even restricted, it must start with Chaucer — not the familiar though largely unread poet of *The Canterbury Tales*, but the far more subtle and satisfying artist of *Troilus and Criseyde* and the highly wrought shorter poems, such as *The Book of the Duchesse*.

Moving on, I nominate Dryden as one of the most gravely under-rated of poets, the master of marvellous musical effects that only Handel or Britten could set with enhancement.

Of novels and novelists grossly under-rated, I list first *The Egoist*, and Meredith altogether as shamefully neglected in an age of enlightened paperback publication. Too clever, witty and contrived for today's lover of untidy novels of 'real' life, he would be a major figure in the literature of any other country lucky enough to possess him.

Altogether lower but still entertaining and not to be despised: Disraeli as novelist, especially as the author of *Coningsby* (though some of his other novels are unexpectedly full of good scenes, characters and dialogue, amid frank tinsel and leaden reflection).

For convincing politics, and politicians, and the only family saga in English literature that really works: the Palliser novels by Trollope. Time passes there, and children grow up, and adults grow old or die, with at least as much conviction as in Proust.

And finally, the Wilkie Collins not of the two so often reprinted novels (fine as they are) but of *Basil*; *Armadale*; *The Dead Secret*, and several more, which the British public can read thanks chiefly to the initiative of American publishers.

∿

The truth is missed by people who say that good writing has no market. That is not the point. Good writing sometimes has a market, and very bad writing sometimes has a market. Useful writing sometimes has a market, and writing of no use whatsoever, even as recreation, sometimes has a market. Writing important truths sometimes has a market. Writing the most ridiculous errors and false judgements sometimes has a market. The point is that the market has nothing to do with the qualities attached to writing. It never had and it never will.
Hilaine Belloc, *The Cruise of the 'Nona'*

∿

Six of the Best

RICHARD HOGGART

Here, arranged by category, are the six books that exerted the greatest influence on me in early life.

Poetry   Swinburne at the age of ten or so, in Hunslet Public Library, Leeds. He bowled me over and from then on poetry was for me the most important literary form. It is sentimental and self-indulgent stuff, much of it; but in love with what language can do as an art form.

Novel   Hardy: *Tess, Casterbridge* for a start. The novel exploring individuals but also setting them in a landscape and a context, historical and cultural. At sixteen.

Social Analysis   *Religion and the Rise of Capitalism*. Found as an undergraduate and introduced me to a remarkable combination of historical research and moral fervour. All in Tawney's fluent and sinewy prose.

Autobiography   A continuing interest. At about the age of twenty, *The Education of Henry Adams* became the great formative text, in particular for its tackling of the problems of distance and tone.

Drama   *King Lear*. Read at university, but only made its impact when I was a soldier in North Africa in the early 1940s. Above all, for capturing the sweep of human grief and love in matchless language. The greatest play I know.

General   A voice which has continued to speak to me: George Orwell. Honesty and clarity and insight, and a prose to match those qualities.

V
Books and
Their Enemies

No argument for the suppression of 'obscene' literature has ever been offered which, by unavoidable implication, will not justify, and which has not already justified, every other limitation that has ever been put upon mental freedom.

Theodore Schroeder,
'Obscure' Literature and Constitutional Law

∿

When Ann Veronica *by H. G. Wells was banned by the Manchester Public Libraries in 1909, the unorthodox economist J. A. Hobson famously remarked: 'If the sun ever shone in Manchester, the Watch Committee would probably prosecute it for indecent exposure.'*

∿

Damn all expurgated books, the dirtiest book of all is the expurgated book.

Walt Whitman, 1888.
Ironically, four years later he sanctioned a bowdlerized edition of *Leaves of Grass* as a favour to a publisher friend

∿

Every South African cannot go out and buy every new book and read it to decide if he will like it. Now we have a body that can do it for him. We study the book and tell him if he will like it or not.

Judge J. H. Snyman,
Chief Censor in South Africa, 1978

∿

Book Burnings

~

The Romans burnt the books of the Jews, of the Christians and of the Philosophers; the Jews burnt the books of the Christians and the Pagans; and the Christians burnt the books of the Pagans and the Jews.

Isaac D'Israeli, *Curiosities of Literature*

~

Ancient China   The Emperor Shi Huang Ti (259–210 BC) is said to have buried alive 460 Confucian scholars in his attempt to control history; more seriously, he burned all the books in his kingdom in 212, retaining a single copy of each for the Royal Library; and *that* copy was to be destroyed before he died. His idea was that if all records of the past were destroyed, 'history' would have to begin with him. The indignant Chinese, who felt that history was going along quite nicely without the Emperor's intervention and anyway were much attached to their books, were accustomed to 'befoul the Emperor's grave' long after his death. The thought of being condemned to lie for years under the shit of angry scholars is not a pleasant one.

The Library at Alexandria   One of the worst examples of book burning was also one of the earliest. The Caliph Omar, who captured Alexandria in AD 640, had the entire 200,000 volumes of the famous library burned. The complacency of his justification for this act of barbarism is a model for book burners right up to twentieth-century religious fundamentalists in America; he observed: 'If these writings of the Greeks agree with the Book of God they are useless and need not be preserved; if they disagree, they are pernicious and ought to be destroyed.' (It is said that the books were at least put to good use, providing six months' fuel for the baths of the city.)

Savonarola's Bumper Burning   In 1947 Savonarola's pulpit propaganda inspired a great burning of 'vanities' in Florence. Bonfires of vanities were not in fact a new phenomenon and St Bernardino had encouraged them, but this time the fires were to be fed with 'lascivious and indecent books and all sorts of figures and paintings which could arouse people to wicked and indecent thoughts', as

Iacopo Nardi called them. Some authors destroyed many of their own works under the influence of Savonarola's puritanical teaching, and the writer G. F. Pico gave up reading poems because it was 'destestable . . . that most poets mixed into their verses the greatest wickedness and impurities'. Popular songs also came under attack, though some of the best, such as Lorenzo de' Medici's '*Quant' è bella giovinezza*' were simply turned into hymns with new and suitably pious words. Paintings and sculptures were burned, some actually brought along by the artists themselves; Fra Bartolommeo and Lorenzo de' Credi, for instance, contributed their drawings of nudes. The bonfire included not only works one might expect, such as those of Ovid, Boccaccio and Propertius, but even those of Dante.

Disagreeable though he was, Savonarola is a fascinating historical phenomenon. In the inevitability of death he saw a powerful weapon to frighten people into obedience, and he pushed the idea relentlessly, encouraging his flock to visit cemeteries, to regard every day as if it was their last, even to take a skull in the hand and contemplate it deeply. His attack on reason and his insistence that the essential human activity was, or ought to be, 'contemplation of God' was a powerful antidote to the worldly and humanistic strains in Renaissance life. Because Savonarola was essentially sincere he lacked the political cynicism to manipulate the forces that he unleashed. His second 'bonfire of vanities' in 1498 led to riots and after that his decline, torture and execution followed rapidly. There was a certain irony in the manner of his end – Savonarola's first great bonfire had filled San Marco and was built higher than the roof of the Medici palace itself; its circumference was 80 metres. On 23 May 1498 in the Piazza della Signoria another vast heap of faggots was lit, this one surmounted by a cross on which hung Savonarola and two of his companions. With him were burned all his writings, sermons, essays and pamphlets.

Tyndale's New Testament   Cuthbert Tonstall, Bishop of London, attempted to burn all the copies of Tyndale's translation of the New Testament into English. In October 1526 he compelled everyone in his diocese to hand over the copies they had, and then burned them at St Paul's Cross. However, the books kept arriving from the continent, where they were printed, and even the ardour of the bishop was insufficient to prevent their circulation. A man called Packington offered to help the bishop by buying up as many Tyndales as he could, and the bishop, who saw in his mind's eye an unending succession of satisfactory bonfires, eagerly agreed. Unfortunately for him, Packington was a friend of Tyndale's and went off to see him at once. Edward Halle in his *Chronicle* tells what followed:

> Augustine Packington came to William Tyndale and said: 'William, I know thou art a poor man, and hast a heap of New Testaments and books by thee, for the which thou hast both endangered thy friends and beggered thyself; and I have now gotten thee a merchant, which with ready money shall dispatch thee of all that thou hast, if you think it so profitable for thyself.'
> 'Who is the merchant?' said Tyndale.
> 'The bishop of London,' said Packington.
> 'Oh, that is because he will burn them,' said Tyndale.
> 'Yea, marry,' quoth Packington.
> 'I am the gladder,' said Tyndale, 'for these two benefits shall come thereof. I shall get money of him for these books, to bring myself out of debt, and the whole world shall cry out upon the burning of God's word. And the overplus of the money, that shall remain to me, should make me more studious to convert the said New Testament, and so newly imprint the same once again; and I trust the second will much better like you than ever did the first.' And so forward went the bargain: the bishop had the books, Packington had the thanks, and Tyndale had the money.

Byron's *Memoirs* In the upstairs drawing room of No. 12 Albemarle Street, still occupied by the distinguished publishing house with which Byron was associated, John Murray the second consigned the poet's *Memoirs* to the flames on 17 May 1824. Present were Tom Moore, to whom Byron had originally given the *Memoirs*; Byron's friend John Cam Hobhouse; Colonel Doyle, representing Lord Byron; Wilmot Horton, representing Augusta Leigh; a Mr Luttrell, who was a friend of Moore's; and John Murray the third, then aged sixteen.

Murray came into absolute possession of the *Memoirs*, which were a decidedly hot property in every sense of the word according to the few who had read them, on the death of Byron. Despite having paid the substantial sum of 2000 guineas for the work, Murray blenched at the thought of letting loose on the world such a candid and probably reputation-destroying document. The meeting was a stormy one, but at length Mrs Leigh's wishes prevailed and the manuscript was burnt in the presence of all. Moore paid Murray back the 2000 guineas (which, not untypically, he had just borrowed from another publisher, Longman), with interest.

Many people were extremely disappointed by the burning of

Byron's *Memoirs*, but not half as disappointed as others were relieved.

Isabel Burton's Bonfire   Although it is not uncommon for protective wives to destroy documents that they feel would read incongruously beside the biographical monuments that they have in mind for the deceased, the wholesale destruction of academic work is less common. Isabel Burton, however, shocked by her late husband's evident interest in oriental attitudes towards sex, destroyed the whole of his 1282-page manuscript translation of *The Perfumed Garden* (second version). Not content with this act of supreme vandalism she (more understandably) destroyed his journals as well. Nor did she neglect some of his priceless rare books of which she happened to disapprove. A list of those of her husband's works that she burned is given in Michael Hastings's biography of Sir Richard Burton:

> Twenty-seven years of his private journals
> Every day-book Burton had kept as long as he'd known Isabel
> MS of *The Perfumed Garden* – 1282 pages
> More Notes on Paraguay
> Personal Experiences in Syria
> Lowlands of Brazil
> South America
> North America
> Central America
> A Book of Istria – more Castellieri
> Materials for Four more Books on Camoëns
> Slavonic Proverbs
> Dr Wetstein's Hauran
> Ausonius, Epigrams
> A Study of the Wali
> A Trip up the Congo
> Ober Ammergau
> Vichy
> Lectures and Poetry
> The Eunuch Trade in Egypt
> Akits as Mirza Ali
> The Ashantee War
> Inscriptions
> Sind-Karachi
> The Adelsburg Caves
> The Neapolitan Muses
> Syrian Proverbs
> Four Cantos of Ariosto

This gigantic and vengeful incineration took place in the garden of the Burtons' Trieste villa after Sir Richard's death on 20 October 1890. Its motive seems to have been an attempt to create posthumously a man to whom Isabel had not been married in real life. A zealous Catholic and a stubborn, dullish-minded woman, she married Burton when he was forty; he was then a man of incredible vigour, insatiable curiosity and the master of some thirty languages; thereafter his decline into a repressed and frustrated individual moving from one minor consulship to another was rapid. The marriage seems to have been without sexual passion on his side, which doubtless made his interest in erotica even more dismaying to Isabel, especially as it was not without cynicism; he once wrote: 'I translated a doubtful book in my old age, and I immediately made sixteen thousand guineas. Now that I know the tastes of England, we need never be without money.'

The Library of Peking   In 1900 the Boxer Rebellion broke out in China, so called from its moving spirit, the secret Society of Harmonious Fists. They were opposed to the extension of western political and commercial influence in China and for a time laid siege to the European legations in Peking as well as killing a number of missionaries and other Europeans. In the co-ordinated retaliation by five western nations and Japan, the Library of Peking, which had taken centuries to create, was burned, an act of wanton destruction which exposed the shallowness of the claims to 'civilization' made by the commercially orientated greedy nations of the West.

***Dubliners* Inflamed**   According to James Joyce in a letter to the American publisher Bennett Cerf in 1932, when *Dubliners* was published by Grant Richards in 1914, 'some very kind person bought out the entire edition and had it burnt in Dublin'.

The Nazi Book Burnings   The victims of this massive incineration were mostly Jewish authors, with a few Communists thrown in. The biggest of the nationwide bonfires was held in front of the University in Berlin on 10 May 1933. Dr Goebbels delivered an address, and it rained, which two phenomena seem to have dampened the enthusiasm of the estimated 40,000 spectators. The authors whose works were committed to the flames in various parts of the country included the following:

Alfred Adler	Emil Ludwig
Henri Barbusse	Rosa Luxemburg
John Dos Passos	Heinrich Mann
Albert Einstein	Thomas Mann
Lion Feuchtwanger	Karl Marx
Sigmund Freud	Marcel Proust
Maxim Gorki	Erich Maria Remarque
Heinrich Heine	Arthur Schnitzler
Ernest Hemingway	Upton Sinclair
Helen Keller	Stalin
Lenin	Leon Trotsky
Jack London	Stefan Zweig

In Salzburg a 'purification bonfire' was held in 1938 under the auspices of the Nazi Teachers' Association. Two thousand volumes were tossed into the flames, with a promise that 30,000 more would go the same way.

King Penguin A remarkable instance of a publisher burning his own books is to be found in J. E. Morpurgo's vivid life of Allen Lane, the domineering and erratic founder of Penguin Books. When Tony Godwin was chief editor of Penguin in the latter part of Lane's career, the personalities of the founder and the young prodigy frequently clashed. Things came to a head over a book of Godwin's by the draughtsman-satirist named Siné, which contained scatological drawings. Many booksellers protested when this book was shown to them by Penguin representatives, and a board-room battle ensued in which Lane, the publisher of *Lady Chatterley's Lover,* illogically adopted a Grundyist line against Godwin's defence of the book. Probably the dispute had more to do with his personal animosity and resentment towards the rising star than with any beliefs he fancied he held. At any rate, the booksellers' chorus of pious disapproval provided him with an argument that the book should be withdrawn in order not to offend Penguin's friends in the trade. This line contradicted most of what Lane had valiantly upheld in a lifetime of publishing, not to mention its inherent illiberality, and the board decided to back Godwin. Although Lane appeared to accept his defeat, he was in fact plotting an extraordinary and possibly unique *coup* in publishing history. He conspired with a trusted member of the warehouse staff and one night loaded the entire stock of Siné's book, *Massacre*, on to a van; then he took it home and made a bonfire of it. Naturally this was not well received by Godwin, but there was little he could do except threaten resignation — a move possibly welcome to Lane. What was really at stake was the reduction of Lane's autocratic power by democracy resulting from Penguin having become a publicly quoted company in April 1961. As his biographer remarks with some asperity, Lane was more used to treating his fellow directors 'in the manner of Abraham Lincoln: "Noes, seven, Ayes, one. The Ayes have it".'

Censorship

~

Obscenity is whatever gives a judge an erection.
American lawyer

~

The censor is like a chameleon, taking on the colour of his surroundings. Sometimes it is indeed impossible for the average person to know that the censor has been at work at all. And it is often easier to recognize — and wax indignant — about the censorship one observes in other cultures, while forgetting a narrow consensus that has silently pulled up the drawbridge in one's own society. Moreover, although 'morals' are the issue that usually hits the newspaper headlines, politics lurks in the background. The now abolished office of Lord Chamberlain, as stage censor, was originally established for political reasons alone.

~

> *It is the Lord Chamberlain's past experience that once a word of this sort is allowed there is a tendency for it to come into popular use. . . .*
> The Lord Chamberlain in the 1930s, explaining why he was insisting on a certain word being cut from a revue sketch.
> The word was 'constipated'.

~

As in everything else, however, there are degrees of censorship. A violent attack by the local watch society or a raid by the police following information received may show a vested interest lashing its tail. But a discreet decision by a publisher, taken on other than literary grounds, that he will not risk publishing a certain book is more insidious, if less dramatic. *Animal Farm* was a case in point.

George Orwell's *Animal Farm*   The manuscript, doing the rounds of publishers in 1944, was rejected by three who would normally have been keen to publish Orwell. Victor Gollancz, with whom Orwell had an option clause, turned it down. He had stomached a great deal of the author's opinions, which were increasingly a direct attack on the 'fellow-travelling' which then characterized his firm and his list (though he couldn't stomach *Homage to Catalonia* either, which exposed the cynical and brutal behaviour of the Communists during the Spanish Civil War). Gollancz extricated himself on a technicality – his option was for a full-length novel and at 30,000 words *Animal Farm* was not full-length.

Faber also turned it down. T. S. Eliot, in an evasive letter to the author, admitted the literary qualities of the book, but he and the other director he had consulted had 'no conviction (and I am sure none of the other directors would have) that this is the right point of view from which to criticize the political situation of the present time'. Presumably this Delphic pronouncement meant that an ally, Soviet Russia, should not be exposed as a barbarous dictatorship even by means of an allegorical satire, if it risked damaging solidarity. Just as in the Spanish Civil War, truth had to be subordinated to the cause. Eliot added some other rather odd comments which seemed to interpret the book as favouring Trotskyism; significantly, this also was a non-literary criterion for rejecting it.

Before Faber the book had been turned down by Cape. This was perhaps the most blatant censorship it met with, for the manuscript had been originally accepted after highly favourable reports from Veronica Wedgwood and Daniel George. All appeared to be settled and Orwell was offered a contract. At this point Jonathan Cape asked the personal advice of a friend in the Ministry of Information (a body whose title now has faintly Orwellian overtones). This friend, not surprisingly, said that the book would be 'very bad for our relations with Russia'. Cape withdrew the contract.

Probably the most disreputable aspect of all this, particularly when one considers the stream of canting rhetoric about freedom of speech so prevalent in English public life, is the way in which illiberal political systems may be permitted to extend their illiberalism into free ones by a species of blackmail. The modern form of this process is the attempt to soft-pedal criticism of those bloodstained régimes in which Britain has substantial commercial or political interests. As Warburg observed in *All Authors Are Equal*, in his account of how he acquired *Animal Farm*: 'It might be argued, and I think it should be argued, that "responsibility", whether political or social or literary, is not necessarily a desirable quality in a publisher.' It should be added that Warburg's wife had threatened to leave him if he published *Animal Farm*.

Private and Official – Lady Waterhouse and the Censors In 1938 Lady Waterhouse submitted to Jonathan Cape her account of six years as secretary to Mrs Baldwin, also covering a time when her husband, Sir Ronald Waterhouse, had been private secretary to King George VI, then Duke of York. The 'revelations' in this manuscript about her husband's activities, though innocuous enough to anyone not as pathologically secretive on the British establishment, aroused all the self-righteous paranoia of the Treasury solicitor, to whom it was submitted. It was returned with numerous passages marked for deletion. An editor at Cape going through it found that everyone seemed to have tried to get their finger into this particular pie – some objections seemed to emanate from the court, others from 10 Downing Street; some had been made on purely party political grounds (a characteristic attempt to misuse the Official Secrets Act), and one or two were simply incomprehensible. In particular, a conversation with King George V relating to Bonar Law's resignation, where Sir Ronald Waterhouse urged the claims of Baldwin rather than Curzon to succeed him, was strongly objected to. In the eyes of the authorities it certainly wouldn't do for the British people to know the processes and influences by which their leader had 'emerged'. The expedient of denying that such a conversation had ever taken place was tried – which not unnaturally exasperated Sir Ronald, who didn't like his veracity being questioned for the self-serving ends of the unscrupulous interested parties. He placed on record the veracity of his wife's account. But Lady Waterhouse did rewrite the chapter, incorporating many of the amendments requested.

When the book was again submitted to the Treasury solicitor, it came back with an embarrassed explanation that, although he had hoped the amendments would remove difficulties, Their Majesties themselves now objected to publication in any form at all. In 1939 rattling the royal sabre would usually have been sufficient for the respectful subject's submission, but Cape and Lady Waterhouse were made of sterner stuff. The Prime Minister was now trundled into action. Sir Horace Wilson, head of the civil service, tried to bludgeon Sir Ronald into withdrawing his wife's book, but Sir Ronald was unmoved, pointing out that he was no longer in the civil service and subject to Sir Horace's jurisdiction; and that in any case the decision lay with his wife, not him. The Treasury solicitor and Sir Horace tried twice more, and a final shot from Sir Horace made open threats that action might be taken under the Official Secrets Act. The book was published in 1942 and no such action was taken, since there was nothing in the book even faintly prejudicial to national security — as the publisher knew — but there was of course considerable public interest, which the authorities wished to suppress.

The steadfastness of Cape, Lady Waterhouse, and perhaps especially Sir Ronald Waterhouse did them as much credit as the authorities' tactics did them discredit. Beginning with the friendly nudge-and-a-wink technique, they proceeded to overt warnings and from there to outright threats. It remains one of the most disreputable examples of attempted suppression by an unholy alliance of court, Downing Street and civil service, and raised some of the issues that were later to be aired in the case of *The Crossman Diaries*.

The Crossman Diaries   One of the less attractive features of British society is the officially maintained secrecy about matters of public interest, always claimed to be in order to preserve national security and good government based on cabinet confidentiality, and always extended, as far as politicians and civil servants can manage, to cover anything that might be an embarrassment to them. When Sir Anthony Nutting submitted his manuscript detailing the actual manoeuvres of government during the Suez affair, the secretary of the cabinet of the day, after going through the book, objected to almost every page until the last twenty (which dealt with Commons debates and Nutting's troubles with his constituency). The usual barrage of threats, always on the grounds of highest principle, was laid down. But it didn't take a genius to see what the real motive was. In his account of the affair given to support the publication of *The Crossman Diaries* he wrote: '. . . as far as I am aware no British records were kept showing the collusion between Britain, France and Israel which led to the attack on Egypt, [and] future historians would find no enlightenment in the archives of the Foreign Office when the official history of those times came to be written'. (Even if there was anything in the archives, the thirty-year rule, which opens to inspection governmental records at the expiry of that time, would probably not have helped. The records are carefully weeded under the guise of removing items prejudicial to 'national security'.)

Nutting resisted most of the semi-formal pressure put upon him, and a slightly altered version of his manuscript was published. The publishers of *The Crossman Diaries* in their turn, and particularly the *Sunday Times* who wished to serialize the book, played a patient cat and mouse game with the secretary of the cabinet office, then Sir John Hunt. The details of the argument were complex, not least because it emerged that the dispute was conducted in a grey area where the legal sanctions available to the would-be suppressors of the *Diaries* were by no means clearly defined. Hunt's opening position was that he 'would not agree' to publication of Volume I and he gave detailed reasoning as to why not, foremost among his reasons being breaches of cabinet confidentiality.

Hunt's position was somewhat undermined by the fact that the Prime Minister he was at that time serving, Harold Wilson, had himself breached the rules his secretary was enunciating in his account of his first administration (*The Labour Government, 1964–1970*), notably by describing the positions of members of his cabinet over the sale of arms to South Africa. Wilson also seemed to have taken a more liberal position than his then secretary of the cabinet, Sir Burke Trend, over the contents of Nutting's book. But there was another telling reason why the smooth suppression of the *Diaries* should not be allowed to proceed. It concerned the hypocrisy of a system whereby cabinet ministers routinely gave non-attributable 'off the record' briefings – notably to the circle of tame hacks known as lobby correspondents – including details of cabinet discussions and often deliberately puffing their own interests. As one ex-cabinet minister said in an affidavit supporting the *Sunday Times* and the publishers (quoted in Hugo Young, *The Crossman Affair*): '. . . I understood full well that [such briefings] . . . would be used by journalists for the purpose of political reporting and comment. The deliberate leaking of Cabinet or Government information is a well-known device.'

In the end the guerrilla war in the courts over publication was won by the defendants, and Crossman's wishes that a little light should be shed (as opposed to a doctored report issued) on the workings of British government were fulfilled. The case highlighted the attitude towards information of government and the civil service, who tend to see it as no more than a weapon in the power game, and of having little or no objective value in a democracy, notwithstanding the cant put out by politicians about 'open government'. Even if some of them genuinely believe in this concept, the civil service does not.

As the former Liberal leader Jo Grimond put it in his submission for the defendants in the *Crossman Diaries* case:

As I understand it, the ban sought in this action would prevent the publication of much material relevant to decision-making, and it is requested for up to thirty years. This is an interference with open democratic government. It is important at this time that it should be resisted . . . the bureaucratic frame of mind, self-regarding, secretive, hierarchical, and averse to open discussion, is a major though perhaps well-intended threat to our society. . . .

Banned or Withdrawn Books

~

If any word or expression is of such a nature, that the first impression which it excites is an impression of obscenity, that word ought not to be spoken, or written, or printed; and if printed, it ought to be erased.

Dr Thomas Bowdler, 1823

~

1557   The *Index Librorum Prohibitorum* was first promulgated; it was chiefly concerned with heresy, the church's unhealthy obsession with sex only gradually establishing itself later. There was, however, an earnest of things to come in the general guidance to inquisitors to prohibit 'books which include the treatment of obscene and immoral subjects'. But the portions of Boccaccio which were condemned were not the 'obscene' ones. By the 1950s there were 4000 books on the list, including titles by Gibbon, J. S. Mill, Pascal, Richardson, Hume, Voltaire, Anatole France, Stendhal and Zola, as well as all of Balzac and all of Dumas.

1739   The bookseller and printer Edmund Curll was obliged to stand in the stocks for publishing such items as *The Nun in Her Smock* − though his technical offence condemning him to the stocks was the issuing of politically sensitive works. In order to avoid being half-killed by the egg and tomato throwers he printed a broadside stating that he had been placed there for 'excessive zeal for the good memory' of Queen Anne. This effectively protected him from the patriotic crowd.

c.1750   John Cleland was arraigned before the Privy Council and his book *Memoirs of a Woman of Pleasure (Fanny Hill)* condemned. Cleland explained that he had written it to alleviate his poverty and the president of the Council, who happened to be related to Cleland, granted him a pension of £100 a year on one condition – that he wrote no more erotic books. Cleland sold the copyright of *Fanny Hill* for a mere £20 and his publisher is supposed to have made £10,000 from it.

1822 and 1841   Shelley was prosecuted for blasphemous libel in 'Queen Mab'. The poet was no stranger to legal tangles: in 1826 he lost the long-running law suit over custody of his wife Harriet's children after twelve years of litigation. Lord Eldon found against him on the ground of his atheistic and immoral opinions, and of the fact that, in the judge's view, he put such opinions into practice. 'Queen Mab' was one of the documents adduced in evidence.

1837   Flaubert was prosecuted for his novel *Madame Bovary*, but acquitted.

1864   Baudelaire was prosecuted for *Les Fleurs du Mal*, considered to be an '*outrage aux bonnes moeurs*'. He was arrested in the cemetery of Montparnasse where he was peaceably reading Boswell's *Life of Johnson*. Defiantly he told a friend: 'I expect reparation to my honour' [from the court]; but was fined 300 francs.

1866   Algernon Charles Swinburne's *Poems and Ballads* was withdrawn after threats of criminal prosecution. Such phrases as 'splendid supple thighs', and 'quivering flanks' were too much for the public. But Swinburne found another – braver – publisher and refused to alter his poems for the prudes.

1877   Charles Bradlaugh and Annie Besant were tried for publishing *The Fruits of Philosophy*, a pamphlet advocating birth control. They were convicted, sentenced to six months' imprisonment and fined £200 each. The conviction was overturned via a legal technicality on appeal. As in the case of Shelley, vengeance of a more personal nature was taken on Annie Besant; her estranged clergyman husband was able to deprive her of contact with her daughter for ten years.

1881   Walt Whitman's *Leaves of Grass* (published 1833) was threatened by the Boston district attorney unless it was expurgated. The furore stimulated enough sales to enable Whitman to buy his Camden home.

1885 W. J. Stead founded the National Vigilance Association and wrote articles in the *Pall Mall Gazette* against the white slave traffic – a major social evil of the time. The exposé was entitled *The Maiden Tribute of Modern Babylon*. However, as Morris Ernst wrote in *To The Pure* (Cape, 1929), 'It is almost a law of their evolution that vice societies arise to deal with tangible evils and then soon turn to imaginary ones.' Within three years the vice secretary of the society was leading the attack on Zola's novels.

1888 Henry Vizetelly, the publisher of Flaubert, Goncourt, Gautier, Murger, Maupassant, Daudet etc. was hounded by the courts for his edition of Zola, notably *La Terre*. This had already been expurgated, but not enough for the severely disturbed judiciary and its supporters. Vizetelly made some alterations, so that the book had now been twice expurgated, republished and was again prosecuted. At the age of seventy he was sent to jail for three months, and financially ruined by the courts; his health was also undermined, and he died five years later. His persecution, ruin and virtual murder by the authorities represents the greatest triumph in recent times of right-thinking people and an ignorant judiciary over freedom of expression. Vizetelly did not endear himself to humourless puritans by publishing an 86-page pamphlet detailing what passages in English classics would require deletion to satisfy the criteria of acceptability they proposed for the Zola novels.

1890–1900 Richard Dehmel's *Die Metamorphosen der Venus* was prosecuted three times. The publisher and bookseller were charged with '*das Scham- und Sittlichkeitsgefühl in geschlechtlicher Beziehung groblich zu verletzen*' – a long-winded German formulation for outrage to public morals. After six years' harassment, however (some of it maliciously inspired by commercial rivals to Dehmel's publisher and personal enemies of the poet), the forces of darkness succeeded in having precisely one poem, 'Venus consolatrix', condemned, and one or two expurgated.

1897 Havelock Ellis's *Studies in the Psychology of Sex*, volumes 1 and 2, were prosecuted successfully in England. The book continued to be printed in America, from where it was imported in substantial quantities into Britain. Ellis was drily philosophical about this, writing in a postscript to the work:

> I supposed that . . . a student [of sexual psychology] was at all events secure from any gross form of attack on the part of the police or

government under whose protection he imagined he lived. That proved to be a mistake . . . I do not complain. I am grateful for the early and generous sympathy with which my work was received in Germany and the United States, and I recognize that it has had a wider circulation, both in English and the other chief languages of the world, than would have been possible by the modest method of issue which the government of my country induced me to abandon.

Dean Inge boasted in the *Evening Standard* that he bought the first two volumes of the *Studies* and burned them.

1908   Boston courts convicted the publisher of Elinor Glyn's *Three Weeks*.

1915   Methuen, the publishers of D. H. Lawrence's *The Rainbow*, were hauled into court and, as they offered no defence to an obscenity charge, the book was destroyed. No one bothered to notify Lawrence of the case. An underlying motive for the attack in this case may have been Lawrence's denunciation of World War I.

1922   John Gott was given nine months' hard labour for publishing a pamphlet in which Christ's entry into Jerusalem was described as a circus act.

1923   At Folkestone harbour 499 copies of James Joyce's *Ulysses* were seized under the Customs Act of 1867 and burned. The book was ruthlessly pursued for another ten years until Judge John Woolsey's judgement in the USA seems to have made it respectable, even in the eyes of the British authorities.

∿

> . . . *my considered opinion, after long reflection, is that whilst in many places the effect of* Ulysses *on the reader undoubtedly is somewhat emetic, nowhere does it tend to be an aphrodisiac. . . .* Ulysses *may therefore be admitted into the United States.*
>
> Judge John Woolsey,
> giving judgement in the case United States v. *Ulysses* and
> Random House Inc., 1933

∿

1928   Jonathan Cape and a bookseller called Leopold Hill, who was offering for sale the Penguin edition of Radclyffe Hall's *The Well of Loneliness*, were summonsed at Bow Street magistrate's court to show cause why seized copies of the book should not be destroyed. This followed a campaign of vilification against it. Cape had ceased to offer for sale copies of their edition after threats from the Home Office, though copies already on sale had been seized. Jonathan Cape himself flew with the plates for the book to Paris, where a new edition was printed, copies of which were then imported into England.

Forty writers, professional people, teachers, academics and clerics were assembled to testify for the defence; among them were Rose Macaulay, A. P. Herbert, Julian Huxley, Leonard and Virginia Woolf, and Storm Jameson. After disallowing an opinion from Desmond MacCarthy on whether the book was obscene or not, the magistrate, Sir Chartres Biron, was informed by counsel for the defence that he had thirty-nine witnesses to call. 'I reject them all', he said irritably. Norman Birkett's fumbling defence did not improve the book's chances and it was ordered to be destroyed.

In America, after 20,000 copies had been sold, an attempt was made to suppress the book. This time witnesses' statements from, among others, Hemingway, Sherwood Anderson, clergymen and doctors were allowed in support of it. The case was dismissed.

All this fuss was over a somewhat turgid novel that dared to discuss lesbianism. It has since been translated into fourteen languages and sold over half a million copies. But when the author died in 1943 her book had still not been republished in her native country.

1929   Jonathan Cape were once more the targets, this time because of *Sleeveless Errand*, written by Norah C. James who worked in their advertising department. It was seized at the instigation of the manic Sir William Joynson-Hicks at the Home Office, and banned at Bow Street. This novel had apparently too many swearwords in the dialogue not to endanger the blood pressure of the moral guardians. It too was republished in France.

1929   D. H. Lawrence's satirical poems 'Pansies' were seized by the Post Office. After questions in the House of Commons they were delivered, accompanied by a note 'recommending' which fourteen poems should be deleted if the publisher decided to issue the work. The publisher took the hint.

1934   Copies of James Hanley's novel *Boy*, which was too frank for the authorities about what can happen to a young boy who has run away to sea, were seized at a lending library in Manchester and the librarian successfully prosecuted. The publishers were also prosecuted and fined £400. Shortly afterwards they went out of business, after a serious work of sexual instruction published by them was condemned in 1935. On that occasion the magistrate was worried, not about the effect that the book might have on children, but about the effect on the working class. In this he was foreshadowing the oafish pomposities of the prosecuting counsel in the trial of Penguin books in connection with *Lady Chatterley's Lover*.

1946 Kathleen Winsor's *Forever Amber* was attacked in the American courts and burned on importation into Britain by the customs. In America it was eventually cleared, the judge observing: 'While it is conductive to sleep, it is not conductive to a desire to sleep with the opposite sex.'

1955 *Malloy* by Samuel Beckett and *Lolita* by Vladimir Nabokov were published in Paris. The British customs seized copies at ports of entry. The works of Jean Genêt — in French — also began to be a target in the fifties.

1959 The Grove Press issued an unexpurgated edition of D. H. Lawrence's *Lady Chatterley's Lover* with a preface by Archibald MacLeish and an introduction by Professor Mark Shorer. The US Post Office declared the book obscene and non-mailable. On 21 July a federal judge overturned the Post Office action and challenged the postmaster general's right to dictate the criteria as to what was or was not obscene.

1960 In the historic trial of Penguin Books on the ground of publishing an obscene book, namely *Lady Chatterley's Lover*, Mervyn Griffith Jones for the prosecution asked the rhetorical question: 'Is this a book you would give to your wife or servant?' Penguin won the case and Lawrence's stepdaughter remarked: 'I feel as if a window has opened and fresh air has blown right through England.' This was not the view of Nottingham City Council, which requested all their public libraries not to stock this work by the city's most distinguished son.

Banned in Boston

This list and its introduction are taken from *To The Pure . . . A Study of Obscenity and the Censor*, by Morris L. Ernst and William Seagle (Jonathan Cape, 1929).

No complete list of books banned in Boston has ever been officially announced by the public authorities. The following list, which appeared in the Authors' League *Bulletin*, indicates the varied types of works which were deemed obscene in 1927:

The Wayward Man	St John Ervine	*In Such a Night*	Babette Deutsch
Dark Laughter	Sherwood	*The Starling*	Doris Leslie
	Anderson	*Pretty Creatures*	William Gerhardi
High Winds	Arthur Train	*The Madonna of the*	Maurice Dekobra
Blue Voyage	Conrad Aiken	*Sleeping Cars*	
The Irishman	St John Ervine	*Dream's End*	Thorne Smith
What I Believe	Bertrand Russell	*Tomek the Sculptor*	Adelaide Eden
Circus Parade	Jim Tully		Phillpotts
The American Caravan;	E. Pettit	*The Plastic Age*	Percy Marks
Move Over		*The Hard Boiled Virgin*	Francis Newman
Oil	Upton Sinclair	*The Rebel Bird*	Diana Patrick
From Man to Man	Olive Schreiner	*The Butcher Shop*	Jean Devanny
Mosquitoes	William Faulkner	*The Ancient Hunger*	Edwin Granberry
Pilgrims	Edith Mannin	*Antennae*	Herbert Footner
Horizon	Robert Carse	*The Marriage Bed*	Ernest Pascal
The Sorrows of Elsie	André Savignon	*The Beadle*	Pauline Smith
Nigger Heaven	Carl Van Vechten	*As It Was*	Helen Thomas
Power	Lion	*Elmer Gantry*	Sinclair Lewis
	Feuchtwanger	*Doomsday*	Warwick Deeping
Twilight	Keyserling	*The Sun Also Rises*	Ernest Hemingway
Black April	Julia Peterkin	*Blinded Kings*	J. Kessel and
An American Tragedy	Theodore Dreiser		Hélène Iswolsky
The World of William	H. G. Wells	*Spread Circles*	F. J. Ward
Clissold		*Little Pitchers*	Isa Glenn
Wine, Women and	John Dos Passos	*Master of the Microbe*	Robert W. Service
War; Manhattan		*Evelyn Grainger*	George Frederick
Transfer			Hummel
Count Bruga	Ben Hecht	*Cleopatra's Diary*	Henry Thomas
Ariane	Claude Anet	*The Allinghams*	May Sinclair
The Captive	Edouard Bourdet	*The Revolt of Modern*	Judge Ben Lindsey
Crazy Pavements	Beverley Nichols	*Youth*	
Young Men in Love	Michael Arlen		

～

Who can define the clear and present danger to the community that arises from reading a book? If we say it is that the reader is young and inexperienced and incapable of resisting the sexual temptations that the book may present to him, we put the entire reading public at the mercy of the adolescent mind and of those adolescents who do not have the expected advantages of home influence, school training or religious teaching. Nor can we say into how many such hands the book may come. . . . If the argument be applied to the general public, the situation becomes absurd for then no publication is safe. . . .

Judge Curtis Bok,
in the case of the State of Pennsylvania *v.*
five booksellers, Philadelphia, 1949

～

Famous Banned Authors

The following list of major writers, scholars and controversialists who fell under a ban at one time or another is, unhappily, by no means complete. The main bannings or destructions are given, but there were many subsidiary examples of local zeal in almost every case. Some of these writers, for instance Luther and Calvin, were very keen to ban the works of others that they considered pernicious.

The last book on this list is Norman Mailer's *The Naked and the Dead* (1949). Since then censorship in the western world, or rather those parts of it that enjoy democratic government, has tended to decline. On the other hand, it is impossible in the space available to list all the authors and works banned elsewhere, and specifically in the eastern bloc. Since the time of Stalin the general principle applied in such countries as the USSR and East Germany has been that all works are banned that are not officially allowed; the publication of a work such as Solzhenitsyn's *One Day in the Life of Ivan Denisovich* (1960), used by Khrushchev to demythologize Stalin, reinforced rather than contravened this principle. Nevertheless, generalizations of this kind can never tell the whole complex story, and some countries − Czechoslovakia in the Prague Spring, Hungary since the 1970s − tolerate quite a wide spectrum of writing that does not toe the official line. Even in a more liberal climate there remain particular taboos of which the most constant are any writing that shows neighbouring Communist regimes in an unfriendly light, and any unnecessarily candid references to the workings of Russian imperialism.

The list is taken from Anne Lyon Haight, *Banned Books* (Bowker, 1955).

			Reason for banning	Censoring authority
250 BC	Confucius	All writings	Political	First Ts' in Emperor
AD 35	Homer	*The Odyssey*	Expression of Greek notions of freedom	Caligula
1140	Abelard	All works	Heresy	Pope Innocent III
1497	Boccaccio	*Il Decamerone*	Vanities, erotic, etc.	Burned by Savonarola
1497	Dante	All works	Vanities	Burned by Savonarola
1497	Ovid	All works	Erotic, impious	Burned by Savonarola
1521	Luther	All works	Heresy	Leo X
1525−6	Tyndale and others	Translation of New Testament	Pernicious merchandise	English Church
1535	Rabelais	*Pantaguel*, parts 1 and 2	Impious, lewd etc.	Sorbonne and Parliament
1550	Erasmus	*Opera Omnia*	Heresy	Spanish Church

			Reason for banning	Censoring authority
1555	Erasmus	*Opera Omnia*	Heresy	Mary Queen of Scots
1555	Machiavelli	All works	Impiety etc.	Pope Paul IV
1559	Abelard	All works	Heresey	Papal Index
1559	Boccaccio	*Il Decamerone*	Unfavourable portraits of clergy	Pope Paul IV
1559	Calvin	All works	Heresy	Papal Index
1559	Dante	*De monarchia*	Questioned Pope's authority	Pope Paul IV
1559	Erasmus	*Opera Omnia*	Heresy	Papal Index
1599	Ovid	Poetical works	Erotic, impious	Burned by Archbishop of Canterbury
1600	Boccaccio	*Il Decamerone*	Condemned for impiety etc.	Sorbonne and Parliament
1624	Luther	Translation of Bible	Heresy	Burned by Papal authorities
1633	Descartes	Some philosophical works	Heresy	Papal Index
1645	Sir Thomas Browne	*Religio Medici* (in Latin)	Heresy	Papal Index
1657	Pascal	*Lettres à un Provincial*	Subversive	French government
1660	Milton	*Pro Populo Anglicano Defensio*	Politically subversive	English Crown
1660	Milton	*Eikonoklastes*	Politically subversive	English Crown
1664	Molière	*Tartuffe*	Ridiculed religious hypocrisy	Louis XIV
1675	La Fontaine	*Contes Nouvelles en Vers*	Politically subversive	Paris police
1676	Cervantes	*Don Quixote*	Impious	Papal Index
1676	Montaigne	*Les Essaies*	Impious	Papal Index
1676	Tasso	*La Gerusalemme Liberata*	Politically subversive	French Parliament
1700	Locke	*An Essay Concerning Human Understanding* (French translation)	Impious	Papal Index
1701	Locke	*An Essay Concerning Human Understanding* (Latin version)	Subversive	Oxford University
1703	Defoe	*The Shortest Way with Dissenters*	Subversive	British government
1703	La Fontaine	*Contes Nouvelles en Vers*	Impious etc.	Papal Index
1734	Swift	*A Tale of a Tub*	Impious and subversive	Papal Index

			Reason for banning	Censoring authority
1734	Voltaire	Lettres Philosophiques and Temple du Goût	Immoral and irreligious	French lay and ecclesiastical authorities
1738	Swedenborg	Principia	Impious	Papal Index
1752	Voltaire	Lettres Philosophiques	Immoral	Papal Index

Voltaire's works, or parts of them, were banned or destroyed over the next two centuries in France, Switzerland, Prussia and the United States (*Candide* was suddenly declared obscene in 1929 by the ineffable US Customs and Post Office, although it had been studied at Harvard for many years as a set book). In 1935, Soviet Russia banned all of Voltaire's philosophical works.

1752	Diderot	L'Encyclopédie	Politically subversive and irreligious	Council of the French king
1755	Richardson	Pamela (French translation by Prévost)	Immoral	Papal Index
1759	Diderot	L'Encyclopédie (Vols 1–7)	Irreligious	Papal Index
1762	Rousseau	Emile	Immoral and irreligious	French Parliament
1763	Rousseau	Emile and Lettres de la Montagne	Immoral and irreligious	Papal Index
1766		Du Contrat Social and Lettre à Christophe de Beaumont		Papal Index
1774	Beaumarchais	Mémoires	Politically subversive	French Parliament
1774	Jefferson	Rights of British America	Subversive	English Parliament
1776	Goethe	Sorrows of Werther	Immoral	Danish lay and ecclesiastical authorities
1781	Beaumarchais	All works	Politically subversive	French Republic
1783	Gibbon	The Decline and Fall of the Roman Empire (Vol. 1)	Subversive	Papal Index
1788	Shakespeare	King Lear	George III's insanity	British government (ban lifted in 1820)
1789	Pascal	Lettres á un Provincial	Impious	Papal Index

Pascal's *Lettres* were burned twice — once in French, and once in Latin

1791	De Sade	Justine and Juliette	Obscene	French government. Papal Index. Later banned, with all other works by De Sade, in the USA

			Reason for banning	Censoring authority
1792	Paine	The Rights of Man and The Age of Reason	Subversive	French and British governments. Papal Index
1793	Kant	Die Religion innerhalb der Grenzen der blossen Vernunft	Irreligious	Prussian state
1806	Rousseau	La Nouvelle Héloïse	Impious and immoral	Papal Index
1819	Sterne	A Sentimental Journey	Immoral	Papal Index
1827	Kant	Critique of Pure Reason	Irreligious and subversive	Papal Index
1832	Hugo	Le Roi S'Amuse	Insulting to Louis Philippe	French government
1834	Casanova	Mémoires	Immoral	Papal Index
1834	Hugo	Notre Dame de Paris and Les Misérables	Immoral	Papal Index
1835	Heine	All works	Subversive	German Bund
1836	Heine	De la France, Reisebilder and De L'Allemagne	Subversive etc.	Papal Index
1841	Balzac	All works	Immoral	Papal Index
1841	Shelley	Poetical works	Immoral and subversive	British courts
1842	Shelley	Queen Mab (privately printed)	Immoral subversive	British courts
1850	Balzac	All works	Immoral	Russian government
1850	Dumas	La Dame aux Camélias	Immoral	British authorities forbade translation and circulation of opera libretto
1850	Hugo	All works	Immoral and subversive	Nicholas I of Russia
1850	Stendhal	All works	Immoral etc.	Nicholas I of Russia
1863	Dumas	All love stories	Immoral	Papal Index
1864	Flaubert	Madame Bovary and Salammbô	Immoral	Papal Index
1880	Tolstoy	Various works	Subversive and immoral	Russian government
1888	Zola	Novels	Immoral	British courts
1890	Tolstoy	The Kreutzer Sonata	Immoral	US Post Office
1891	Hardy	Tess of the D'Urbervilles	Immoral	British circulating libraries
1892	Ibsen	Ghosts	Subversive	Lord Chamberlain refused performance in Britain

			Reason for banning	*Censoring authority*
1894	George Moore	*Esther Waters*	Immoral	British circulating libraries
1894	Zola	All works	Immoral	Papal Index
1896	Hardy	*Jude the Obscure*	Immoral	British circulating libraries
1898	Havelock Ellis	*Studies in the Psychology of Sex*	Obscene	British courts
1898	Kipling	*A Fleet in Being*	National security	British government
1911	D'Annunzio	Love stories and plays	Immoral	Papal Index
1914	Balzac	*Droll Stories*	Immoral	Canadian customs
1914	Maurice Maeterlinck	All works	Immoral and irreligious	Papal Index
1915	Margaret Sanger	*Family Limitation*	Immoral	New York courts
1918	Joyce	*Ulysses*	Obscene	US Post Office. Irish authorities. Canadian authorities. British customs.
c. 1920–31	Boccaccio	*Il Decamerone*	Obscene	US treasury and customs
1922	Anatole France	All works	Immoral	Papal Index
1923	Margaret Sanger	*Family Limitation*	Immoral	British authorities
1925	Darwin	*On the Origin of the Species*	Irreligious and immoral	State of Tennessee

In fact a teacher was convicted for having taught evolution in a high school. The State passed a law forbidding any theory to be taught that conflicted with the biblical story of divine creation.

1926	Darwin	*On the Origin of the Species*	Immoral	Soviet government
1926	Descartes	All philosophical works	Subversive	Soviet government
1926	Tolstoy	All works	Immoral, subversive etc.	Hungarian government
1927	Lenin	*The State and Revolution*	Obscene and subversive	Boston authorities in USA. Hungarian government
1927	Sinclair Lewis	*Elmer Gantry*	Obscene	Boston authorities
1928	Kant	All works	Politically unsound	Russian government
1928	Lenin	*Proletarian Revolution in Russia*	Subversive	Canadian government
1928	Radclyffe Hall	*The Well of Loneliness*	Obscene	British authorities
1929	Conan Doyle	*The Adventures of Sherlock Holmes*	Occultism	Soviet government
1929	Ernest Hemingway	*A Farewell to Arms*	Frank account of Caporetto	Italian government
1929	Joyce	*Ulysses*	Obscene	British courts

			Reason for banning	Censoring authority
1929	D. H. Lawrence	*The Rainbow* and *Lady Chatterley's Lover*	Obscene	British authorities
1929	Ovid	*Ars Amatoria*	Erotic	San Francisco authorities
1929	Rousseau	*Confessions*	Impious and immoral	US customs
1929	Zola	All works	Immoral	Yugoslav government
1930	Ernest Hemingway	*The Sun Also Rises*	Immoral	Boston authorities
1930	Aldous Huxley	*Antic Hay*	Obscene	Boston authorities
1930	Aldous Huxley	*Point Counter Point*	Immoral	Irish government
1930	Swedenborg	All works	Politically unsound	Soviet government
1931	Will Durant	*The Case for India*	Politically subversive	British government
1931	Sinclair Lewis	*Elmer Gantry*	Obscene	Irish government. New York State Post Office
1931	Marie Stopes	All works	Immoral	Irish Free State
1932	Adolf Hitler	*Mein Kampf*	Politically subversive	Czech government
1932	Aldous Huxley	*Brave New World*	Immoral	Irish government
1932	D. H. Lawrence	*Lady Chatterley's Lover*	Obscene	Irish government. Polish government
1933	Casanova	*Mémoires*	Immoral	Irish government
1933	Dreiser	*The Genius* and *An American Tragedy*	Immoral	Nazi government
1933	Lion Feuchtwanger	All works	Subversive and semitic	Nazi government
1933	Ernest Hemingway	All works	Immoral etc.	Nazi government
1933	Erich Maria Remarque	All works	Subversive	Nazi government
1933	Upton Sinclair	All works	Subversive	Nazi government
1933	Trotsky	All works	Subversive	Nazi government. Soviet government
1935	Casanova	*Mémoires*	Immoral	Mussolini's Italian government
1935	Darwin	*On the Origin of the Species*	Immoral and irreligious	Yugoslav government
1937	Darwin	*On the Origin of the Species*	Immoral and irreligious	Greek Metaxas dictatorship. Papal Index
1937	Adolf Hitler	*Mein Kampf*	Politically subversive	Palestine government
1939	Goethe	All works	Immoral	Franco's Spanish dictatorship
1939	Ernest Hemingway	*A Farewell to Arms*	Immoral etc.	Irish government

			Reason for banning	Censoring authority
1939	Ibsen	All works	Immoral and subversive etc.	Franco's Spanish dictatorship
1939	Kant	All works	Politically unsound	Franco's Spanish dictatorship
1939	Stendhal	All works	Immoral etc.	Franco's Spanish dictatorship. Papal Index
1944	Balzac	*Droll Stories*	Immoral	US Post Office
1948	Descartes	*Meditations* and six other works	Heresy	Papal Index
1948	Sartre	All works	Subversive	Papal Index
1949	Norman Mailer	*The Naked and the Dead*	Obscene etc.	Canadian customs. Australian authorities
1952	Gide	All works	Immoral etc.	Papal Index
1953	Balzac	All works	Immoral	Franco's Spanish dictatorship
1953	Anatole France	*A Mummer's Tale*	Immoral	Irish government
1953	Ernest Hemingway	*The Sun Also Rises* and *Across the River and into the Trees*	Immoral	Irish government
1953	Alfred Kinsey	*Sexual Behaviour in the Human Female*	Obscene	South African censor. Irish government
1953	Margaret Sanger	*Happiness in Marriage* and *My Fight for Birth Control*	Immoral	Irish government
1953	John Steinbeck	All works	Subversive and immoral	Irish government
1953	Zola	All works	Immoral	Irish government
1954	William Faulkner	Most works	Immoral etc.	Irish government

From the above selection certain facts emerge, most notably that zeal in censorship is recurrent rather than continuous. At certain periods whole societies are cowed by the malign interference of the state in their intellectual freedom; in other societies this is more or less to be expected throughout their history because of the autocratic nature of the usual governing system. Even allowing for the latter, however, the 'censorship terror' under Tsar Nicholas I of Russia, lasting from the early 1830s until his death in 1855, was remarkable for its thoroughness, no work being safe from interference if it had religious, political or sexual content. More difficult to explain is the supine acceptance by the American people and, often shamefully, by publishers and libraries, of curtailment of intellectual liberty in the worst period of that nation's Grundyism. From the passing of the Comstock Act in

1873, which enlarged the Post Office's powers to seize matter disapproved of, until about 1948, book after book was seized after complaints from busybodies or pressure groups such as the New York Society for the Suppression of Vice. In 1948, however, the persecutors over-reached themselves when a Vice Squad patrolman seized twenty-five books from a Philadelphia store, including works by James T. Farrell and William Faulkner. A raid on fifty-four bookshops followed and the owners were all indicted. The judge threw out the case contemptuously in 1949, as did the superior court of Pennsylvania; the tide seemed to have turned. Unfortunately Grundyism was followed by McCarthyism.

In England the period of prudery lasting from mid-Victorian times until after World War II is well known, though the vindictiveness of the persecutors varied in intensity. The landmark trial of Penguin Books for publishing an unexpurgated version of *Lady Chatterley's Lover* in 1960 seems to have brought this period to a close.

Complacency is not justified, however. The irrationality and malevolence embedded in the censorial mind cannot be underestimated. One should not forget that in 1933 a book containing a plate of Michelangelo's *The Last Judgement*, made from the original Sistine Chapel fresco before the figures were given additional covering, was seized by the US customs on the grounds of obscenity, and only released after public ridicule forced the Treasury Department to capitulate. It was clear that the customs officer concerned had never heard of Michelangelo.

But some censors have remained constant to their dubious calling through thick and thin. And here one can only applaud the persistence and zeal of the Irish authorities whose labours on behalf of lies, ignorance and prejudice have probably exceeded even those of the Soviet or South African censors. No doubt they take their cue from the greatest monument to the closed mind and hostility to freedom of the intellect ever raised by supposedly civilized people: the *Index Librorum Prohibitorum* of the Roman Catholic Church. Created in 1559 by Pope Paul IV, it is still theoretically in existence.

∿

To put thought in leash to the average conscience of the time is perhaps tolerable, but to fetter it by the necessities of the lowest and least capable seems a fatal policy.

Judge Learned Hand,
in the case of United States *v.* Mitchell Kennerley and
Daniel Goodman's *Hagar Revelly*, New York, 1913

∿

Six of the Best

SIR ALFRED AYER

The six books that influenced me most in the period when I first became attracted to philosophy are:

Bertrand Russell, *Sceptical Essays*. This was the first philosophical book that I read for pleasure, at seventeen or thereabouts. It is one of his more popular works, but displays his penetration and wit.

W. H. Lecky, *A History of European Morals from Augustus to Charlemagne*. This two-volume work is probably now out of print. It was recommended to me by my headmaster when I confessed my agnosticism to him, and provides splendid ammunition against the early and medieval church.

Voltaire, *Candide*. Speaks for itself.

David Hume, *A Treatise of Human Nature*. A cornerstone of empiricism. I sometimes wonder if we have progressed beyond it.

J. S. Mill, *Autobiography*. My introduction to the Utilitarian movement.

Ludwig Wittgenstein, *Tractatus Logico-Philosophicus*. My reading of this work when I was an undergraduate put me on the road to logical positivism.

Authors Tortured, Mutilated or Killed on Account of Their Books

c. **250 BC** The first Ts'in Emperor burned not only all Confucius's works, but buried alive hundreds of Confucius's disciples.

1415 Jan Huss, the Protestant reformer of Bohemia, was led before the Bishop's Palace to witness the burning of his works; when this was complete he was led on to another pyre on which he himself was burned. The burnings followed a rigged trial conducted according to the best traditions of Christian vindictiveness (Huss was allowed no defence, either by himself or on his behalf), and his murder provoked the Hussite wars that lasted for another thirty years. Like so many victims of hatred and intolerance, Huss was immeasurably superior as a human being to his persecutors, and ignored their childish rancour. As he observed his books going up in smoke, he remarked drily on the 'folly of people burning what they could not read'.

1498   Savonarola, after being tortured on the rack, confessed that it was heretical to expose the rank corruption of the Church and Papacy. He was hung on a cross and burned in the Piazza della Signoria in Florence, together with all his inflammatory writings.

1536   William Tyndale was imprisoned, strangled and burned, together with his translations of the Bible, in Vilvorde Castle in the Netherlands. Standing on the unlit faggots, Tyndale raised his eyes to Heaven and cried out, 'Lord, open the King of England's eyes.' The King of England, Henry VIII, was not likely to be impressed by this, though with characteristic capriciousness he had declared himself delighted with Tyndale's *The Obedience of a Christian Man and How Christian Rulers Ought to Govern*.

1553   Michael Servetus, author of *Christianismi Restitutio*, which denied the tri-personality of the Godhead and eternity of the Son, was burned at the stake. Calvin demonstrated his personal brand of Christian charity by working hard to get Servetus condemned, and later writing a book misrepresenting the theologian's views as a *post hoc* justification of his judicial murder. He was also extremely active in having the works of Servetus incinerated.

   Servetus was burned at the stake after a rigged trial. It is said that green wood was used and straw and leaves sprinkled with sulphur placed on his head. His book was tied to his arm.

1579   John Stubbs's vitriolic attack on Queen Elizabeth for contemplating (as he supposed) a matrimonial union with the French Crown was condemned. The pamphlet, entitled *The Discoverie of a gaping gulf where into England is likely to be swallowed by another French marriage*, was burned. As for Stubbs, his right hand was cut off in a barbarous manner, presumably to discourage it from penning any further seditions. Stubbs responded by raising his hat with his left hand and shouting: 'God Save the Queen!'

1597   Giordano Bruno was burned by the Inquisition. A friend of Sir Philip Sidney, Bruno was a brilliant philosopher who wrote an unwise polemic (*Spaccio della Bestia Triomphante*) against the malign superstitions and fatuous dogmas of the Catholicism of the day. He remarked to his judges: 'You pronounce sentence upon me with greater fear than I receive it.'

Sixteenth Century Tommaso Campanella was thrown into a Neapolitan dungeon at the behest of the Inquisition, where he languished over twenty-five years. The cause was his *Atheismus Triumphans*. The malice of the scholastic philosophers, whose works he attacked in his books, together with the natural barbarism of the Inquisition, ensured that he was treated with the utmost bestiality, being put to the rack seven times. No one except professional apologists of the Church now has any doubt that the Inquisition indulged in a lot of sadism for its own sake, and that the real motive for its activities became the perpetuation of its own power. Its reaction to those who demonstrated this rather proved the point; for example, the way in which they treated Antonius Palearius. He wrote in his *Inquisitionis Detractator* that the Inquisition was a dagger pointed at the hearts of literary men. The Inquisition judged him a heretic because he spelled his name Aonius instead of Antonius, thus showing that he abhorred the sign of the cross in the letter T. An indication of the truth of his works may be inferred from the severity of his butchering by God's police — he was hanged, strangled *and* burned in 1566.

1625 *De Republica Ecclesiastica*, by a Jesuit of twenty years' standing, was burned by order of the Inquisition. Its author was a man called De Dominis, sometime Archbishop of Spalatro. He retired to England to concentrate on writing, and such as he wrote incurred the wrath of Pope Urban VIII. Although he retracted his 'errors' in person before the Pope — the errors chiefly consisting in the advocation of charity and tolerance, which were rightly considered to be very unchristian principles — he was thrown into Castel Sant' Angelo and probably poisoned. This greatly frustrated the Inquisition who were consequently unable to burn him together with his books, as they wished to do; instead they exhumed his body and burned that.

1628 Dr Leighton, a Scottish divine, wrote *Syon's Plea against Prelacy*. This attack on bishops was not well received by the latter, or by the Crown, and he was dealt with by the Star Chamber in 1630. The punishment deemed adequate was a fine of £10,000; committal to the Fleet Prison for life; committal to the pillory; whipping; the cutting off of his ears and slitting of his nose; and branding on his face with the letters SS, signifying 'sower of sedition'. There is a certain irony in the fact that Leighton's son, Robert, became an archbishop.

1633 William Prynne published his vitriolic *Histriomastix; or, the Player's Scourge*, a violent attack on all stage plays, which he regarded as irreligious and evil. This might not have mattered much had he not extended his strictures to the court, where masques and dancing were very much part of the royal recreations; and to the Church. Hauled before the Star Chamber, Prynne was sentenced to have his ears cut off – and the book was to be burned by the public hangman. For good measure he was also condemned to the pillory, fined £5000 and imprisoned for life. It is a measure of Prynne's incorrigibility (and of the poor psychology of sadistic-minded conservatives, such as Archbishop Laud) that the culprit took the opportunity of enforced leisure in prison to write another scorcher, *News from Ipswich*. He was summoned again before the judges, and the latter were annoyed to discover that he still possessed considerable portions of his ears. 'My Lords,' said Prynne. 'Here is never a one of your Honours but would be sorry to have your ears as mine are.' On being rebuked for his sauciness, he mildly replied: 'I hope your Honours will not be offended. I pray God give you ears to hear.' Later, after the victory of the Parliamentary party, Prynne became an MP.

1643 Urban Grandier was burned together with his book, *Contra Caelibatum Clericorum*, in the marketplace of Loudun. This famous event, which has been treated in a novel by Aldous Huxley and on film by Ken Russell, was largely the result of Grandier's indiscreet attack on Richelieu in *La Cordonnière de Loudun*. As is well known, the Ursuline convent in Loudun was suddenly overwhelmed by a collective frenzy which had elements of sexual hysteria; under its influence the nuns imagined themselves tormented by devils. Grandier was accused of casting an evil spell on them, but this charge was dismissed by the Archbishop of Bordeaux. Richelieu saw his opportunity and sent an inquisitor to reopen the case; Grandier was unjustly condemned for adultery and witchcraft. As he mounted the pyre a fly was seen to be buzzing round his head; this was Beelzebub himself, the pious onlookers told themselves, ready to convey Grandier's soul to his domain.

1683 Algernon Sidney was beheaded in the Tower. Sidney's republican views – far more radical than anything Cromwell espoused –

made him a target of the authorities after the Restoration; but it was not until the Rye House Plot to assassinate Charles II and James Duke of York in 1683 that the government was able to move against him. He was convicted by a bribed jury on the word of a traitor, and also the 'evidence' of his unpublished *Discourses concerning Government*; the trial was presided over by the judicial murderer, Judge Jeffries. His *Discourses* were finally published posthumously in 1698. They enunciated such principles as freedom of assembly and speech, and somewhat rashly pointed out that a general rising could not in logic be described as a rebellion, for: 'it is the people for whom and by whom the Sovereign is established, who have the sole power of judging whether he does or does not fulfil his duties'.

1696   Molinos, the Spanish founder of Quietism, died after eleven years' imprisonment by the Inquisition. His book on Quietism (*Conduite Spirituelle*) was found to have sixty-eight heretical propositions (the authorities were always precise in such matters), and was of course burned. His ideas regarding mental and physical absorption of the self in God, to the point of indifference to the body, had much in common with those of the Hesychasts on Mount Athos, who believed that prolonged contemplation of the navel would reveal an image of the divine light that irradiated Mount Tabor.

Seventeenth Century   Pierre Petit was among the many victims of ecclesiastical vindictiveness and barbarism in the France of his day. The young man wrote licentious poems, none of which had been published when he left the window of his room open one day, while briefly absent. A gust of wind carried sheets of manuscript into the street below and a passing priest read them. Finding that they contained impious matter, he self-righteously denounced the unfortunate poet, whose rooms proved to be full of material equally likely to raise the blood pressure of the pious bloodhounds. Notwithstanding the attempts of influential friends to save him, Petit was hung and then burned.

1702   Daniel Defoe published *The Shortest Way with Dissenters*, which ironically recommended that this troublesome minority be exterminated. The sentiments were so near to those of the more rabid amongst the High Church party that the pamphlet was much applauded on its appearance by men who were the targets of its satire. When the name of the author was made known, they realized their mistake and the applause turned to abuse. Parliament ordered the book to be burned by the hangman; Defoe was fined and imprisoned, before which he was to spend three days in the pillory; on that institution he wrote a witty poem which was distributed amongst the spectators for their edification and entertainment; perhaps, however, they would not have been inclined to lessen the flow of rotten tomatoes by such lines as:

> *Here by the errors of the town*
> *The fools look out and knaves look on.*

Hall of Infamy

James Douglas Columnist of Express Newspapers during the twenties, and then editor of the *Sunday Express*, Douglas was an anxious puritan who exposed his preoccupations in violent denunciations of books containing (as he thought) too explicit a handling of sex. He managed to do a certain amount of damage by his malevolent attacks on numerous worthwhile books, but was happily counterproductive in the case of others; it was clear that a part of his readership watched out for his attacks, then hastened to buy the offending work on the following day. Douglas was assisted, or accompanied, in his endeavours by his dog 'Bunch'. It was Douglas who wrote of Radclyffe Hall's *Well of Loneliness* in the *Sunday Express* of 19 August 1928 that he would rather put a phial of prussic acid into the hands of a healthy girl or boy than the book in question. He challenged the Home Secretary to have the book suppressed, and indeed suppression followed. Douglas himself wrote a novel somewhat luridly entitled *The Unpardonable Sin* (1907) and also a book about his wretched dog, *The Bunch Book* (1932).

William Joynson-Hicks Known, not affectionately, as 'Jix', he was Home Secretary 1924–9. A man of strong religious convictions, he held Church posts such as president of the Church League as well as political ones. During the period in which he graced, or disgraced, the office of home secretary, busybodies and puritans found it easy to gain the support of the law in attacking books that offended them. Active in the particularly absurd and vicious persecution of Radclyffe

Hall's *Well of Loneliness*, he personally wrote a threatening letter to Jonathan Cape, who had to withdraw the book.

The Rev. Charles Coughlin 'The American radio priest' frequently attacked books in his broadcasts. He was violently anti-semitic, and there were some books he did approve of, notably the fraudulent *Protocols of the Elders of Zion*, which described the supposed Jewish plot to subvert the world.

Alfred Noyes The versifier deserves a prominent place in the Hall of Infamy for his vigorous attack on *Ulysses* carried out in an unholy alliance with the then head of the Publishers' Association, James Blackwood. In his disingenuous and self-righteous account of the affair in his autobiography, *Two Worlds of Memory*, Noyes praises Lord Darling's suppression of the book in the courts and remarks *en passant* that it had been 'introduced into England by a traitor now in a lunatic asylum'. He then explains how Blackwood contacted him to say that a talk analyzing *Ulysses* was to be given on the BBC and how this must be stopped on the grounds that it represented an attempt by 'a government organization' (*sic*) to 'override the decision of the law courts and induce booksellers to break the law'. (How this could be known in advance of the talk is not explained; considerations of freedom of speech are raised in his remarkable exposition, only to be airily dismissed.) Noyes called a meeting of influential people and it was decided that he should write a belligerent letter to *The Times*. This he did, backed up by one from Blackwood, in reply to objections to it, which claimed that *Ulysses* 'would make a Hottentot sick'. (The objectors to Noyes's attempt to suppress free speech included Shaw, Hugh Walpole, the headmaster of Eton and a bishop. Noyes is witheringly sarcastic about the first two of these, but sadly puzzled by the last two.) Noyes winds up by describing with satisfaction how the broadcast was suppressed.

But the world of the censor is full of little ironies. In 1938 Noyes wrote a book on Voltaire, apparently unaware that as Voltaire's works were on the Papal Index, he should, as a Catholic, first seek permission to write about him. He was anonymously denounced to the Holy Office, the book was withdrawn and a new edition issued with a grovelling preface by the author professing the historical and religious opinions required by the censors.

John S. Sumner This man, who succeeded Anthony Comstock (see below) as the secretary of the New York Society for the Suppression of

Vice, was an equally relentless libracide, but had less success. 'The sincerity of purpose of any writer', he declared, 'does not justify the thing he writes. As a matter of fact, if the subject matter is obscene at all, it is only made all the more immoral by more capable presentation.' Using, again, the arbitrary Post Office mailing regulations, Sumner attacked anything he considered obscene (and if he considered it obscene that made it so — there was no room for alternative opinions), including *Ulysses*, *The Well of Loneliness*, Marie Stopes's *Love in Marriage*, and (repeatedly) *Mademoiselle de Maupin* by Théophile Gautier. Sumner's powers of seizure were so sweeping that they amounted to a sort of lynch law for books, and it was difficult to fight back. However Horace Liveright, who had published a translation of *The Satyricon* of Petronius Arbiter, decided to do so when a lower court failed to uphold Sumner's seizure of the book. He filed a libel suit of $25,000 against the secretary, hoping to wear down the society with expensive litigation. Sumner was aided and abetted by the district attorney, who kept trying to revive the indictment against Liveright. When the case went to a grand jury, Liveright had the book read out to them. The hours of droning recitation soon exhausted the jurors who, rather than sit through any more, adjourned without an indictment, literally bored into submission.

Sir Archibald Bodkin   Not a character in a Sherlock Holmes story, but the Director of Public Prosecutions from 1920 to 1930; there is, of course, much competition for the title of worst government law officer ever, but Sir Archibald must be a strong contender. He it was who only agreed not to prosecute *A Young Girl's Diary*, published by Allen and Unwin, if booksellers supplied it only to members of the legal, medical and educational professions, and even then recorded the name, address and occupation of each customer. This must rank as the silliest proposal of censorship ever, but reflects the snobbery and intellectual vanity that is so often a feature of censors. Later, at a conference in Geneva devoted to obscene publications, Sir Archibald distinguished himself by convincing his colleagues that no definition of obscenity was possible, saying that it did not exist in English statute law, but boasting that he himself had got two people sent to prison none the less for privately exchanging 'indecent' books.

Anthony Comstock   One of the least attractive puritans in history, the severely disturbed Comstock died in 1915 having destroyed more than 160 tons of books and pictures in his career. His weapons were the so-called Comstock Act of 1873, forbidding the mailing of 'obscene' literature, and the New York Society for the Suppression of Vice, of which he was the founder and first secretary. The Comstock Act brought even contraceptive literature within the sphere of obscenity; and to enforce it Comstock himself was appointed a special agent of the Post Office with wide powers of seizure. He was thus able to indulge his neuroses at public expense and went into battle under the slogan 'Morals, not Art or Literature'. He claimed — as have many self-appointed censors since — that his only concern was the possible harm to children. An indication of his character may be seen in his boast that some of those whom he persecuted had been driven to suicide. As with all purity censors, his position was ultimately illogical; Theodore Schroeder wrote of him: '. . . for thirty years he has "stood at the mouth of the sewer", searching for and devouring "obscenity" for a salary; and yet he claims that this lucrative delving in "filth" has left him, or made him, so much purer than all the rest of humanity that they cannot be trusted to choose their own literature and art until it has been expurgated by him'.

Dr Thomas Bowdler and Henrietta Maria Bowdler   In 1807 the *Family Shakespeare* was obscurely and anonymously published in Bath. Its preface claimed that it removed from Shakespeare's work 'everything that can raise a blush on the cheek of modesty' — or about 10 per cent of everything the playwright wrote. The mind and eye that had busied itself with the purification process was actually that of Dr Bowdler's sister, Henrietta Maria, but this was a well-kept secret for over 150 years. It must have been a painful process, for she was a woman of exquisite delicacy: she once told the Earl of Minto at a dinner party that she never looked at the dancers in operas but kept her eyes shut the whole time — they were so 'indelicate' she could not bear to look. She was also an intellectual — her anonymous sermons were so impressive that the Bishop of London wrote, care of her publisher, offering the author a parish in his diocese.

In 1818 the ten-volume *Family Shakespeare* appeared. A notice from Lord Jeffrey in the *Edinburgh Review*, declaring confidently that it made all other editions of Shakespeare obsolete ('what cannot be spoken, and ought not to have been written, should cease to be printed'), gave it a good send-off, and sales began to multiply. By 1894 the poet Swinburne (*sic*) was saying 'No man ever did better service to Shakespeare' than Dr Bowdler, and he was apparently not joking.

Dr Bowdler's *Family Gibbon* failed to catch on, however, despite the editor's assurance in the preface that Gibbon himself would have been pathetically grateful for the doctor's work in 'laying aside [the] former editions of his history'.

Bowdler was at least open about what he was doing, and it is perhaps not fair to blame him personally for all the pernicious effects that his pioneering (or nearly pioneering – there had been others less well known) efforts were later to have. Noel Perrin, in *Dr Bowdler's Legacy* (Macmillan, 1970), shows how open bowdlerizing gave way to surreptitious, the brazen declaration being superseded by the pious and furtive lie. Numerous editions appeared that pompously trumpeted their critical thoroughness while silently removing great chunks of the text.

Nine Clues to Racism and Sexism in Children's Books

The following list was drawn up by Judith Stinton and published in the book she edited entitled *Racism and Sexism in Children's Books* (Writers' and Readers' Publishing Co-operative, 1979). The vexed question of racism was brought into sharp focus when in 1972 Chatto and Windus republished Helen Bannerman's *The Story of Little Black Sambo* (1899), together with her six other children's stories. A sensitive article in *The Times* by Brian Alderson subsequently raised the whole question of censorship of children's books thought to embody undesirable attitudes. The discussion polarized into two camps whose more extreme pronouncements contained elements of absurdity; for instance, the Central Committee of Teachers against racism complained that 'black people' are shown as greedy in the book because Sambo eats 169 pancakes. Right-wing letters to *The Times*, on the other hand, produced arguments of varying implausibility liberally laced with self-righteousness, to demonstrate the impossible: that *The Story of Little Black Sambo* does not purvey a view of black people that is at best patronizing in the extreme, and at worst unpleasantly racist. The nine 'guidelines' that follow illustrate the attitudes of the new would-be censors – and perhaps some of the problems inherent in trying to subject such works to a litmus test of cultural desirability (look, for instance, at the question-begging contained in guideline 7):

How to Look for Racism and Sexism in Children's Books: A Guideline

1 Check the Illustrations

(a) Look for stereotypes: happy-go-lucky banana-eating Black Sambos, inscrutable slant-eyed yellow orientals, the cottage-loaf mother, the demure doll-loving daughter.

(b) Look for tokenism: if there are non-white characters shown, do they look like whites except for their tint or colour? Do all minority-group faces look the same — or are they depicted as genuine individuals?

(c) Who's doing what? Are black or brown characters, or females, shown in leadership and action roles?

2 Check the Storyline

(a) Standards for success: is success in the white-dominated society projected as the only ideal? Does a black person have to have outstanding qualities to be accepted? In friendships between white and non-white characters is it the non-white who does most of the understanding and forgiving?

(b) Resolution of problems: are minority people treated as 'the problem'? Are the reasons for poverty explained, or accepted as inevitable? Is a particular problem faced by a minority person resolved only through benevolent white intervention?

(c) Role of women. Are female achievements due only to good looks? Could the same story be told if the sex roles were reversed?

3 Look at the Lifestyles

Are minority people and their setting unfavourably contrasted with the unstated norm of white middle-class suburbia? If the illustrations and text attempt to depict another culture, do they go beyond oversimplification to offer genuine insights into another lifestyle? Look for inaccuracy and inappropriateness in the depiction of other cultures.

4 Watch Relationships

Do the whites in the story possess the power, take the leadership, and make the important decisions? Do non-whites and females function in essentially supporting roles?

How are family relationships depicted? In black families, is the mother always dominant? If the family are separated, are social conditions — unemployment, poverty — among the reasons for the separation?

5   Heroes and Heroines
When minority heroes and heroines do appear, are they admired for the same qualities that have made their white counterparts famous or because what they have done has benefited white people? Whose interests is a particular figure really serving?

6   Consider the Effects on a Child
Does the book counteract or reinforce a positive association with the colour white and a negative with black?

What happens to a girl's self-esteem when she reads that boys perform all the brave and important deeds?

In a particular story, is there anyone with whom a minority child can readily and positively identify?

7   Check the Author's Perspective
No author can be wholly objective. All authors write out of a cultural as well as a personal context. Look carefully to see whether the direction of the author's perspective weakens or strengthens the value of her written work.

8   Watch for Loaded Words
Examples of loaded adjectives (usually racist) are *savage, primitive, inscrutable,* and *backward.*

Look for sexist language, and adjectives that exclude or ridicule women: look for the use of the male pronoun to refer to both males and females. The following examples show how sexist language can be avoided: *ancestors* instead of *forefathers, community* instead of *brotherhood, manufactured* instead of *man-made.*

9   Look for Copyright Date
Books on minority themes – usually hastily conceived – suddenly began appearing in the mid-1970s. There followed a growing number of 'minority experience' books to meet the new market demand, but most of these were still written by white authors, edited by white editors and published by white publishers. They therefore reflected a white point of view. Only very recently has the children's book world begun even remotely to reflect the realities of a multi-racial society. And it has only just begun to reflect feminist concerns.

The copyright dates, therefore, can be a clue as to how likely the book is to be overtly racist or sexist, although a recent copyright date, of course, is no guarantee of a book's relevance or sensitivity.

Masterpieces Written in Prison

Boethius – *The Consolations of Philosophy* Ancius Manlius Severinus Boethius (*c*. 470–524) was a Roman philosopher whose *De Consolatione Philosophiae*, dubbed 'the last work of Roman literature', was favourite reading in the Middle Ages. Theodoric the Great, the Ostrogoth ruler of the period, made Boethius a consul but he was later accused of treachery and imprisoned at Pavia before execution. In prison he wrote his great work, which was to have an influence that endured for some 900 years after his death; both King Alfred and Chaucer translated the book into English. The five books of prose and verse meditate, appropriately enough given the unhappy circumstances of the author, on the fickleness of fortune, the vanity of worldly power, and the benefits of rational philosophy.

Cervantes – *Don Quixote* Cervantes had a colourful and often miserable life, during which he was twice imprisoned, once by Algerian pirates, and once after being accused of fraud in his native Spain while serving as a government tax inspector. During this latter spell of imprisonment he began to write *Don Quixote*, the first part of which was published in 1605. An instant success, it was also instantly plagiarized and imitated, so that Cervantes had to struggle to produce further parts one step ahead of the pirates. The second part was published in 1615, the year before the author's death.

Sir Walter Raleigh – *History of the World* This great work, albeit the product of considerable outside collaboration, is generally attributed to Raleigh, who worked on it during his eleven years' imprisonment in the Tower. The book was written for Prince Henry. Literary-minded fellow prisoners are supposed to have assisted with references, and research was undertaken by his chaplain, Robert Burrel. Ben Jonson was also pressed into service, causing him to remark drily that: 'The best wits in England were employed in making [Raleigh's] history.' After three-quarters of a million words had been written, the period covered only reached 130 BC and there the book came to a halt. Even that was nearly lost owing to an unfortunate incident related in Granger's *Wonderful Magazine*. Looking out of his prison window one day, Raleigh saw two men quarrel and one of them actually murder the other. Shortly afterwards two friends of his entered his room and described what had occurred, both giving decidedly different versions. Sir Walter, having witnessed the whole event himself, saw that both these two eye-witness accounts were, in important respects, erroneous. He provided a third. Realizing that three people who had all seen the same thing happening, only a few minutes before, could genuinely and dogmatically disagree as to the facts, Raleigh was overcome with rage and frustration — if it was impossible to verify what went on under one's nose, what was the point in trying to relate events of the distant past accurately? He seized the volumes of his manuscript and threw them on to a large fire. The adroitness of one of his friends rescued two volumes from the flames, but the rest was consumed.

Richard Lovelace 'One of the handsomest men in England,' wrote John Aubrey. 'He was an extraordinary handsome Man, but prowd. He wrote a Poem called "Lucasta".' An ardent Royalist, Lovelace was unfortunate enough to spend two periods in prison, the first for presenting the Kentish petition in favour of the King in 1642; it was then that he wrote his famous poem 'To Althea from Prison':

> *Stone walls do not a prison make*
> *Nor iron bars a cage;*
> *Minds innocent and quiet take*
> *That for an hermitage:*
> *If I have freedom in my love,*
> *And in my soul am free,*
> *Angels alone that soar above*
> *Enjoy such liberty.*

Lovelace was actually in prison for only seven weeks and released after giving an undertaking that he would not continue his anti-Parliamentary activities. However, in 1648 he was again in prison — this time for ten weeks. He put the hours to good use once more, preparing for the press his other famous poem, 'To Lucasta, Going to the Wars', together with odes, sonnets and songs. His reputation, perhaps unfairly, rests on these two lyrics alone. In his personal life, too, he was unfortunate, for it was reported that he was killed fighting in France; consequently his betrothed, Lucy Sacheverell (Lucasta), married another man. Perhaps, also, she was a bit fed up with Lovelace, who put military duty before passion:

> *True, a new mistress now I chase,*
> *The first foe in the field;*
> *And with a stronger faith embrace*
> *A sword, a horse, a shield.*

Yet this inconstancy is such
As you too shall adore;
I could not love thee, dear, so much,
Loved I not honour more.

John Bunyan – *Pilgrim's Progress*   Bunyan was a zealous puritan, his zeal apparently stimulated by that of his wives, who became a popular preacher with the labouring classes after he joined the Bedford Baptist Congregation in 1653. As such he became an object of suspicion to the newly restored monarchy, which arrested him in 1660 for unlicensed preaching. His first imprisonment lasted twelve years, during which he studied Foxe's *Book of Martyrs* and wrote a spiritual autobiography (*Grace Abounding*, 1666). But it was during his second imprisonment, which began in 1675, that he started on his masterpiece: *Pilgrim's Progress* (Part I, 1678; Part II, 1684), which presented the Christian attitude to life in allegorical narrative form.

The success of *Pilgrim's Progress* was not only due to its being written with a 'pen of fire'. The Puritans were denied the pleasures of novels and plays, which were condemned as impious, but a strong storyline that appeared in the guise of a narrative tract was an agreeable substitute. (Even so, the more extreme Puritans condemned the work as 'a vain story'.) The fame of the work spread outside Puritan circles. The language has the virility and vividness of the King James Bible, and the story a dramatic simplicity and intensity that has appealed to generations of readers. Indeed it became known as 'the lay Bible', and ninety-two editions of it appeared in the hundred years after its publication. He followed it up with *The Holy War* (which Macaulay considered superior to *Pilgrim's Progress*) and *The Life and Death of Mr Badman*. Of his writing he said: 'I have not for these things fished in other men's waters; my Bible and my concordance are my only library in my writing.'

Oscar Wilde – **'De Profundis'**   The circumstances of Wilde's trial and arrest under the Criminal Law Amendment Act in 1895 are well known. The case arose directly from his foolish decision to sue the Marquess of Queensberry for libel, the aristocrat having hoped to provoke him to do precisely that by leaving a card for Wilde at his club which suggested that he was homosexual. The further motive was to detach his son, Lord Alfred Douglas, from Wilde's influence. After being sentenced to two years' hard labour, Wilde wrote during his imprisonment his remarkable apologia, 'De Profundis', which detailed the effect of suffering on his spiritual development. 'De

Profundis' strikes an uneasy balance between self-pity and lofty ideal-
ism. Not untypical is the magnificently expressed passage about
Christ, whose attraction for the author was that he was 'the supreme
individualist'.

Wilde's other — and better received — 'prison' writing was 'The
Ballad of Reading Gaol'. But this was written after his release, when
he had gone to France, and published in 1898.

Last Laugh to the Publisher . . .

In his memoirs of his career as a publisher Sir Stanley Unwin tells the
remarkable story of how he helped to save a distinguished Viennese
art publishing house from the hands of the Nazis. In the mid-thirties
Unwin was visiting Vienna and noticed that Jewish publishing houses
in Germany became officially 'Aryanized' if they were purchased by
non-Jews. Armed with his non-Jewish pedigree, Unwin persuaded the
head of the Nazi publishing organization that a house purchased by
himself would be 'Aryanized' and extracted an assurance to that
effect in writing. He then bought all the stock and copyrights of the
art publisher Phaidon, and urged its proprietor, Dr Horovitz, to take
refuge in England. Dr Horovitz nearly left it too late, and was in Holland on his way back to Vienna, after seeing Unwin, when the Nazis
walked into Austria. A Nazi official was soon in the Phaidon offices,
and on calling for particulars of the business at first refused to believe
that Dr Horovitz was not proprietor and owner of the assets. He was
further thwarted when all the printers and binders assured him that
Allen and Unwin had owned the stock for more than a year. 'The dis-
appointment of Nazi art publishers,' records Unwin with satisfaction,
'who had thought they would acquire the business for a song, was
great.'

Unwin added insult to injury by obtaining consent to publish the
now 'Aryanized' Phaidon books in Germany (where they had hitherto
been banned as 'Jewish' publications) under the Allen and Unwin
imprint.

. . . and Last Word to the Poet

~

. . . as good almost kill a man as kill a good Booke; who kills a man kills a reasonable Creature, God's Image; but he who destroys a good Booke, kills reason itself, kills the Image of God, as it were, in the eye.

John Milton, *Areopagitica*

~

Acknowledgements

Nicholas Parsons and Sidgwick & Jackson extend their thanks to those authors and publishers who have given their permission to reproduce extracts from works still in copywright, listed below. If anyone has been unintentionally omitted the publishers offer their apologies and will be pleased to rectify it in future editions, provided that they receive notification from the copyright holder.

Pages 64—6, Early Bestsellers in America, from Alice Payne Hackett and James Henry Burke, *Eighty Years of Best Sellers*, Bowker.

Pages 78—82, The Most Popular Fiction in Britain 1578—1930, from Q. D. Leavis, *Fiction and the Reading Public*, Chatto and Windus.

Pages 157—9, Leo Tolstoy's List of Books That Made the Most Impression on Him, from R. F. Christian (ed.), *Tolstoy's Letters*, Athlone Press.

Pages 160—1, The Hundred Books That Most Influenced Henry Miller, from Henry Miller, *The Books in My Life*, New Directions Publishing Corporation.

Pages 162—4, Cyril Connolly's Hundred Key Books of the Modern Movement, from Cyril Connolly, *One Hundred Key Books from England, France and America*, André Deutsch/Hamish Hamilton.

Pages 164—9, Frederic Raphael and Kenneth McLeish's Choice, from Frederic Raphael and Kenneth McLeish (eds), *List of Books*, Mitchell Beazley.

Pages 170—2, Anthony Burgess's List of Best Novels, from Anthony Burgess, *Ninety-nine Novels, The Best in English since 1939*, Allison and Busby.

Pages 177—81, Fifty Works of English and American Literature We Could Do Without, from Brigid Brophy, Michael Levey and Charles Osborne's book of the same name, originally published by Rapp and Carroll.

Pages 207–13, Famous Banned Authors, from Anne Lyon Haight, *Banned Books*, Bowker.

Pages 225–6, Nine Clues to Racism and Sexism in Children's Books, from Judith Stinton (ed.), *Racism and Sexism in Children's Books*, Writers' and Readers' Publishing Co-operative.

Verse on pages 3, 5, 11, 13 and 17 by W. H. Auden, Hilaire Belloc, E. C. Bentley, Noël Coward, Cecil Day-Lewis and Richard Le Gallienne.